War memories - Primary Source Edition

Croy, Marie, Princess de, 1875-

Nabu Public Domain Reprints:

You are holding a reproduction of an original work published before 1923 that is in the public domain in the United States of America, and possibly other countries. You may freely copy and distribute this work as no entity (individual or corporate) has a copyright on the body of the work. This book may contain prior copyright references, and library stamps (as most of these works were scanned from library copies). These have been scanned and retained as part of the historical artifact.

This book may have occasional imperfections such as missing or blurred pages, poor pictures, errant marks, etc. that were either part of the original artifact, or were introduced by the scanning process. We believe this work is culturally important, and despite the imperfections, have elected to bring it back into print as part of our continuing commitment to the preservation of printed works worldwide. We appreciate your understanding of the imperfections in the preservation process, and hope you enjoy this valuable book.

WAR MEMORIES

MACMILLAN AND CO., Limited
LONDON · BOMBAY · CALCUTTA · MADRAS
MELBOURNE

THE MACMILLAN COMPANY
NEW YORK · BOSTON · CHICAGO
DALLAS · ATLANTA · SAN FRANCISCO

THE MACMILLAN COMPANY
OF CANADA, LIMITED
TORONTO

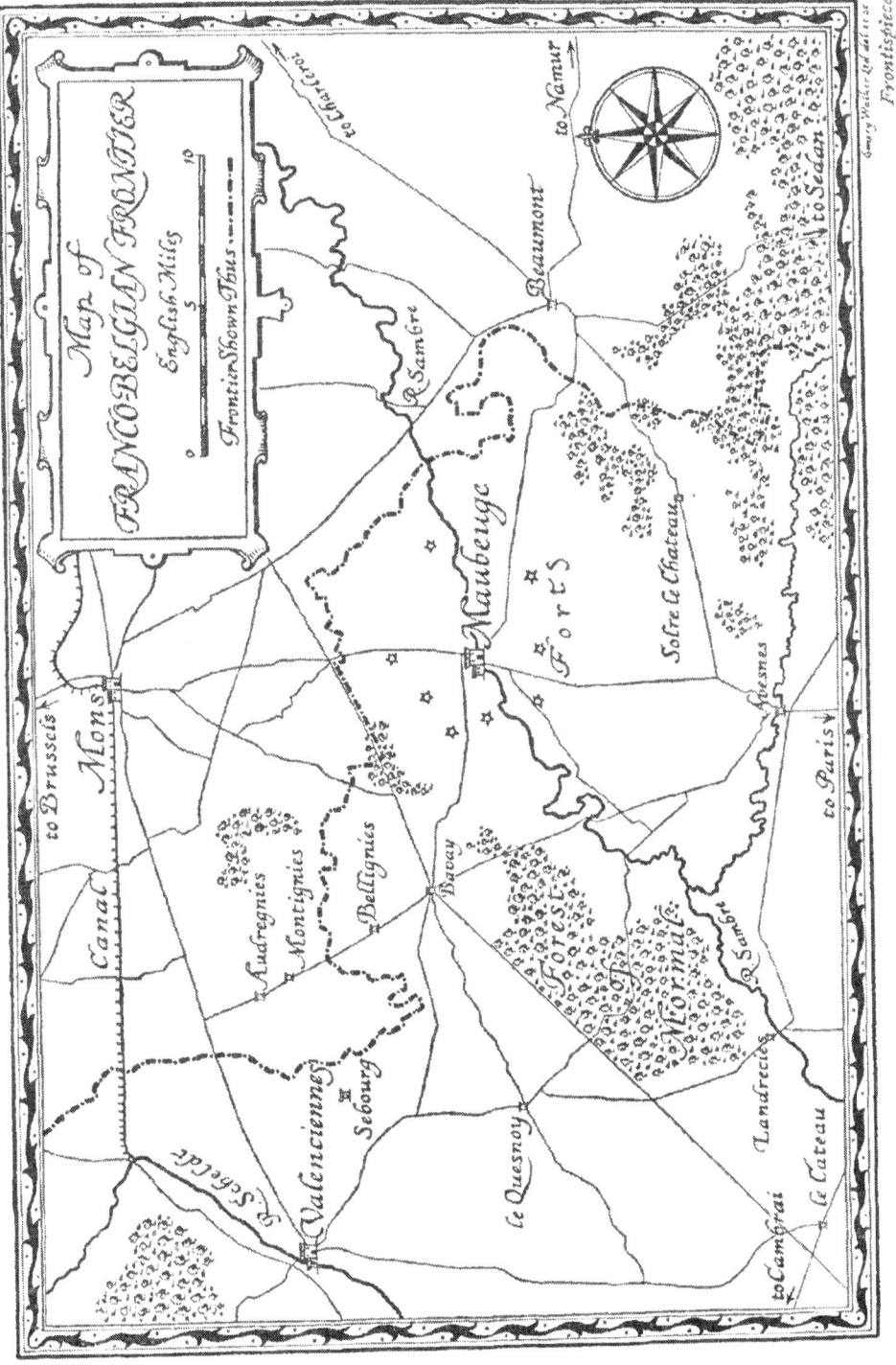

WAR MEMORIES

BY
PRINCESS MARIE DE CROŸ

MACMILLAN AND CO., LIMITED
ST. MARTIN'S STREET, LONDON
1932

COPYRIGHT

PRINTED IN GREAT BRITAIN
BY R. & R. CLARK, LIMITED, EDINBURGH

FOREWORD

LIKE my country, I was forced into the War. Everyone who knew Belgium up to 1914 will agree that it was a peaceful, industrious and hospitable country. Except for the brutal aggression of which it was the victim, it would have, doubtless, been so still. And I also lived a peaceful, busy life, with friends of every nationality. The war lost me some on whom I thought I could count; in compensation it brought me others whom I least expected. Modern warfare spares neither age, nor sex, nor profession, nor situation; it is this which constitutes its chief horror. For twelve years I have refused all solicitations to publish my experiences, and if I do so now it is because my silence has allowed various fables to circulate, and I am sometimes quite surprised when I read of adventures which are attributed by imaginative journalists to me and mine. From the beginning of hostilities I wrote down regularly the small happenings of the day. They were hasty notes, written at odd times, giving the facts as we thought to know them then. Much was modified later, of course. I do not write to please anyone in particular, neither to do harm to anyone; I only try to write the truth as I saw it, as objectively as possible. It is the mass of the experiences of an epoch which forms notes for future history. Much has been written from the military and political points of view, but less is known of the life of the inhabitant in occupied territory, where often one had no choice between risking imprisonment, or worse, and betraying a cause of whose justice we were all absolutely convinced, or leaving fellow-countrymen and allies in danger for want of help. From the day when our King, voicing the mind of his whole people, showed us that our duty lay in resistance to an unjust aggression, I think a burning desire to help in the cause of right possessed us all. But I imagined at that time that my share would confine itself to nursing the sick and wounded, and helping and consoling my poorer neighbours. I neither sought adventure, nor cared for it; I tried only to do the duty which presented itself, as I saw so many doing around me.

BELLIGNIES, 30*th December* 1931

LIST OF ILLUSTRATIONS

Map of Franco-Belgian Frontier . .	*Frontispiece*	
		PAGE
Princess Marie de Croy	*to face*	74
Miss Edith Cavell	,,	128
The Château de Bellignies . . .	,,	300

WAR MEMORIES

BELLIGNIES, my home, is on the Franco-Belgian frontier, between Valenciennes, Mons, and Maubeuge. The little neighbouring town of Bavay was the capital of the Nervii, whom Julius Caesar found so warlike and brave. Some historians suppose the name of Bellignies to be derived from "Bel Ignis" (the fire of Bel or Baal), and truly war and fire have played a great part in its history.

In 1914 my family consisted of my eighty-four-year-old grandmother, Mrs. Hellyar Parnell (of a family now extinct, from the west of England), my two brothers, and myself. We had many friends in England, my father having been attached for years to the Belgian Embassy in London, where my brother Reginald has also been Secretary or Counsellor for the last ten years. I was staying with my dear friend, Miss Violet Cavendish-Bentinck, and her mother when the clouds began to gather on the political world. About the 29th of July, a telegram from a well-informed friend told me, "If you are going home, go at once". Notwithstanding the protestations of my friends, who would not even contemplate the possibility of war, until they got a great shock on receiving from the military authorities orders for sending their dearly-loved horses for census taking, I started on the 1st of August, and although at that time the "man in the street" in England had not yet begun to realise the seriousness of the situation, the trains were crowded with Germans leaving for home, and by the time we got to Calais the least observant could see that grave events were imminent.

A little anecdote will illustrate the English mentality at the time. At Victoria, my friend, who had come to the station with me, anxious at my travelling in bad health, asked a fellow-traveller to look after me on the journey. He was an elderly gentleman, whom we found comfortably installed in a corner of the carriage I travelled in, surrounded with portmanteaux and dispatch-cases, and amply provided with literature. I put him down in my mind for a family lawyer, or the head of some well-established firm. On my enquiry what was his opinion of the situation, he answered with conviction that Sir Edward Grey would never let it become too serious, that he had every confidence the situation would soon become peaceful. On my remark (I had bought *The Times* and looked through it) that I saw the German frontier was closed, he said, "Well, I am going to Germany myself, on business, and if that is so I shall have to hire a motor from the frontier to Cologne." I have often since wondered what was the fate of my companion.

At Calais the Rapide for the north was under

steam, and, fearing to lose it, I approached the *Chef de gare*, who was on the platform, told him where I lived and begged him to order my luggage to be put on board at once. He acquiesced civilly and told me at the same time that the frontier was closed, but that French troops were being rushed up as near to it as possible. Either he or one of the Customs officials whispered to me that it was known that war would be declared next day. My anxiety to get home was great, and I scarcely felt the discomfort of an overcrowded carriage, for we must have been twelve or more people in it, mostly officers, and I was the only lady. I had English papers with me, and at once the officers began asking about public opinion in England, and if there was any hope of her coming into the war. I passed my *Times* and *Telegraph* to the one who seemed best able to read them, and he translated aloud, frequently asking my help, until he returned me the papers and begged me to read them in French. All the way to Valenciennes I translated the papers to an anxious audience. At Valenciennes my brother Reginald had come to fetch me in the car, and as we left the crowded station we met Monsieur Maurice Dupas, who told us he had just seen his eldest son off for an unknown destination. Jacques Dupas was a fine young fellow of twenty-two, who had been educated on Anglo-Saxon lines at the Collège des Roches, and had done his military service in the Cuirassiers. His father told us that even the station-master did not know the destination of the train; that an officer had got on to the engine and would give orders to the driver outside the station. Monsieur Dupas never saw his son again.

Everyone seemed to be in the streets, but the crowds were orderly, rather serious than sad. In Bellignies we heard that all the men belonging to the reserve had received orders to join their regiments next morning. We were anxious about my elder brother Leopold, who was on a yachting cruise in the Baltic, and had been in Cronstadt and Petersburg when we last had news of him. The last letter received described the fêtes in honour of President Poincaré and the latter's departure, and had announced his intention of going on to Moscow before leaving Russia. But that same evening of my return, Leopold arrived also, having come from Brussels by the most unorthodox ways, partly even on foot, and, of course, without any luggage. He told us that at a banquet given by a Grand Duke, I believe the Grand Duke Dimitri, the English Ambassador, Sir George Buchanan, had warned him and the rest of the yachting party that if they were thinking of leaving Russia it would be wise to start that night. They took the hint, and left at midnight, and heard that the port was mined before morning. On coming through the Kiel Canal they had been astonished to see the German Fleet taking in coal at full speed, even piling it on to the decks, and on signalling for information, were informed it was "the grand manœuvres". But still they were so far from realising events that their chief interest was to know if Madame Caillaux, who had been tried in Paris for the shooting of Calmette, was condemned or acquitted. Off Ymuiden they were astonished at being brought under a powerful searchlight, and when the pilot came on board and told them it was war, all were aghast. The Frenchmen left at once to rejoin their respective regiments. Leopold also took the train for Brussels, where friends told him of the rumour of an imminent German aggression against Belgium. They all decided to volunteer next day, but in the meanwhile he came home, where I had just arrived, and told us of his decision.

That night no one went to bed. We talked together and tried to make plans for the future, but who could know what the future would be? We tried to hide the truth from my grandmother, whose age and many sorrows had made us anxious to shield her from further care, and we persuaded my brother Reginald to await events and not volunteer also at once.

Next morning at daybreak Leopold left us. I saw no more of him for over four years, and he never saw our grandmother again.

I had obtained my diploma after a course of nursing in Paris, and we at once offered our home to the French Red Cross to be used as an ambulance or field hospital. The Marquis de Vogüé telegraphed accepting it as a French hospital for officers, which made us think we were not expected to be occupied by the enemy. The different householders in the village and the owners of the marble works were all called to their posts in the army, and their wives decided to follow where they could keep as far as possible in touch with their husbands; but before leaving they told us to dispose of beds and bedding from their houses for our ambulance. The whole village wished to help, and even those whom we scarcely knew brought some contribution, a mattress, a pair of sheets, and an offer of help when there should be nursing to do. So I made a list and arranged for shifts of eight hours, in each of which some of the village ladies and one of ourselves should be on duty. Alas! for goodwill, when the enemy arrived nearly everyone had fled, except our Curé, his housekeeper, and the foreman of one of the factories, an elderly man, a militant Socialist, and antagonist of the Church. But before a common danger, Jean-Baptiste François forgot all, except that he was a Frenchman and a patriot, and became our useful and devoted helper.

At the neighbouring little town of Bavay all parties, united under the presidency of the Mayor, and the effective direction of Mademoiselle de Montfort, daughter and sister of French generals, and head of the Red Cross in the region, had prepared the College of the Assumption to receive wounded soldiers. While all this preparation was going on we heard no news. But as we were extremely anxious about Leopold, Reginald determined to try and reach Antwerp to get news of him. He started, and managed in some way to find the regiment, the First Guides, who, while doing their training, were lodged in a barn at Beveren-Waes. With Leopold were Robert d'Ursel, Robert de la Barre, Baudoin de Ligne, Renaud de Briey, and many others.[1] Robert d'Ursel and Leopold had pulled some handfuls of hay out to lie on, but the younger men had climbed on to the top, and, playing games up there, often made those below fear they would fall on them. Just about this time, some of them, among whom was young Ligne, distinguished themselves at the battle of Haelen. Leopold has told me since how ardently Baudoin wished to do some extraordinary deed of valour, often saying, "The war will be over in three weeks; this is my *one* chance, perhaps in a lifetime". Alas, a few days later, driving his auto-mitrailleuse into an ambush, this ardent young warrior of eighteen fell for his country.

Leopold's experience, when he went to enlist, was a curious one. After passing three hours in a queue of people who also were enlisting, when he arrived before the officer he was at once asked for his certificate of "bonne vie et mœurs". He had carried his birth certificate, and thought this to be sufficient. Fearing the want of the document would cause great delay, he was hesitating what to do, when a small boy scout touched his arm and said: "Is there anything you want, Monsieur?" In his perplexity, Leopold said to the youngster, "Yes, I want a certificate of 'bonne vie et mœurs' and don't know where to get it". Immediately the little fellow

---

[1] The Duc d'Ursel, Comte Robert de la Barre, Prince Baudoin de Ligne, Comte Renaud de Briey, etc.

pulled out a small notebook and a pencil, asked for name, address, and other details, which he noted down, and saying, "Wait here", trotted briskly away. To Leopold's amazement, he returned in a short time bringing with him the necessary document, on presentation of which Leopold became a soldier of Belgium until six months after peace should be declared.

The few papers that arrived were so severely censored that, apart from wildly exaggerated accounts of Belgian victories, we knew nothing of events. The French Army might have been non-existent as far as we were concerned. Of course, most of it had been concentrated towards the East frontier.

At last, on Friday, the 21st of August, news came that British troops were arriving, and orders were given that everyone must be prepared to lodge or feed them. My brother and I motored into Bavay. As we entered the town we met the British Expeditionary Force marching up the hill towards the Grand' Place amidst the enthusiastic welcome of the population. At once I was hurried to the College hospital, for casualties had been brought in and an interpreter was required, and my brother was kept busy helping with billeting, translating, and so on for the Staff. He made the acquaintance of Sir Charles Fergusson and Lord Graham, who were lodged at Mademoiselle de Montfort's. The general impression the army gave was that, though individually the men appeared worn-out, on the whole they looked orderly and business-like, very confident and even cheerful. Many wore flowers that the French girls had given them, and an admiring population was proffering drinks, cigarettes, and chocolates.

As soon as I could leave the hospital, having heard that troops were marching to Bellignies, we hurried home and met a company of the Middlesex Regiment entering the gates. The officer in charge, a tall, tired-looking lieutenant, asked for some boiling water to make tea for his men, saying that they had had scarcely anything to eat for twenty-four hours. In those days in the country one kept big stores, and so without letting them get out their emergency rations we were able to provide a substantial tea for the men, who sat around the edge of the lawn to eat it. While all we volunteers cut and spread bread and jam, the officer stood in the conservatory door and, as man after man came forward with his mug, kept order, murmuring gently, "No wolfing", if some seemed too eager in their hunger. At last I begged him to sit down and rest, and leave us to work, but he said, "If I sat down I could not get up again", and a glance at his drawn face showed me that he only told the truth. On my asking if a room could be got ready for him that night, he answered that no one must think of sleeping, that they had the roads and bridges to guard between us and the Belgian frontier, and perhaps might have to blow up the bridges. So he went off with guides we provided, and posted his men, and only when all was done came back for the meal prepared for him. We left him quite alone that he might rest, and when a little later he came to say "Good-bye", his words were, "I believe you have saved my life".

The Middlesex Regiment was dreadfully cut up at Mons; many, many of its men lie in the little cemetery on Mont Panisel.[1] I often wonder, when I walk between their head-stones, which of those who lie there ate their last meal sitting in the evening sunlight on our quiet lawn. Had it not been for a low rumbling sound like that of distant thunder, nothing would have seemed farther than we were from "battle, murder, and sudden death".

August 22.—At daybreak the next morning, Saturday, my maid called me to the window to see a strange sight. In the middle of the lawn lay long khaki-clad figures studying maps stretched on the dew-laden grass. The gates were open and a group of orderlies held horses near them. I soon dressed and went out, and an officer asked me if I could give them any maps of the region. He held in his hand a map of the Namur country, and from that I suppose that they had hoped to get so far. These were, I believe, part of General French's Staff, and they soon left on the way to Mons with the motoring maps we were able to give them. All that day and the next the battle raged. We heard the troops pouring down the hill going northwards; all the

---

[1] I heard later that our young Lieutenant, Audrey Albrecht, was reported missing.

men left in the village, among them our old coachman, stood in the roads admiring the beauty of the horses and the perfection of their harnessing and equipment. At that time, to our inexperienced eyes, the army seemed immense, but later on, in comparison to that of the enemy, it was as a stream to a great river.

August 24.—Soon we heard that wounded and sick men were lying in farm-houses and on the roadside, so my brother and the chauffeur started out to bring them in. All the rooms were ready, and I had a large provision of food cooked in readiness for emergencies. The first wounded that came in were so exhausted from want of food that I had jugs of milk and glasses ready by the door to give them before they were lifted down from the cars or horses which brought them in. One officer arrived between two troopers who held him on his horse, and when the glass of milk was lifted to his lips it was immediately red with blood. He had been shot through the palate, splinters of which were running into his tongue. Having removed these and filled the hole with a tampon of wadding, we were able to get the poor fellow into bed and attend to other cases. Attracted by the Red Cross flag which flew from the tower, they came, some for food and rest, some to have wounds dressed. Now and then a doctor would arrive, and I took him around the wards to ask his advice. One malaria case worried me very much. Many of the old regulars had been for years in the colonies and were subject to fever.

The young doctor, evidently inexperienced too, worn-out and confused at being in a foreign land, told me to give so much quinine, using the English measure, which, even if I had known it, no one here would have possessed the weights of. Seeing he knew nothing of the metric system, I begged him to tell me about how much was a dose. He stammered, "Gi-gi-give it until you see signs of p-p-poisoning".

About this time a car brought in a superior officer accompanied by a doctor. He was a Major of the Gordon Highlanders, who had a bullet in his shoulder which could not be extracted at once. He had lost much blood, and must have a night's rest and be sent by special train to the English base at Amiens next day, the doctor told us. After the coat sleeve had been cut off, the wound dressed and a sleeping draught administered, I saw the doctor preparing to leave, and asked him, "Who will give orders for the special train to-morrow?" "You must," said he, as if it were the most natural thing in the world, and before I got back my wits he was gone.

Feeling like a character out of *Alice*, I went back to my work until my brother called me to the front door. There was a long ammunition car, on which lay two sorely wounded men, an artillery officer and his driver. I handed a glass of milk to the officer first, but he took it and gave it to his man to drink. It was a thing I noticed often, that the British officer's first care was for his men. But these two looked so very bad that, having no doctor in the house, after a consultation with my brother, we decided it would be wiser to send them on to Bavay, where we knew there was a large British ambulance. So Reginald got up by the driver of the car, and drove off with him to Bavay Hospital, and on arriving met the two Princes, Pierre and Antoine d'Orléans, who were on General French's Staff, for, being members of the French Royal family, they were not allowed to serve in their own army. Before many weeks, Captain Preston, the wounded officer Reginald had taken away, was to come back to us and have a terrible experience.

I had been too busy to leave the house, and none of those who came in seemed to have any very clear idea of the events that they were taking part in, so I felt a shock when I heard that the army was now marching southward, *up* the hill instead of *down*. My brother had not come back, the unwounded had gone forward, the wounded were sleeping the sleep of exhaustion, so I went out into the high road and watched the troops go by. But even to my eyes the order was far different to what it had been at first. Regiments were mixed up, and only that the men seemed perfectly unconcerned, I should have guessed at once that they were in full retreat. I spoke to one or two non-commissioned officers, who all assured me that they had given the enemy "a proper dressing". I asked for an officer, and was informed that "one would be along soon". I have since realised what great numbers of the English officers were killed or wounded at Mons. At last one made an appearance, and I begged him to stop a minute, saying the house was full of wounded, and I wished to know if there were any danger of the enemy coming. Before answering me, and looking at the little group of villagers who had crowded around, he asked, "Can anyone understand English?" On my assuring him that they could not, he said, "Do not tell them that the enemy is close behind, as we *must* keep the roads free. I fear the Germans will be here in a few hours, and you must send away the wounded as soon as possible, and had better leave too, for we shall probably have to blow you up." After this he hurried on, and I went back to the house.

It was very quiet, and as my brother had not yet returned I went up to the senior officer, hoping to get directions. He was sleeping the heavy sleep opium gives, and his wounded shoulder made it impossible to shake him awake. As no amount of calling had any effect, I fetched some strong black coffee which I got him to swallow by pouring it down his cheek, much as one doses a dog. Upon which he opened his eyes and said, "What day is it?" "Still Monday", I answered; "but the Germans are coming." "Do not let them take me", said he, and fell asleep again. In despair I went down to send a messenger after my brother, when I met at the door a young neighbour, Marthe de Pas, who had come up with her little English maid to say good-bye. Her parents, fearing to be cut off from their four soldier sons, had made up their minds to leave their home, the Château de Rametz. They had dropped her in passing while the car went on to fetch her married sister, Baroness de Witte, who lived at the Château de Gussignies, about a mile away. I requisitioned both girls to come and help to get the wounded ready by the time the car came back. When Reginald returned, we lifted the men, wrapped in blankets, two by two on to the car, and he drove them on to Bavay. He went forward and back until late that night, taking the sick and wounded, and handing them over, when fit to travel, to anyone who was going south; but he left those who could not stand the journey at Bavay ambulance. By the evening all were, as we thought, in safety, except four men who were not fit to be moved.

My brother and I thought it would be right to put our grandmother in safety too, so we called in the chauffeur, a faithful servant, who was too young to be left behind the lines, and told him we were going to confide her to his care, that he was to try and join the Countess de Pas and her family, travel with them, and, if possible, get into touch with Leopold. The latter was the motive we gave to induce my grandmother to consent to go. The idea that my brother had no one to look after him, if ill or wounded, was enough, and we knew that if cut off from all of us, many friends' homes would be open to her.[1] Taking a stock of petrol and all the

---

[1] I heard later that our good friend the Marquise de Lespinay, anxious on our account, had persuaded the Préfet de la Vendée to

money she dared, for, the banks being closed, we did not know when we should be able to get any more, my grandmother left us about evening, dreadfully worried in mind, not for herself but for us. Some hours later the car came back; they had got in the midst of the retreating armies, the roads were so crowded with guns, men, and material that they were impassable, and all the country lanes were filled by refugees taking their cattle and goods into safety. The poor country folks had lost their heads entirely, and some carried quite worthless objects, while losing their children or their parents. My grandmother seemed so relieved to be back that we could not regret her return, but we thought it better to let the chauffeur try once more to get where he could do his duty to his country, as well as put the new powerful car out of reach of the enemy. So armed with recommendations he started off again and eventually attained the Belgian Army, where he served for the rest of the war. The car also did good service until it was destroyed by the enemy during the advance on Bailleul in 1918.

August 25.—That night was extraordinarily quiet after the noise and confusion of the last days, and only an occasional shell disturbed the peaceful air. When early in the morning we made a round of the village, it seemed like a deserted place; not a creature

---

telegraph to the Préfecture du Nord to get news of us, and offer to take us all in. The answer that the Préfecture du Nord kindly sent announced that we were already cut off from all communication

was to be seen. About eight o'clock we heard the noise of horses trotting, and saw two Uhlans, holding their lances stretched before them, go by the gates. Nothing can describe the feeling of revolt, of nausea almost, that the first sight of the enemy in one's country provokes. Although we are Belgians, our family had been settled here for centuries, before the modern Kingdom of Belgium was constituted. Under Burgundian or Spanish or French domination we had been here. And the common danger had united Belgium and France so closely that one heart seemed to beat between them. A Belgian woman, once in our service, and who lived in a cottage near the frontier, made her appearance that morning. She said she felt she must come to see what we thought of the situation. I was often to remark at that time that the simple people turned naturally to us, confident that we should be able to counsel and console them. She had heard that Liège and Namur had fallen, but "What does that matter? Belgium will not be conquered until every Belgian is dead", were her brave words.

We walked up to the gates with her, and there met Baron de Witte, our neighbour of Gussignies, walking down the deserted streets in the most unconcerned way, followed at a short distance by a whole German regiment. A very stout officer in front stopped his horse to ask the way to St. Waast, and the troop went slowly by, looking sullenly at our little group, who no doubt looked with as little favour back at them. De Witte told us that his wife and the servants had left with her parents, as his sister-in-law, Marthe, had told me they intended doing. He had never done any military service, having outgrown his strength when young, but he tried, as soon as war was declared, to volunteer. His wrath against the official in Valenciennes, who had repeatedly said, "Go home and wait until you receive your mobilisation papers", was great, and he chafed under inaction until he found work, and dangerous work, later. He returned to the house with us, and while we were talking together, a long grey motor-car came quickly to the door, and an officer sprang out of it, saluted, and said in guttural French: "In an hour you will receive an Army Staff which you must lodge". Not waiting for an answer, he drove away as rapidly as he had come. As all the rooms were ready, just as they had been in use for the British, we went to tranquillise our wounded men, who by now were very nervous, and to put their arms and equipment out of reach of the enemy.

Several days before this an order had come from the *Mairie* telling us to send all arms, sporting guns, etc., down to where they would be locked up in safety until the end of hostilities, after which they were to be restored to us. We had obeyed the order, but now the soldiers' rifles were a new problem, and so, after a rapid discussion with the English sergeant, a long-service man, we decided that the safest thing to do with the soldiers' rifles was to throw them down an old and very deep cistern. It was hard to induce the men to give up their well-kept rifles, or rather let us take them from under their beds, but as time was short and we had been told that anyone found with firearms would be shot, de Witte, my brother, and I took them one by one and carried them down to the cistern. During this while, watch was kept by our Curé, Monsieur l'Abbé Vallez, and Jean-Baptiste François, our Socialist helper. I may say that the two latter made up all old differences during this anxious time, and remained friends until death parted them. Suddenly the servants came in to say that someone was knocking violently at the doors that gave on to the highroad from the stableyard, but they dared not go to open, whereupon Reginald hurried to the spot and unlocked the door. A wrathful German was there at the head of a waiting regiment, asking rudely why the doors were not opened at once, and demanding drinking water. The men poured in and were about to fill their cans from taps with water used for cleaning carriages, when Reginald humanely told them that this water was not fit for drinking, and showed them the only tap of clean water. This was small, and the filling of cans went very slowly. The fuming officer asking rudely why we had no more and bigger taps, Reginald told him curtly that, if he preferred, they could drink the other water and get poisoned, on which he became silent until, finding they did not move off rapidly enough, he began kicking his men about as if they were a flock of sheep.

When my brother came back and we were standing talking near the drawing-room, now turned into a ward, we saw, through the open front door, come gliding in at the gate a whole procession of long grey cars, each with a high steel blade erect in the front of it. They made one think of the early Norseman ships as they must have appeared coming up the rivers of France and England. A few days later, when I asked the object of the steel blade of a German officer, he answered: "To cut the wires that your Belgian compatriots stretch between the trees, and which cut the heads of our brave soldiers off when they motor past".

Almost at once the first car was at the door; two superior officers got out and saluted us. The first, a stoutish, bearded man, speaking good French, presented his companion as "General von Kluck". The latter, tall and thin, grey-haired and serious-looking, said, "And this is our Empress's brother, the Duke of Schleswig-Holstein". In the meanwhile the other cars discharged more officers, and just as the Duke and General were going up to their rooms, they perceived through the open door the soldiers lying in their beds. "Englische Soldaten", they cried excitedly, and at once asked me if there were any officers. I answered quietly, but with inward delight, "No, the last had left us yesterday". Giving an order that I did not catch to a blue-uniformed, pompous-looking doctor, whom they named "Generalarzt", the Duke went upstairs.

We passed before our little chapel, which is on the

landing of the first-floor staircase, where out of precaution (a wise one as we saw later) Monsieur le Curé had brought the Blessed Sacrament to the house from the church. Knowing it was useless to send for servants, who were far too terrified to appear, my brother and I showed the Duke and the General to two communicating bedrooms. Their first precaution was to examine the fastenings of the door, and the solid locks must have satisfied them. They retired, saying that they were weary after a very long march and were going to rest. We returned downstairs, but almost at once the Duke descended again and, saying to Reginald that he wished to see the "prisoners", went in with the doctor to the ward, where they began dragging the bandages off our poor wounded men. One, whose broken leg had been only set the day before, fainted from the pain of being made to stand on it. On my violent intervention the doctor calmly answered that he wished to make sure that the men were really wounded, and were not shamming with the intention of getting up in the night to cut all their throats, as English officers had been known to do before. The Duke asked Reginald where were their arms, and requested that they should be delivered up. On my brother's protest that they had no arms, as this was merely a hospital, he said, "I am sure they have knives and they must give them up," and he collected them himself, going from bed to bed. Taking hold of one of these pocket-knives and leaning over a man whose state had caused us great anxiety, as he appeared almost moribund, the Duke said, "These are the things we hear you fellows use to kill off our wounded." George Goodier was still sufficiently conscious to realise what he meant, and his indignation roused him and, I believe, saved his life. He suddenly opened his eyes and said, "Whoever told you that told you a damned lie." From that moment he began to pick up. We were allowed at last to bind up the wounds again, and put our poor fellows back to bed in comfort.

Slowly the house settled down, and at last Granny, Reginald, and myself, as de Witte had gone home, had a cup of tea, our first meal that day. The silver had been buried, and we were served in an earthenware service prepared for the soldiers. In the middle of tea, down came the Duke of Holstein again, this time accompanied by his nephew and aide-de-camp, Prince Georg of Saxe-Meiningen. The Duke presented his tall, young nephew politely, and, hearing my grandmother speak English, in that tongue, which he spoke perfectly, he began a conversation as if the circumstances were quite normal. According to him, King Edward had been the instigator of the war. His jealousy of his nephew, whose Empire was getting too big in comparison with that of the British, had made him form an alliance with France and Russia, the natural enemies of England. But it would probably be fatal to the British Empire, as her coloured troops could never be brought to fight against white troops, and would doubtless revolt against their Suzerain. We answered that

General French's Staff had assured us that the Indian Princes were sending their Home Troops to the aid of their Emperor, that many were even on the way. He questioned us eagerly about the British Army, and the officers whom we had seen. I doubt whether the answers he received, which I own were rather exaggerated, can have been very pleasant hearing. As to Belgium, he spoke despisingly of the country, and especially of its King, notwithstanding that he himself had married a granddaughter of King Leopold II. He ended by saying that now the country was conquered. I repeated to him the words of our Belgian compatriot quoted before. The conversation continued for some time "aigre-doux", and the Duke's temper appeared to have changed for the worse by the end of the meal. His nephew was evidently uncomfortable, but remained polite and courteous.

The rest of the afternoon was taken up by calls in every direction, terrified villagers arriving to say their houses were invaded and food demanded at the pistol-point. Generally they were made to taste any food provided before the Germans would eat it. Now and then shells burst at no great distance, aeroplanes flew by overhead, and in one case one appeared to graze the roof of the house. We were standing just then near a group of officers who had been examining some prisoners in the courtyard. In an instant a hundred rifles were fired at the 'plane, and bullets came falling around us. I did not realise any danger, my brother and I both wishing that the aviator would throw a bomb, which, while certainly it would have killed us, would have wiped out the whole Staff of the First Army. There was a general *sauve qui peut*, and in one moment all were in the house watching from open windows the progress of the English 'plane. It appeared for an instant to have been hit, as it dipped towards the ground, but in another moment was rising rapidly and flying due south.

In our relief my brother and I clapped our hands, which made all the Germans pull in their heads and shut the windows violently. Shortly after this, to our dismay, we saw a tall Frenchman, with his arms tied behind his back, and a rope round his neck, being dragged down the drive between two Uhlans. In an instant he was surrounded by soldiers who began pulling his clothes off roughly to search him. The sight of one unarmed man among many gesticulating, insulting enemies was too much for me, and I went out and stood beside him and protested against this treatment. By this time the Duke and General had arrived on the scene, and on seeing me the former said violently, "Into the house, Madame, this is no place for you." "I beg your pardon, Monseigneur," I answered, "this is a Red Cross hospital and I am its Head; no one shall be maltreated here." Waiting until I saw that orders had been given to treat the prisoner more humanely, I returned to the house and watched the scene from the windows. Some papers found in a satchel carried by the Frenchman were carefully examined, and he was marched off between a guard of soldiers to an unknown destination. The calm, brave look on the man's face haunted me for a long time. I was never able to know if he had been shot as a spy or merely retained as a prisoner, but the sound of a volley during dinner left anguished doubts.

The aide-de-camp had told me that there would be twenty-two officers for dinner, and heard me order twenty-two places to be laid. We determined to have our own meals anywhere rather than sit at table with our enemies. A few minutes before dinner was served, as I was crossing the hall to relieve my brother, who had been on duty in the ward, I met the Duke of Schleswig-Holstein, who seemed in a towering rage. "I hear, Madame, you will not dine with us. No doubt you wish to poison us all."

"I am here to save life, Monseigneur, not to take it, as you know", I answered.

"Well, then, you will have to take the consequences if you wish to be treated as enemies. I will begin by sending your brother as a prisoner of war to Germany."

Our controversy was broken into here by some new prisoners arriving who had to be examined, and the Duke, crimson with rage, went out to the courtyard. Almost at once his nephew, Prince Georg, came to me, and in the kindest way begged me not to anger his uncle "for all your sakes and for the sake of the village and its inhabitants". On my asking what his mother and sisters would do if the rôles were reversed, and the enemy in his country, he looked distressed and said, "I understand, but I beg you for all your sakes to sit at table". Turning to my brother, who had come in, the Prince asked him as a personal favour that we would dine with them, and Reginald answered that there was no reason to do him a personal favour as he came in circumstances which made it out of the question: he added, however, that as the Duke had suggested we wished to poison him, we were quite prepared to sit at table so as to reassure him. So two more places were added, and a few moments later we sat down to dinner, my grandmother remaining in her room.

The Duke sat on my right, and General von Kluck on my left. Ostentatiously, we, Reginald and myself, took one mouthful of each dish. The conversation was strained, both sides trying to obtain information while giving none, but the General was rather silent, and I was grateful to him for only being coldly correct; it was more soldierly. But I soon discovered that the Germans really knew very little about general events, and seemingly nothing of the situation outside Germany. On our mentioning happenings in Italy and in the United States they asked whence we got the news, and were astonished to hear that our post had arrived regularly until the previous morning, in proof of which letters lay, I told them, on my desk which had been posted only a few days ago from Rome. I left these letters purposely where indiscreet eyes might see them: the assurance that the whole of public opinion in Italy was on the side of the Allies cannot have been very pleasant reading. Also letters from America were full of indignation at the violation of Belgian neutrality, and wishes for our speedy victory. Even the German Staff had received no correspondence for many days, their rapid march forward being the cause of this. My brother repeated, for the use of the Staff in general, the information we had given about the imminence of the arrival of Indian troops. We noticed an expression of dismay on all the faces: indeed, Germans appeared terrified at that time of being opposed to natives of whatever race, their special terror being the French "Turcos". To calm this effect, the General said, "They will hardly have time to arrive. In a week we shall be in Paris, and in six weeks peace will be declared."

"According to the English, war will not *begin* for six months, and may last from three to five years." The officers who came to us during the retreat from Mons had reported these to be the exact words of Lord Kitchener. I hasten to say that happily at that time we did not believe them.

"With the present means of destruction *no* war can last six months," asserted von Kluck. "Besides," said the Duke, "our army is far greater than the enemy is prepared for. France knows we have four and a half million soldiers, and believes we may have six, but we can put ten million in the field." However, the General turned to the officers and said in German, "Please do not discuss the war." This showed me, for the first time, a thing which I noticed very often afterwards, that the German is singularly impressionable, and easily takes a pessimistic view, where a Frenchman would shrug his shoulders.

The scene that evening round the house would have been picturesque if one had had the heart to contemplate it with a detached eye. Groups of soldiers sat around the lawn and under the trees eating their meal, their rifles stacked near them, beside fires on which they were stirring their pots and pans containing chiefly chickens and rabbits looted from the farms. Every hole and corner was requisitioned for a sleeping-place, straw was being carried about for bedding, and buckets of water used for toilet purposes. Every now and then a car would arrive, out of which an officer sprang to go and report to the General. In the meantime, in the back hall, long tables had been set up on which telephones and typewriters were already in use. The organisation seemed as perfect as anything could be. Still the distant guns roared and an occasional aeroplane went by, but otherwise the scene appeared very peaceful, the soldiers being too worn-out to move more than necessary.

Late that night a messenger brought important news. We saw the officers conferring together in the hall, which, with the dining-room, formed the only rooms downstairs not turned into hospital wards. Presently the Duke of Schleswig-Holstein came and asked me where was the Château de Rametz, as they had decided to go on there at once, having heard that the English army was in full retreat. Indeed, so many stores, especially oats, had been left behind, that the retreat must be almost a *débâcle*. Our hearts sank at hearing this, but we managed to keep a serene countenance and to watch the hurried departure of our uninvited guests. The men, who had had only a few hours' rest, instead of the good night they expected in comfortable quarters, were very loth to leave. During that night the guns seemed nearer and their noise more and more violent.[1]

August 26.—Next morning we could be sure that a terrible battle was raging not far off. Many volunteers came to help clear up the evidence of last night's invasion, but the poor lawns were badly cut up by the motor-wheels, and straw and refuse lay everywhere. After a busy and anxious day, when we hoped at last for a little rest, a whole new Staff arrived, having at its head General von Bauer and accompanied by its Sovereign, the Grand Duke of Mecklenburg-Strelitz, in person. This time there were only ten officers, with twenty-five non-commissioned officers and orderlies. Dinner had to be got again, and the beds remade. The Duke, a handsome young man of thirty-four, appeared most anxious to spare us trouble, and the whole Staff were well-mannered and discreet. There was an aide-de-camp with a French name which I have unfortunately forgotten, who told us he was of

---

[1] Sir John French said the 26th August was the most critical day for the British Army.

French descent, and whose politeness conciliated everyone.

A few hours previously Monsieur le Curé had come to tell us that the troops that passed the day before had committed great damage at the neighbouring village of Houdain. They had stabled their horses in the church, taking altar-cloths and vestments for them to lie on, while they must have had a regular orgy there themselves. The worst of all was that they had sacrilegiously thrown the consecrated wafers in every direction, while a great many things belonging to the altar had disappeared altogether. There was no doubt that this was done out of pure malice, for they had destroyed, by tearing them into small pieces, the books containing records of births, deaths, and marriages of the parish. On hearing of this from us, the General and Staff of the Mecklenburgers seemed profoundly annoyed, and the Grand Duke at once sent officers to have cleared up, as far as was possible, the devastation in Houdain Church.

I heard the officers talking in low tones to each other about the excesses that the preceding troops had committed. In the shops all the groceries that they had not consumed had been emptied in a heap on to the floor, where sugar, flour, soap, etc., were saturated with oil and vinegar from the barrels whose taps were set running. Jam was emptied into the beds, which were carefully covered over again, and the empty jam-pots, filled with offal, were restored to their places in the cupboards. At our neighbours' home, the Château de Rametz, the cellars had been opened, and empty bottles and jewel-cases strewed the ground. In the daughter's room, where their attached old German governess, on her hurried departure at the outbreak of war, had left books and papers, these had been ruthlessly torn into tiny bits, and filth emptied over them. In another neighbouring château, a notice was found nailed to the table, signed by a German name, saying that the writer had once been a servant here, and now was master. As soon as the officers were out of sight, the rowdy elements among the troops took possession and destroyed all that they could not use.

When the rest of the Staff had gone to work or to rest, the Grand Duke came down and asked if he might visit the sick with us. He spoke in the kindest fashion to the English soldiers, gave them cigarettes and, to their great joy, some *Daily Mirrors* which he had procured in Belgium. Seeing my grandmother preparing to descend the stairs, he ran up and offered her his arm, brought her down and installed her in an arm-chair, saying, "I have an English grandmother, too, whom I love dearly." In the conversation that followed, he told us that he was only accompanying his men, as he considered a Sovereign should, but that he hated the war, and had most of his best friends in England and France. Later on the General and some of the other officers came in and joined in the conversation. They also were in absolute ignorance of events, did not even know which Staff had preceded them, and heard with great astonishment from us of the death of the Pope. They told us that, according to the last news they had received, revolution had broken out in Russia, and her army was marching back to Moscow.

We had heard of an English soldier lying dead not far from our gates, and Monsieur le Curé came down to ask my brother to go and help to bury him. With the aid of an old man, and carrying a ladder as a stretcher, they fetched the poor fellow, as well as a French peasant who had also been killed, no one knew how, and carried them to the cemetery where they put them in hastily dug graves. They took from the Englishman his army papers, which we sent later on, with many others, through the American Embassy in Brussels to the War Office.

Some time later, the American Minister, Mr. Brand Whitlock, forwarded a letter he had received for us from the British Government, thanking us for the services we had rendered to the army. Reginald placed this in his desk and forgot it, but it was to cause trouble later on.

A few days afterwards we met a young countryman who told us that he had been digging potatoes in a field on the way to Bavay on the 25th of August, at a spot where the road is sunken, and a hedge at right angles to it shuts off the view in our direction. Suddenly he had seen two English soldiers climb up the bank and kneel down behind this hedge. He heard horses trotting in the road beneath, two shots were fired, and the Englishmen jumped down the bank again. He dared to creep along under cover of the hedge, where he saw two dead German soldiers lying (doubtless the first Uhlans whom we had seen pass by), while the Englishmen, mounting the Germans' horses, trotted briskly away. Fearing to be made responsible for the death of these Germans, this boy of seventeen had hurried to the little farm where he lived, only to find it empty; the whole family had fled with their waggon and horses, but not being able to get far they eventually returned home again. The two Uhlans were buried where they lay, their pointed helmets marking the spot, on which was also stuck a board with the words: "Here lie two brave German soldiers". They remained there many months, and we saw the grave every time that we passed on our way to Bavay, but they were removed later.

All our hope at this time centred in the fortress of Maubeuge. We believed the place to be very strong, and knew large quantities of troops to be concentrated there, and wondered if they were well informed about what was happening around. We could see that spies and traitors were helping our enemies. Frequently cars arrived, in which, with a German officer, were people who seemed to belong to the country, and young girls and men came in on bicycles, and were immediately surrounded by officers who appeared to question them eagerly. I remember especially a boy of about twelve whose arrival caused much interest. We heard that the first German regiment marching down the road from Malplaquet to Bavay had had an officer killed near the entrance to the town. A patrol of French cyclists were ambushed near there, and doubtless one of these fired. But the Germans, evidently thinking it was a "franc-tireur", seized on a man who was sitting peeling potatoes outside a house by the roadside and shot him. He happens to have been, if not an idiot, at least simple in mind, which is why he was not serving in the army, and he certainly had done no one any harm, but an immediate victim was necessary.

On Thursday, the 26th of August, we had a visit during lunch from Prince Georg of Saxe-Meiningen, whose brother had just been reported missing from near Maubeuge, only his horse having been found. That morning, one of the villagers, who had managed to get into Maubeuge on foot, had brought news that a German prince was reported to be lying wounded in the hospital there, having been shot through the head by a patrol the day before. We promised Prince Georg to try and obtain further information, and he left us after lunch, but came again very shortly bringing with him a sick German officer. He asked us to nurse the latter, saying he was confident we would treat our enemy in the same humane way we treated our Allies. Towards evening, an ambulance brought six German wounded men, and we put them in a ward by themselves, next to the room where the English lay. At first we noticed that they shrank from us every time we approached them as if frightened of being ill-treated. After having with much difficulty removed their clothes and boots, the hard leather top-boots especially having stuck to their swollen feet and causing great agony when pulled off, we got them into bed, where in a few minutes all were sleeping the sleep of utter exhaustion.

That night General von Bauer told us that the English had fought magnificently at Mons, but that they personally had only seen a few French soldiers for the first time on the previous day. The French regiments that had fought on the Meuse were in retreat on the English right flank, and did not come further west than Maubeuge during their retreat from Namur and Charleroi, so that it was natural that those Germans who had fought at Mons should not have seen them. Also, of course, the greater part of the French Army was on the eastern frontier. The General assured us to our dismay that the forts at Liège had fallen, and that he had visited the ruins of two of them himself. He also was deeply incensed at reported remarks of King Albert, which showed us that everything was being done on the German side to arouse feelings of hatred and revenge in their army against our beloved Sovereign and his people. I had on their arrival asked the Grand Duke rather stiffly if he also, like his predecessor, the Duke of Schleswig-Holstein, enforced our presence at table with him. With a pained look he answered that on no account would he force our feelings in any way, but that he would feel greatly honoured if we might dine together.

During the whole night cars were coming and going and the lights were kept lit. Every now and then messengers arrived and ran up to the General's room to report. Even during a thunderstorm, when the lightning lit up the scene outside, the activity never ceased; but the next day, Friday, was comparatively quiet. We heard big guns firing at intervals and a large convoy went by the gates. The sick and wounded kept us busy, especially one Englishman who was in high fever and made us anxious, as in his delirium he kept speaking of the battle in which he had taken part near Boussu Wood. He had been one of fifteen crack shots posted along the outskirts of this wood to prevent the enemy passing. He had fired every time a horseman came in sight between trees in front of him, keeping count of every one who fell. His voice and those of his companions counting "fourteen — fifteen — sixteen", were ringing in his ear, and he kept saying, "It's men I'm killing".

August 28.—In the midst of this we were fetched to the big farm at the entrance of the village to find the farmer Prévost, who had tried to fly with his numerous family, but had been overtaken by the German Army and obliged to return home, had been run over by a motor-car on the way back. We found several ribs were broken and running into his lung, and realised at once that he was dying. We washed and bound up his wounds, and tried gently to prepare his wife, sending word at the same time to the Curé to come at once. While the priest was administering the last Sacraments, Reginald and I attended to the children, of whom several were lying in hysterics in the courtyard of the farm. On our way back we met a man from the village returning from a round on foot; indeed, half the village seemed to be making these rounds to see what was happening, although they ran great risks in doing so of being killed by stray shots or arrested as spies. This man, greatly excited, told us of an aeroplane battle that he had witnessed near Cousolre, a French 'plane flying around a large German one, the officer in it shooting repeatedly until he killed the German aviator, or so Carpentier thought. At that time, as far as we could understand, the Allies, not being prepared for war, were very inferior to the Germans in military aviation. As soon as we arrived home we had a visit from our good doctor from Bavay, with his wife and sister-in-law, who had been visiting various wounded men on the way out to us and came in to see ours too. I took him upstairs to see Lieutenant Thörl, Prince Saxe-Meiningen's friend, whose fever had been rising, and who had developed double pneumonia. I shall quote now textually from my notebook, which, of course, being written daily, is in the present tense.

"The German soldiers downstairs, most of whom have been sleeping for 24 hours, still shrink every time we go near them. Vicky (the little fox-terrier) having followed me into the room, I spoke to her in English and saw that one of the Germans understood. But pretending not to notice, I went on speaking English to Reggie, expressing pity for these poor men, who like ourselves are the victims of German militarism. Then we left the room for a few minutes and on my return smiling faces met us, and it was, 'Schwester, look here,' or 'Please, Schwester, come to me,' with perfect confidence. When I asked them why they had appeared so frightened at first, they told me that they had heard that Belgian ladies cut out the eyes of their wounded! They are all imbued with the idea that Belgium is full of sharp-shooters, 'franc-tireurs' they call them, although they own that none of them have seen any, but all have heard of dreadful doings. Now, with proper care and food their strength is returning, their spirits are rising, and their independence of mind is asserting itself. Two or three are Socialists, and speak disparagingly of their Government, saying they would never have fought if they had not believed Germany to have been attacked.

" As soon as they are well enough to leave their beds, they go into the room where the English are, and smoke and chat together, one German acting as interpreter. This afternoon Reginald took two Englishmen and two Germans out to lie on the lawn at the back, where they seemed perfectly happy, until hearing a car coming I called them in to prepare for a doctor's visit. It was comical to see the haste with which they jumped into bed, not wishing to appear too well for fear they should be sent to the front again. The Germans even jumped into bed with their boots on. As the windows of their ward do not look on to the front, they asked me to warn them next time the doctor is coming."

(A few days later.) "Dr. Jacquemart (our French doctor) came. After I had given the promised warning, the German sergeant said, with an amusing smile of complicity, 'It doesn't matter about *him*; it's *our* doctors you must warn us about.' However, I must say that generally speaking the German doctors seem both humane and conscientious. One of them told me that his chief preoccupation is the excesses both in eating and drinking of his officers."

After the Grand Duke of Mecklenburg and his Staff left us, we had a few quiet days, during which we were kept very busy nursing. Lieutenant Thörl's illness had not yet come to the crisis, and it was a great responsibility when I saw the fever rising and feared for the strain on his heart. He was very heavy to lift when putting on cold compresses, and when Reginald was not available I took an elderly woman-servant with me. One day in his half-delirium he shook her off so violently that she bruised herself against the wall, after which I was obliged to get other help.

On the 2nd of September we were invaded by another Staff, that of General von Kühne, with many officers and innumerable men. They soon settled down, and annexed the ground-floor rooms in the left wing for offices, and in a short while were telephoning to Berlin.

I go back to my notebook: "Happily they provide their own food, as our poultry-yard has very much decreased, and food is getting scarce in the village. There has been terrible waste in this respect, the Germans killing cattle and pigs from which they take only the best pieces, leaving the carcasses to rot in the fields. The villagers are afraid to touch this meat, fearing that it may have been poisoned. Often the only parts of a pig taken are the hams and head. The doctor who has come in with the Staff has sent away some of our men, both German and English, much to the latter's dismay, but we could not protest as they were undoubtedly fit to be removed. We gave the English a little money, telling them to hide it if possible on their persons." (These were the days of the big French five-franc silver pieces which the Englishmen called cart-wheels.)

"Last night a German soldier was brought in, shot through the face, and another one shot through the foot. The head of the one who was shot through the face has swelled out to abnormal proportions and his face has gone black. It is almost impossible to see his features, which are mere creases in this black balloon. I helped the Staff doctor to dress these wounds, while Reginald gave the patient a little red wine and water by teaspoonfuls. He does not seem to suffer much, and when we say, 'Wie geht's, Atterman' (his name is in his pointed helmet), he answers cheerfully in his Rhenish accent, 'Hoot' (gut). The other man's wounds had been insufficiently bound up, and we have had to stanch blood all day and most of the night. Hearing sobbing in the hall, we find a Staff Lieutenant there who has just heard that his brother has been killed to-day. He had been at the telephone taking down lists of casualties when the name of his brother came through with those of five other officers killed. Reginald and I console the young man, while the others go and dine, and we hear them laughing and joking. After dinner one of the officers asks for a bouquet for the Captain, whose fortieth birthday is to-morrow.

"We hear that this army is besieging Maubeuge, and, indeed, the noise of the guns gets louder and louder, and more and more wounded are brought in. Even on Sunday neither of us can go to Mass; we are kept busy dressing wounds and arranging for food. The cook has her work cut out. Breakfast is ordered between 5 and 6.30. Some of the officers require tea, some coffee, some chocolate, all want eggs in various manners. Then comes the hospital breakfast, then ours and our helps', while orderlies are coming all the time with various demands. Some want lunch to carry away to the old mill, whence the artillery fire on Maubeuge is being directed. Others of the Staff lunch here, twelve or more dine each night. On the 6th they celebrate the Captain's birthday, lighting forty tallow candles which, so the servants told us, melted and mingled with the icing on the cake. The gardener gave them a wreath for the funeral of Lieutenant Schwartz, who was buried to-day with another officer killed at the same time, whose luggage the doctor has confided to our care as well as his watch and papers." (These I forwarded some time later by the orderly of another officer who was returning home to Paderborn, the town whence the dead man came. I hope they reached his mother safely; he was the only son of a widow.)

One morning, Mademoiselle Carpentier, the brewer's sister, came in looking very excited, saying she had met two English troopers with their horses in a lane near her house. She had hurriedly hidden them between the trees of the little nursery plantation or *pépinière* near our back gate, the young trees screening men and horses from the Germans who passed on the road a few yards away. Reginald and the Curé went out to them at once, and found the men feeding their horses with loaves of bread. No one thought that Maubeuge could be taken, and so it was decided that the English troopers had better go there, where they believed some English troops still to be. Monsieur le Curé offered to creep near the lines and guide the men as close to Maubeuge as possible, passing through Houdain Wood and trusting to darkness. The brave priest, having bound up the hoofs of the horses to prevent noise (he had tried in vain to induce the men to kill them and escape on foot), guided them through fields and lanes until they were within reach of the fortress. Passing quite close to a German bivouac in Taisnières Wood, he had had the greatest difficulty to prevent the Englishmen rushing forward when they heard what they took to be "God save the King" sung by soldiers sitting round a fire. Of course, in reality it was "Heil, dir im Siegerkranz", and only the horrified tones of the Curé saying, "Germains, Germains", saved them.[1] When poor Abbé Vallez got back to us, what with fatigue and nervousness he looked as if he had tumbled into a pond." (Undoubtedly, had they been discovered, he would have been shot at once, the fate of so many priests in Belgium who had done nothing compared to this.)

"The Staff doctor has brought in four more wounded men, among them Lieutenant von Hartmann, who has been shot through the head and is a ghastly sight. The bullet went in just above his eye and came out behind his ear; the blood has run into his beard and saturated his uniform. It took me several hours, after the wounds had been dressed by the two doctors who brought the case in, to wash off the blood. The orderly who has come in with him tells us that this officer is a nephew of the Archbishop of Cologne, and son of the Regierungs-Präsident (Prefect). Before leaving, the army surgeon told me that Lieutenant von Hartmann's life hung by a thread, that a violent movement would cause the artery to burst out bleeding and bring on sudden death. As he is light-headed I am almost unable to leave him. He evidently takes me for a relation, and is comforted at

---

[1] This German national song has the same tune as "God save the King".

feeling me near. If I am absent I hear him calling, and his long arm (he seems to me gigantically tall) comes searching round the room until he can catch my arm or feel my dress. Both eyes and ears are bandaged, but his speech, though rather wandering, is quite clear.

"Whilst I am attending to this and other cases upstairs, Reginald comes up to tell me that he has just heard that all these Germans were brought here as it is thought likely the French will make a sortie from Maubeuge and shell Bavay, in which case the hospital would be burnt. Of course, we were both indignant that they should put their sick in safety while leaving ours in danger. It is decided that Reginald shall go in the doctor's motor out to the mill where the General is, and ask for all wounded, of whatsoever nation they are, to be brought here. We express our indignation in no measured terms, and the officers agree to allow Reginald to go to interview the General on condition that his eyes are bandaged. The driver of the doctor's car is so terrified that he declines to start until we give him a Red Cross flag to put in the front of the car. All the men here seem convinced that Turcos are among the garrison of Maubeuge, and talk of it continually.

"Reginald found the General at the old mill, around which trenches were being hastily dug. The whole detachment are evidently in great apprehension. The General, after hearing Reginald's request, explained that, according to information they had just received, Maubeuge would be unable to hold out any longer, and that everything indicates that the garrison must try to make their escape through the besieging army in the direction of Lille and Calais. He pointed out smoke in the distance to my brother, saying, 'Maubeuge is burning, and the French troops will have to abandon it.' However, permission was given for the Allied soldiers to be brought from Bavay here, but in the meantime Dr. Jacquemart has telephoned that they are not transportable." (We discovered afterwards that the Red Cross authorities in Bavay, who knew nothing about the state of affairs at Maubeuge, imagined this to be a German manœuvre to get all the wounded into their hands.) "While these negotiations are going on by telephone between Bavay Hospital and ourselves, German officers come forward and back, giving orders in the most excited way, and prepare their men for instant flight if necessary. Several have asked me if we will be responsible for their sick and wounded, assuring me that one of their officers was found yesterday mutilated by the French outside Maubeuge. We naturally protested against such a mischievous calumny, and give them our assurance that their wounded are perfectly safe here."

September 8.—That evening the white flag was put up at Maubeuge, and almost at once all the valid troops left us, except for the telephone operators, who worked all night in the office downstairs. On the morning of Tuesday, the 8th, more sick arrived, but as we had no doctor, and the state of Lieutenant von Hartmann was very grave, we sent to Bavay to ask Dr. Jacquemart to come. He sent back word that his motor-car had been requisitioned, that he hoped to have it returned shortly and would then come at once. Some time later the doctor and Madame Williot came and helped to dress these terrible wounds, out of which scraps of the skull and cellular tissue were working.

"While attending to this I was called downstairs to an officer who had been sent by the General to present his adieux and thanks, and to ask for a picture post card of the place". Later in the war, an old and honoured friend of ours, the Countess de Spangen, was placed in the same situation. This Belgian lady, who was 90 years of age, had also lodged a General and Staff, and before leaving her château in Flanders, the General had asked to be allowed to present his adieux and thanks. Leaving her room and speaking from the landing to the officers in the hall below, the valiant old lady said, 'Gentlemen, it is not necessary to thank me, for I had not invited you,' whereupon she returned to her room. The General's delegate told me they had made 40,000 prisoners at Maubeuge. Later in the day we heard from refugees that the number was greatly exaggerated and that they were mostly Territorials, also that they had burnt all cars, petrol, and anything that could be of use to the Germans before surrendering Maubeuge, and had given out quantities of stores to be divided amongst the townspeople.

I turn to my notebook again. "There is, of course, the usual talk of treachery; it is even said that one of the French Generals met and drank with German officers every night during the siege. This is only one of the wild stories going about. Some of our neighbours are even being accused of crimes against their country, and people seem unable to distinguish truth from fiction and are ready to believe any nonsense. However, one thing is certain, that a considerable number of the garrison escaped before Maubeuge surrendered, several cars even getting away yesterday by Jeumont. One of our Bellignies men, Oscar Descamps, had his two legs blown off by a shell, and we hear that another, Segers, was killed. Dr. Jacquemart came to-day to visit all our sick and wounded, and was highly indignant at the fall of Maubeuge. He has become very popular with the Germans; the men tell me they much prefer to be treated by him than by their German doctor. Of course he can't order them back to their regiments, which may partly account for this preference.

"During the day we had a visit from Monsieur le Curé, who brought the Dean of Bavay with him to announce the nomination of a new Pope, Benedict XV. I tried to tell this news to Lieutenant von Hartmann, who seems to understand, but finds his words with difficulty. He always says 'Danke' politely for everything we do for him, and 'Gott sei Dank' when his wounds have been dressed. The orderly tells us that the army that was here is off by forced marches to Antwerp. This makes us anxious for Leopold, who was in garrison there when we last heard of him. All the wounded who are sufficiently well to be moved have been sent on to Mons, both English and Germans thanking us profusely and promising to send us photos later on. Only seven Germans and three Englishmen are left, and the house feels almost empty.

"Lieutenant Thörl came down to-day for the first time. He is still extremely weak after his severe illness, but shows eagerness to regain strength and return to his military duties. He says that he is one of seventeen brothers and cousins in the field. I suggested his coming up to see von Hartmann, but he told me that he cannot bear to look at wounds. Most soldiers seem the same in this respect. When I told our German wounded how kind the English officers were towards their men, they answered that it was not the same with theirs. They all fear, and some even hate, their own officers.

"The house feels quite different without some of the enemy in every hole and corner, and in the whole village the atmosphere seems to have cleared. People come in continually to complain of the loss and destruction in their homes. Deburge (the farmer at our gate) has received a broken old waggon in return for the new one borrowed from him. Bassez has had more than ten thousand francs' worth of goods taken from his farm. Everywhere crops, cattle, and material have been requisitioned, and a scrap of paper given in exchange, which the

Germans call a *Zettel*, on which are scribbled a few words no one can understand. Some of these papers have been brought in to me for translation. On one of them was written, 'There are pretty women in this village', on another, 'Get your English friends to pay you'."

Wednesday, September 9.—"Reginald went to Bavay this morning to try and persuade the authorities there to send a telegram to Lieutenant von Hartmann's parents, as he is anxious that they should know of his whereabouts. The orderly, who is also ill in bed and quite useless to his master, tells us that the father is a 'Regierungs-Präsident'. Having given the telegram to some officers who promised to send it off, Reginald went in to the hospital, where he found a great number of French wounded who have been brought in from Louvroil, where the hospital was destroyed by shell-fire. He heard much gossip at the hospital, and the usual wild rumours about the concrete gun positions that are supposed to have been prepared for the use of the enemy, and of the people who are said to have given them money to have their homes spared. In the meantime people are puzzled at seeing the regiments which had started for Antwerp returning again and going southward. Evidently something unexpected has happened, as the enemy appear anxious and perplexed. While Reggie was away Laurentiaux's daughter came in here to tell me about the siege of Maubeuge and of the burial of the young Prince of Saxe-Meiningen, who was only nineteen. I took Lieutenant Thörl around to see all the wounded, and then he lunched with Granny, Monsieur le Curé, and myself."

September 10.—"A car came from Maubeuge to-day bringing two doctors, a French and a German one, the latter wishing to go through the lists of our wounded and examine those who are left. While they were occupied, I had a conversation with the French driver of the car, who, although he wore a very shabby *poilu's* uniform, told me he was a priest (*le bleu horizon* had only just, I believe, been invented and certainly never been seen at that time in our region; all the soldiers still wore the red trousers of pre-war days). I must own that Monsieur l'Abbé's sentiments smacked very much of the Church militant, and his spirits were not in the least affected by his being a prisoner, so this whispered conversation cheered me greatly. They have taken Lieutenant Thörl away with them. He seemed almost sorry to leave us, thanked us profusely and promised to try and send news to our aunt in Switzerland from his home in Germany, where he is going to spend his convalescence. The car had scarcely gone when another came bringing a German surgeon with a brain specialist to examine Lieutenant von Hartmann. After a long consultation they came to tell me that they were going to arrange to have him transported to a German surgeon's house in Mons. I objected that our doctor thought it would be fatal to move him, and that we had sent for his parents, so after a further discussion they agreed to leave him a few days longer in our hands, which we realise is a great responsibility; if he dies we shall undoubtedly be accused of not having taken proper care of him, or even worse."

September 12.—"Lieutenant von Hartmann is distinctly better; he called Vicky on to his bed to-day and fondled the little dog and talked quite normally. He asked Reginald as a favour to play the piano, which he willingly did, and we left the door of the room open on to the gallery surrounding the hall in which is the piano. While Reginald played some Chopin and Schumann, we sat in the twilight listening until I heard the piano being roughly shut and wondered why he had stopped so suddenly. He told me later that it was because two or three of the soldiers, who had been listening from the next room, came in, and thanking him gratefully, asked him to play 'Deutschland Über Alles', not realising the tactlessness of this request. It is the first time the piano has been opened since war was declared; the roar of the cannon has been the only music we have heard; during the siege of Maubeuge it was so loud and incessant that one could not hear oneself speak. However, one gets used to anything, and we only noticed it when the great silence fell after Maubeuge put up the white flag. When the noise and confusion was at its worst, I missed my grandmother and found her at last in the cellar in the midst of a group of women and children. These had taken refuge from their little houses under our massive vaults, but whenever a shell whistled or exploded in the neighbourhood the poor folks cried out in terror. Calm and unmoved, my grandmother quieted them with a gesture of her hand, and soon I left them, the women saying the Rosary and the children sleeping round her feet."

September 13.—"Late last evening while we were dining, and during pouring rain, a mysterious car arrived driven by a civilian and bringing two officers and an orderly whose uniform bore no sort of mark. The officers entered the dining-room through the conservatory, and asked for dinner and a night's lodging, also for news of the officers we have been nursing, whom they imagined to be both still in the house. I took them up to see von Hartmann, but he showed no interest whatever in them, and it is evident that it is not on his account that they have come. The chauffeur told the servants that they have come from Liège to-day, but mentioned no names. From the extreme deference one showed to the other we supposed him to be an important personage.

"When we got up in the morning, we found that last night's visitors had disappeared as mysteriously as they came.

"We have had a visit from Mademoiselle de Montfort (our kind neighbour who was the head of the Red Cross in Bavay). She brought with her Simone du Sartel, who has returned after spending some time at Le Quesnoy, where she had gone during the English retreat with a transport of wounded. She described the hurried march from Bavay to Le

Quesnoy, where artillery and infantry were mixed up, and the fleeing population impeded the march, while 'planes overhead gave battle. When they arrived at the station she had been entrusted by the English with the organisation of the last hospital train to leave there, which was fired on as it left. Then, with their wounded and the town authorities, they took refuge in the hospital, on which three shells fell." But whereas Le Quesnoy was a very strong place in the days when Charles the Bold lived there, and had been fortified later by Vauban, who surrounded it with three rows of ditches and bastions, it could not be defended at the present day, although the armoured casemates were most useful in protecting the wounded and the inhabitants from artillery fire.

"Simone told me that her mother had left for Blois on the 24th of August, the last day on which civilians could travel. Of course her two brothers, Jean and Gaëtan, are in the Army (her two sisters were nuns), and on Simone therefore falls the whole care of their property. She has hidden most of the valuables at Potelles (their old moated château, which had sustained many a siege since its erection in the thirteenth century) and has given herself up now to the care of the wounded. Her decision, common sense, and energy will be of great use to Mademoiselle de Montfort, who is looking far from strong."

After the fall of Maubeuge the whole countryside was overrun with refugees, many soldiers having escaped in civilian clothing and returning to their homes. Some of the stories they told were both thrilling and very amusing, but one had to be careful, as undoubtedly there were spies among them. A night or two after Maubeuge surrendered, when our house was still crowded with von Kühne's Staff, a small boy came in to say that the servant who had been left in charge of the Joseliers' house was ill, and wished to speak to Reginald. Monsieur Joselier was the owner of one of the marble works in our village, and was on the Staff driving his own car as automobilist at Maubeuge. His family fled on the approach of the enemy, Madame Joselier sending me her favourite dog, a very fine borzoi, which she implored me to care for. I had the poor beast shut up, and tried when I had a moment free to console it, but it refused to eat and, being released by a German soldier, returned to its home, where it died of grief a few days later.

While the Staff went to dinner, Reginald followed the boy messenger, and to his great surprise found Monsieur Joselier himself hiding in his house, accompanied by his friend Monsieur Gouverneur, Director of the Pelgrims' Works. He heard from Monsieur Joselier that 200 French artillerymen had escaped just before Maubeuge capitulated, hoping to reach Calais or Dunkirk. By this time we had got a fair idea of where the German troops lay, and Reginald was able to advise Monsieur Joselier as to the best route to take. We heard later that he reached Dunkirk safely, having passed between the German lines, and found there the artillerymen with their commandant. About this time also, one day Reginald met two unwounded English R.A.M.C. officers in Bavay Hospital, who had managed so far to escape detection, and had found their way into the hospital to ask for a meal and for information. Knowing that the safest direction for them to take was that of Lille, from whence they could get to the sea coast, he explained with the aid of a motoring map a short cut through lanes to Sebourg, a village in the region of Valenciennes, where there was a château belonging to the Baron de la Grange. Reginald gave a word of introduction to Baron Louis, who lived with his father, and who we were sure would consent to give the refugees a day's lodging, as of course they must travel by night. Some time later when Monsieur de la Grange came over to see us he told us that his lodge-keeper had seen at daybreak one morning two English officers reading the German notice posted up at his gates. This notice threatened with death any inhabitants who should give shelter to French or Allied troops, and the Englishmen, having read it, turned away and disappeared, doubtless not wishing to put anyone in danger. Baron de la Grange was distressed as to what could have been their fate.

Louis de la Grange came over on foot a few days after the fall of Maubeuge to ask Reginald to go with him to see the town. They got into it without much difficulty, visited the hospital there, where some English Red Cross ladies, I believe from Mons ambulance, had paid a call the day before and caused enormous excitement, the Germans believing the French Red Cross to have connived at their *fugue*. The adventurous Englishwomen returned to Mons, and were sent, I believe, later on to England via Sweden or Denmark. Louis de la Grange and Reginald came back fearfully depressed by the sight of the enormous amount of booty, guns, and ammunition that had been collected by the Germans ready for transport. Both Maubeuge and the villages around it were filled with wounded, and eighty more men were brought to Bavay Hospital in a terrible condition from neglect.

Another day Monsieur de la Grange came with Reginald to meet me at Bavay Hospital, where I had done a night's watch, as the few soldiers we had left at home were out of danger, and all the Red Cross ladies were getting worn out with over-work. They asked me to go on with them to see the villages of Vieu-Mesnil and Hargnies, which we heard had been burned by the Germans during the siege. It was a terrible sight to see these peaceful little villages in which hardly a house was left intact. We called on the Curé of Vieu-Mesnil, who told us how it had happened. Daily some French soldiers had arrived from Maubeuge, as a sort of outpost in the village. One day a sergeant with three men, instead of stopping at the top of the hill outside, came in to take a glass of beer at an *estaminet* (small inn). While they were drinking the sergeant went upstairs and looked through an attic window, whence he saw a whole company of German soldiers headed by two officers entering the village street down below. He hastened alone along the backs of the houses to where an old tree commanded the road, and from behind the trunk he fired directly the Germans came in sight. He killed one officer and wounded the second, after which all the men beat a hasty retreat, but only to return shortly in force to the village, from which by this time the four Frenchmen had retired. Removing their dead and wounded officers, and still fearing a surprise, the Germans began firing in every direction at anything they saw moving, chiefly women and children, of course. One young woman, who had been keeping her own baby and three of her neighbours' children while they worked in the fields, was shot down in her own house and left for dead among the crying babies. The soldiers then set the village on fire—after which they retired.

It was only some hours later that Madame Caillaux was found and removed to hospital at Hautmont, where she lay on straw among French and German soldiers for forty-eight hours. Her sister then obtained permission to bring her to her home near us, where I promised to go daily to dress her dreadful wounds. Five inches of her femur had been shot away, and the wound was badly infected. I had to chloroform her every time I dressed it. Now and then the doctor got leave to come, but more often

I had only an old woman who lived next door and the village harness-maker, a gentle old man, to help lift the poor, suffering creature. Luckily one of the German doctors had given me a provision of antiseptic dressings which I found very preferable in such a case to the merely sterilised dressings that I had had from the Red Cross, but for weeks I smelt of iodoform, so the family told me.

September 14.—On the 14th of September, we had a surprise visit from Prince Saxe-Meiningen, who came to ask after Lieutenant Thörl. He told us that he had lost his father as well as his brother since war began, and that all the members of the Staff with whom he had been here at first had been wounded during a terrible battle that had taken place near Chauny. Three of the officers of the Staff had been killed, he himself had been slightly wounded, and they had lost many thousand men. This was the first we heard of the battle of the Marne, as it was called later on, and the news cheered us considerably. The young Prince was now on his way to Brussels, where he had been appointed to serve under General von der Goltz. He told us that the Germans had found dum-dum bullets on English soldiers, but that he had not seen them. This was a story we were often to hear at this time, and which they evidently believed. I retorted by showing the instrument a German soldier had left behind in the village, and which he had explained was for cutting off the point of their bullets, causing them to expand. Another of my arguments was that their wounded got well at once, while ours did not. Before the Prince left, we took him to see von Hartmann, but he could hardly understand what the latter, whose head was still bandaged, said. Before leaving he promised to do all he could for us in the way of messages. Among other items of news we heard that the *Kaiser Wilhelm der Grosse* had been blown up by the English in a neutral port, and that "the Germans are convinced that after this war is over France will be ruled by an emperor again. They do not say, however, who the emperor is to be."

Next morning two German ambulances arrived and took away von Hartmann and all the other wounded who were fit to be removed, all thanking us gratefully on departure. The doctor who came with them said that Prince Georg was still in Maubeuge, but that his brother's body had already been removed to Germany. Louis de la Grange arrived again one day on a bicycle, having come by quiet lanes, and brought a smuggled French newspaper which gave details of the victory of the Marne, and also of a Russian victory in Austria. While lunching he told us how he had been taken as a hostage on August 25th and kept from 6 A.M. till 2 P.M. and made to march in front of the troops who occupied the village, and threatened that he would be held responsible in his person in case of any attack on the troops. This must have worried his old father very much, and another source of agitation had been the destruction of their beautiful terraces and well-kept garden, which were overrun by the horses. However, he told us that this was the only damage done to the place so far. Old Baron de la Grange was eighty-eight at this time and a remarkable old gentleman. He was the father-in-law of the Baroness Ernest de la Grange of la Motte au Bois, who is so well known as the "mother of the British Army".

One day Reginald and I went over to Sebourg and Monsieur de la Grange told us how, when the German Commandant had said that by the 15th of September they would be in Paris, he had raised his hand towards heaven and answered, "Si Dieu le veut, Messieurs".

Lille had been occupied for two days by the enemy, but their detachment was not strong enough to hold the town, and it had been retaken by the French. But neither on the French nor on the German side was the surveillance very good, as the following incident will show. Our postmaster, Monsieur Moret, having walked the fifty miles to Lille and managed to pass through the lines both going and coming, brought us back, as a pleasant surprise, a large packet of letters which he had found accumulated there. On his way home he had taken from his daughter's house in Valenciennes a child's perambulator, in which he put his packet of letters and French newspapers, and walked the fourteen miles back to Bavay pushing this in front of him. Naturally so many letters for the neighbourhood, as well as the French papers describing the battle of the Marne, gave unbounded joy to the population.

The German authorities happily never knew of this journey, but one day Monsieur Moret's post office was invaded by soldiers who accused him of having corresponded by a secret telephone with the garrison of Maubeuge during the siege. They made him go down with them into the cellar, where they knocked at the walls and dug holes to find this buried wire, which never existed except in their imagination. Not finding it, they notwithstanding kept him prisoner, and a day or two later he was brought, among others, to Bellignies, and though we were not allowed to approach the prisoners, they were given the food sent out to them, after having fasted for two days. At the same time the Curé of Taisnières-sur-Hon had been arrested, for no known reason, and we saw him standing for some hours in the courtyard surrounded by soldiers. At last I sent out a maid to ask if he would not like some breakfast. With an irritated look around him he answered, "J'en ai déjeuné et soupé aussi". (The equivalent of "I am fed up enough already".) The prisoners were taken away and shut up until, in the excitement which followed the surrendering of Maubeuge, their guards left them, on which they all jumped out of the window and returned to their homes. This incident showed us that the Germans thought that evidently some means had existed of informing the Commander and garrison of the fortress of what was happening in the vicinity, and undoubtedly if France had expected and prepared for war these wires would have existed.

Having once succeeded in getting in and out of Lille, Monsieur Moret could not rest until he tried again, and so he started off on the following Sunday, loaded with letters and telegrams to send off from Lille. However, this time he only got as far as Valenciennes, where he meant to spend the night, and was within a few yards of his daughter's house and safety when he was surrounded by soldiers and dragged to a neighbouring guard-house, where his clothes were removed and, of course, the packet of letters and telegrams seized upon. The next day he was judged by a court-martial which sat at the Hôtel de Ville at Valenciennes. His trial took place in German, questions and answers being translated, and at the end of it he was told that he would be shot. He asked to be allowed to write to his family, but this was refused and he was thrown into a prison cell and left another day without food. But on the third morning the cell door was opened and the Governor of the town, Major von Kingler, announced to him, "You, Postmaster, have been condemned to death by the court-martial, but I exercise my right to commute your sentence, as you bore neither arms nor military intelligence. In consequence of your disobedience to our laws, you will go to Germany until the end of the war." It was only nearly a year later and after falling very ill that Monsieur Moret was released from his prison at Rastadt and sent to Switzerland.

On the day before his arrest, Abbé Delbecque, the Curé of Maing, near Valenciennes, had been arrested also for carrying letters. Having been to Dunkirk on his bicycle, he had brought back all those he found addressed to his parishioners. Among them were letters of mobilisation and a note of instructions from the Governor for the reservists. These caused the Curé to be condemned to death; his trial took place in the station waiting-room and he was shot at once and buried along the high road, where his feet were seen sticking up through the earth. The notices announcing this execution were posted in all public places, and one was shown to M. Moret on his way to trial.

(From my diary.) "We hear from the Bellevilles that the convent at Audregnies, which has been turned into a field hospital, is still crowded with English wounded, and Marie, Jeanne, and their nephew Eric are kept busy nursing there all day. It seems that the Germans forbade the villagers to leave their homes or the village for several days after the battle, and so the wounded lay untended and many died who could have been saved. The chaplain of the convent with his niece crept out at night against all orders, and found some of the wounded lying in the beetroot fields; one poor fellow had had both legs shot off and died as soon as they brought him in. I believe the chaplain got him on to his back and crawled most of the way home on all fours in the darkness. Marie and Jeanne had met an English soldier not far from their house while sharp fighting was still going on. He had lost most of the buttons off his uniform and made signs that he wanted a needle and thread. While one of them fetched these and began sewing on a button to the man's trousers, the other brought out a cup of tea for him, when around the corner suddenly appeared some Germans, who fired straight at them. The Englishman fled in one direction, while Marie, Jeanne, and the tea-pot retired hastily into the house. They had not realised at all that a modern battle is not like those one sees in pictures, and that they had been in the midst of it. They worked at the hospital for several weeks, even carrying the poor soldiers on to the operating table themselves. Their nephew (a boy of seventeen at that time) was of great use as he is able to speak English."

September 17.—"We had a visit from Eugénie (a former maid who lived near Mons) and she told us of the battle at Hyon-Ciply. She said the noise of the shells whistling overhead made a sort of weird music, and that many men had been killed round M. Bourlard de St. Symphorien's château. She had herself fetched in from the field an English major whose leg was shattered, and said that the same shell had taken off his horse's nose and his orderly's head! She told us also that M. Gendebien's house was completely wrecked. It had been full of English wounded when it caught fire during the battle, and the whole family helped to get the men out and were unable, therefore, to save any of their own valuables. For three days the dead lay about in the fields until the population obtained leave to bury them, which they did where they lay.

"All motor-cars and bicycles have been ordered to be surrendered and naturally everybody tries to hide theirs. The doctor took his motor out to the forest, put it in a ditch and covered it over with brambles and sods. Also an order has gone out that anybody found keeping carrier pigeons will be shot, and as there are hundreds in the country and many of them of much value, these also are being hidden, but at great risk. When we can get hold of a clandestine newspaper (of course there are no others, and anyone found with one of these can be imprisoned at once), Reginald takes it down to the village council, and has it passed on to those whose discretion can be counted upon."

September 20.—"Reginald and I went to lunch at Sebourg, and took coffee upstairs afterwards with old Baron de la Grange, who is quite wonderful for his eighty-eight years, and was keenly interested in all we told him. On the way there, we passed by the Château d'Eth, where the caretaker showed us the damage and destruction done to his master's house. Cupboards that had been left locked were smashed open by hatchets, the marble tops of the furniture in the dining-room had been broken into small pieces, and all the contents had disappeared. Clothes taken out of the wardrobes had been evidently worn; a favourite evening's amusement with the German troops seems to be dressing up as women and dancing. In Madame de Beaugrenier's room, laid out on the bed, was a tiny French uniform, which, I suppose, belonged to the child she lost in babyhood. I promised the conçierge to try and send over Simone du Sartel (the Beaugreniers' niece) who will put in safety whatever valuables have not been carried away, but I took myself a small pocket Kodak I found lying in a corner, as in any case it would be confiscated if found. I can give it back to them one day. (This camera was produced as evidence against me at the court-martial.) On the way back we passed through Roisin. Although Monsieur and Madame de la Saudée have fled to Biarritz with the children, the place has been turned into an ambulance, and the servants who have remained behind seem to be keeping very good order. (We heard afterwards that the faithful cook had buried even her household stores, and brought them out triumphantly when her masters returned in 1919.)

"Among the letters smuggled from Lille was one from Madame Desjardins (wife of the Deputy of the Aisne) enclosing one from her sister, the Marquise de Chambray. The latter is frantic with anxiety about her husband, who was last heard of some weeks ago in our neighbourhood. She begs me, if I can find him and he is wounded, to see that everything is done that is possible for him. Alas! how can I find him if he really is near here? Reginald and Monsieur de la Grange have made rounds in all directions, and collected all available information about both dead and wounded, either

French or English. Reginald has got long lists of English names, which he will try and forward by some means later on; the French lists are naturally handed over to the Red Cross. Continually we hear rumbling in the distance, and evidently fighting is going on in several directions. Daily troops are passing and new orders of all sorts are posted up in the villages. Some Germans who passed here in plain clothes boasted that they were deserting."

September 29.—"About a thousand Bavarians, mostly oldish men, have arrived, and are quartered in the school-house. One man's rifle exploded while he was cleaning it and his arm was badly hurt. Reggie was fetched to dress the wound, and said the poor fellow lying on the floor was so fat that he looked like a barrel from which blood and groans were oozing. This company say they have been on the march for a fortnight, but as yet have seen no fighting. They had heard that Paris had fallen a fortnight ago, and evidently believed it.

"While we were out in the courtyard preparing our last batch of wounded for leaving us, a big transport passed on the high road, composed of long waggons covered with white awnings on which was a red cross and accompanied by ambulance men. I noticed that the horses seemed to be drawing a heavy load, and I counted the waggons as they passed by the gates. After having counted over a hundred, I said to the officer who stood near me, 'What a big transport! Is it all Red Cross?' Turning quickly and looking up at the gate he said in rather a confused way, 'Yes, all Red Cross.' But one of the soldiers whom we had nursed, and who had told me he was a Socialist from Bremen, whispered while passing between the officer and myself, 'Artillerie'.

"The other day when we were walking around the lawn after lunch with Monsieur de la Grange, who often comes over now, two girls who were standing near the gate came and asked to speak to Reginald. After a few minutes' conversation he called me up and told me that they were from St. Waast (the village two miles away). One was Mademoiselle Moriamé, the brewer's sister (he is fighting), and the other is her neighbour, Mademoiselle Louise Thuliez, a schoolmistress from Lille, who was spending her holidays with relations in the village when war broke out. These two had come over to ask us what they shall do with several English soldiers whom they nursed for slight wounds in August, and have kept hidden in Mademoiselle Moriamé's house ever since. Notices are posted up everywhere ordering all inhabitants to declare at once any French or Allied soldiers who have remained behind the lines. The penalty for disobedience is death. These young girls seem to have rendered good service during the passage of the British troops, making and baking bread, as the village baker has gone to the army, and otherwise helping to feed and billet the men. As we still hope to see our victorious armies come driving the enemy back within a few weeks, we told them the chief thing to do was to keep these soldiers quiet, and give out in the village (if any one knew of their presence) that they have run away, and in the meantime Reginald promised to find a safe hiding-place for them."

A few miles distant from us is the great forest of Mormal: 30,000 acres of magnificent wood in which were occasional keepers' houses and woodmen's cottages. We thought that the soldiers would be perfectly safe for the moment in one of these, if the owner would harbour them on our promising to pay for their food. Taking Dr. Jacquemart into his confidence, Reggie visited with him some of these cottagers on the Obies territory, and they agreed to take in the six or seven men between them. The girls guided them out one night, and bit by bit other stragglers were found and added to the little troop. Although all concerned had promised to keep the strictest secrecy, somehow it got about that we were ready to take charge of any stray soldiers, and in consequence every now and then we were informed of the hiding-place of one or more, or they were even brought straight to us by the peasants who had taken them in. Reginald went out at regular intervals to pay the expenses of our refugees, and warn them to be careful; but the comparative quiet of the country at this time, and the hospitality of the peasants, who all wanted to receive the Englishmen at their table, made them often very imprudent.

Mesdemoiselles Thuliez and Moriamé still continued to take the keenest interest in their little band, visiting them and doing washing and mending for them; and the two girls began also to make long walking tours in the district to look for more stray men. They got into touch with some responsible person in every village: more often it was the Curé, but sometimes the Mayor or a manufacturer. This was such good training for them that very soon they thought nothing of undertaking a twenty-mile walk. Reginald also, who had never appeared to care much for walking exercise, developed extraordinary powers in this way, and beat the country along the Belgian frontier, to collect information about the missing and the fallen. As many of these were buried in fields or along the roadside, often a helmet laid on the grave being the only intimation that a soldier was buried there, it was urgent that all details that could be acquired should be collected at once. Soon the lists grew very long. Where possible he reclaimed the pay-books or identity discs from those who had buried the men, and some of the souvenirs taken from the corpses were very touching. A few letters, a photo, sometimes a prayer-book or a rosary, must have been very precious to the family to whom they were forwarded later.

At Bavay too the hospital was full of both French and English. Whenever we had a spare moment Reggie and I used to go in to act as interpreters, hear the news, and cheer up the soldiers by giving any good tidings we were able. The hospital became a sort of centre where all the town authorities met daily. The head of the College, the Chanoine Lebrun, knew a little classical English. Besides himself, we used to meet the Mayor, Monsieur Dérome, the notary M. Tréca, and many others who used to come in daily and help Mademoiselle de Montfort and the other ladies of the Red Cross. On our first visit we had been astonished and sorry to recognise Captain Preston, the officer who had passed at Bellignies early during the retreat, and whom Reginald had taken on to Bavay when we heard that the Germans were coming. He told us that on the morning after his arrival at the hospital there had been a sudden alarm, and that the whole R.A.M.C. had left hurriedly, taking away in their ambulances all the men who were sufficiently well to get up. But he, Captain Preston, together with Lieutenants Marston and Moore, had been forgotten and left behind, and so had been made prisoners. However, Preston confided to Reginald that he would soon be able to use his leg again, and that he meant to escape. Reggie at once offered him to come and hide at Bellignies until he felt quite strong; by then we hoped to know of the safest route by which he could travel.

So far the lines were not established uninterruptedly between the Swiss frontier and the North Sea, as they were later on, and one imagined that with a little luck they could get through into free territory. Lille was still in French hands, as far as we knew. So Preston settled with Reggie that he would arrive on the Friday night, but, of course, neither of them said a word to any one at the hospital about the projected escape. Therefore on that Friday night Reggie and I waited up, keeping the gates unlocked and walking up and down the road in the direction of Bavay. When at last towards daybreak Preston had not arrived, we got very anxious, fearing he had been taken. Reginald made his usual visit to Bavay next morning, and on going the round of the sick beds at last came to Preston's, who told him he had given up his plan of escape on learning that the Red Cross authorities had just been made responsible by the Germans for the wounded, all of whose names and regiments had been noted down.

October 7.—About a week or so later, a little after two one morning, I was awakened by hearing gravel thrown at my window, and on opening it very gently I heard the gardener begging me to come down at once. Hastily putting on a wrap and calling my brother, I went down to hear that an English officer was up at the lodge. He had just arrived, and had managed to awaken the gardener and had begged him to call us. Without making any light or noise we went up to the lodge, where we found Captain Preston looking dreadfully pale and exhausted, and being cared for by the gardener's wife, Juliette. He told us that two days previously Bavay hospital had been taken over by a German guard, who posted a watch at each door. Once every hour they entered the wards and counted the beds, and seeing that now the French Red Cross could no longer be considered responsible, Preston determined to carry out his previous plan of escape. He wrapped up his coat and put it in his bed with a cap on the pillow, so that in the dim light it looked as if a man lay there, then he let himself out of the window into the Chanoine's garden over which one side of the College looks. I believe he had questioned the good Canon about the topography of this garden, and its relation to the Bellignies road, and he found a chicken-run placed handy against the wall, by the aid of which he climbed on to the ramparts. But even then he had to creep on his stockinged feet between the sentries who guarded the entrance to the town. It was so dark that he feared to walk into one of the men, and it took him more than an hour, creeping a few inches at a time, to get on to our road. In his wounded state the two-mile walk to our gates was a great ordeal, and he had much difficulty in waking the gardener to get let in without causing an alarm.

We held a little council of war while he was resting and taking some coffee, and agreed that it would be unsafe to keep him here that night, as the Germans were sure to suspect all those who were in the habit of visiting the hospital. The safest place we could think of was the de Wittes' home, the Château de Gussignies, off the high road, surrounded by woods, and deserted by all but its owner and one man-servant. Reginald and the gardener César started off, supporting Captain Preston, so as to get to Gussignies before daylight. While Preston and César hid in the wood below the château, Reginald managed to waken René de Witte and explained the situation to him. He at once came down and guided them to an old quarry, much overgrown, in the wood, where between them they prepared a bed for Preston, and René promised to bring him food regularly. Preston spent the first few days there, going into the château sometimes at night to eat a warm meal, and at last when the hue and cry died down, they brought him back to us, and he stayed here until we were able to arrange for his escape through Belgium and Holland, which was not until the last day of the year. We still had in the house two English soldiers whom the Germans had allowed us to keep until such time as the fever left them. The temperature of one of them went up every time a German doctor visited him, and it was thanks to this that he was not taken away sooner. He had served in Africa and was subject to bad fits of malaria, and the slightest nervous tension brought one on.

As soon as we got Preston back in the house it became urgent to find a safe hiding-place for him, and Reginald had a brilliant idea. The old tower, around which the house has been built at various periods, dates from the Middle Ages, or even, according to tradition, from Roman times, and its walls are three yards thick. Some years previously we had discovered a disused staircase in the wall, the entrance to which started from a window embrasure on the ground floor, and it had been walled

PRINCESS MARIE DE CROŸ
standing before the window of the old tower containing the hidden staircase used as a hiding-place by British and Allied soldiers.

up above. Our two Englishmen were handy with tools, and under my brother's direction turned the entrance to the staircase into an apparent cupboard, the panelling at the back of which was easily removed. Two shelves on which bottles and glasses were kept, made it look like a very innocent medicine cupboard. On the slightest alarm Preston could retire inside the panelling, which he pulled into place after him, and hide on the stairs until we let him know that danger was over. This old end of the house was rarely used, and the ground-floor tower room, which had been a hospital, still contained several beds, so Captain Preston lived in it, keeping the wooden shutters closed and being always ready to dart into the *cachette*.

We had not dared to go to Bavay at first after his escape, but we heard that there had been a tremendous uproar there. Among other extraordinary stories that flew about, one was that of how an English *milord* had bribed the German sentries to help him to escape. As a matter of fact, two sentries really disappeared that night, and we supposed that they had bolted in their fear of being made responsible for the escape of a prisoner. We were very careful not to let anyone at Bavay know about the presence of Preston here. It was safer too, but hard not to be able to calm the anxiety all felt about him.

Mesdemoiselles Thuliez and Moriamé, whom for safety in my diary I always wrote down as Girl Guides, or G.G. for short, frequently came to report on what they had heard on their rounds. One day they said that they had come across a large group of French and English soldiers hidden in the vicinity of Englefontaine, a village in the middle of the forest, and that there was an officer among them. Reginald had left just before this, having been solicited by the Mayors of our Arrondissement to try and obtain flour, etc., from the American Committee in Brussels, as foodstuffs were getting very short. He was given a permit for Brussels, where he negotiated the food question, and then managed to obtain a pass for Holland, in the hope of hearing news of Leopold there. Some time previously a badly printed clandestine news-sheet had reached us from Belgium giving information about the fighting around Liège and Antwerp, and in the lists of the fallen was our brother's name. Although we felt the news was not at all reliable, we were extremely worried, and Reginald decided to try to get to Holland or even further, if possible, so as to put our minds at ease. The excuse he gave for this journey was one which the Germans generally accepted at this early stage: the need to procure money. All local banks were closed, and in Brussels only very small sums could be obtained, nobody paid any rents, and our agent had fled in August before the invading army with his whole family. Money was required, not only for daily expenses, but for the innumerable fines the enemy imposed. And our refugee soldiers had to be lodged and fed too.

On arriving in Holland, Reginald immediately

wrote to Mr. and Mrs. Preston telling them in guarded language that their son was safe, but giving few details and begging them to keep the matter secret. Then he left for England with the Albert de Lignes (Prince Albert de Ligne was Counsellor at the Belgian Legation at The Hague), and went on with them to Havre, where the Belgian Government had taken refuge at Sainte-Adresse. On arriving at La Panne, he found the Guides, Leopold's regiment, resting after going through the horrors of the battle around Dixmude, where the dykes had been opened and the land flooded, arresting the advance of the enemy, but drowning all the unfortunate men and animals that lay wounded there. The news of Reggie's arrival from occupied Belgium, and of his intention to return to it, spread like wild-fire, and from all sides he received messages, from people both known and unknown to him, asking his help to find missing dear ones. The wives and mothers of Englishmen unheard-of since Mons besought him to try and find them. Refugees from our neighbourhood, and soldiers in the French and Belgian Armies, gave him messages for those at home, and knowing the impossibility of remembering all these, or of bringing the letters back with him, with the aid of friends he condensed the contents of each and made out long lists, which he entrusted to a regular military secret agent with a promise of a reward if these lists were handed to him in Brussels. Of course, from the moment he said good-bye, we knew nothing of him, for even had there still been a post, it would have been impossible to communicate with anyone outside occupied territory.

Reginald spent twenty-four hours in London on his return journey and looked out the Prestons in the telephone-book. Having called them up, he found that his letter, which had been held up by the censors, had only reached them that morning, nine days after he had posted it at The Hague. They were naturally so anxious for news of their son that they insisted on coming to town from Ealing to hear the whole story. They told Reginald their son had been promoted to the rank of Captain at the moment of his disappearance. He himself knew nothing about it.

Meanwhile, here at Bellignies, on talking over with Preston the news the girls had brought in, I saw he was very eager to get into touch with the officer in the forest, as well as to learn the numbers and regiments of the men hidden with him. He seemed to hope it might be possible, if their group were sufficiently numerous, for them to fight their way through in the direction of Lille, where we had heard both French and English troops still were. So it was decided that I should go myself to the forest. We had an old mare, who occasionally did light work in the garden and whose age had spared her from being taken for the army. I had her harnessed to a dog-cart, and not daring to take a man-servant with me, I asked Mademoiselle Carpentier, whom I have already mentioned, to go, as she knew all the side roads, and had proved her courage in the matter of the two cavalrymen. I filled the cart with all available stores and several English books, and dressing very simply, started off for the forest. But carriages of any sort had not been seen for so long that the dog-cart attracted attention, so Mademoiselle Carpentier proposed to ask a countryman whose cottage we passed to put up the horse and cart in his grange, and lend us his little donkey. He accepted, and we started off once more with an unkempt animal dragging a dirty little carriage with much-mended harness. However, even in this we should have been stopped, had I not thought of addressing the patrol we met in German, and asking the way to the "Kommandantur". Pleased at hearing German spoken, they directed us willingly, and we continued along the Chaussée Brunehaut until we were out of sight, when we plunged into the forest.

At last after several hours' slow going we reached the village of Englefontaine, one long rambling street surrounded by woods. I knew that the Chanoine Flament, the right hand of the Archbishop of Cambrai, lived here, as he had often been to see me about social work, and happily his house was the first we reached. Stopping the donkey before his little gate, I knocked, and was very suspiciously received by the housekeeper, but the Canon came himself to the door and recognised me, notwithstanding my peasant's disguise. He took me in and let me explain the object of my visit. He said that until a few days previously he had frequently visited the English troop in their hut, and had carried them food, but they had been driven farther off by an arrival of Germans, who were quartered in the village. He thought that a Paris Government schoolmistress, whose home was there, still knew of the whereabouts of the Englishmen. He offered to send a message by his housekeeper, begging her to meet me in the orchard behind his house, saying that as she was not a Catholic she might prefer not to come in.

Shortly afterwards the old housekeeper returned and made signs for me to go out, where under an apple tree I saw a tall, young girl waiting. I said to her, "Mademoiselle, I know you are a good patriot and have been helping Allied soldiers. I have been doing the same and wish to consult with those in the forest. Will you take me to them?" She answered, "I cannot, I promised my father not to go out any more. He told me he would not risk my being shot." I said, "Go and ask your father to give you back your word for once. When you have shown me the way you need never go again." She hesitated a little, got pale, then red, and said quickly, "I will break my word to my father and go with you now, and tell him afterwards." I could have kissed her in my relief, and we started at once, taking baskets and bags with the provisions on our arms, and leaving the poor donkey to rest, we struck into the forest on foot.

After walking some way we met German officers

out pheasant-shooting, and we felt very nervous in case they should ask what we were doing, and search us. But I am sure my two companions were not nearly as nervous as I was, because, unknown to them, I had hidden about me letters from Captain Preston and other Englishmen which the doctor had entrusted to me, as well as a quantity of cartridges. However, the sportsmen let us go by, evidently taking us for a forester's family returning from marketing. In a sector where the undergrowth was very high, our guide struck into a track that was scarcely visible between the trees, and after winding in and out among them for some time she touched a piece of twine twisted between the branches, and a tiny bell, like that of a dog's collar, tinkled some way off. Seeing something move between the trees, I called out gently, "It's a friend," in English, and a Tommy stepped out and said, "Stay where you are, please." After a little parley, he agreed to go and ask his officer's leave for us to advance. When he returned, we followed him through more thicket, where a second string gave warning of approach, into a clearing where a curious sight met our eyes. At one end of this was a sabotmaker's hut, in the doorway of which stood an English officer, clean and smart as if he had just come off parade. Near him were two men of a certain age, sergeants, and around in groups were many French and English soldiers, the former still wearing the red trousers of the old uniform.

My two companions stopped to talk to the

Frenchmen, while I advanced to Lieutenant Bushell, Second Dragoon Guards or Queen's Bays, as he told me. I gave him Preston's letter and asked if I could do anything to help. His first words were "Get us arms. We have only a few rifles and rounds of ammunition between us; get us arms to defend ourselves with." I promised to do what was possible, and handed him the fifty or more rifle cartridges which I had brought hidden in my dress. He told me how he had been cut off from his regiment while carrying a message, and had lain for three days and nights on a railway embankment, hidden among nettles, while the German army marched by on either side. Then he had crept down to a cottage, whose owner hid him for several days. From there, hoping to fall in with some of his own troops, he had wandered into the forest, where bit by bit other stray men had grouped themselves around him. On several occasions they had nearly been surprised by the enemy and had to run for their lives. He said that, a few days before, a woman wearing spectacles had been to see them, and although as far as he could understand, not knowing French, she professed to be a friend, some had doubts that she was a spy in the pay of the Germans. I imagined that this was very probably Mademoiselle Thuliez, and found later that my surmise was correct.

They had just finished making a dug-out which would contain the whole troop, and whose entrance was cleverly hidden by brambles. The Lieutenant showed me where it was, and no one would have suspected that this was the entrance to a hole where fifty men could take refuge if necessary. A double row of sentries, as we had seen, made them as safe as possible in the circumstances. They tried to keep excellent discipline, not allowing the men to leave the wood, or do any shooting, trusting to the generosity of the few natives who knew where they were for their food. But some of the men had made friends in the village, and now and then one disobeyed orders and risked the safety of all by going out at night to visit them. That day they had tried one of these delinquents who had returned the worse for drink, and had even discussed the necessity of shooting him. However, the sentence had been commuted to a day's punishment, the man standing tied to a tree without any food for twenty-four hours. It was wonderful to see the prestige this young officer had acquired, and the respect with which he was treated by all. There were among the British troops men from the 11th Hussars, the Manchester Regiment, the Royal Artillery, Argyll and Sutherland Highlanders, Gordon Highlanders, Scots Greys, Munster Fusiliers, Connaught Rangers, Royal Irish Rifles, King's Own Scottish Borderers, etc. I stayed talking some time and then returned to the Chanoine Flament's house, where I parted from and thanked our brave young guide. After arranging to have provisions left daily in a spot on which we had agreed with the officer, and whence he could have them fetched at night, we started for home, fearing to be caught on the road after nightfall. No one was allowed to be out after 7 P.M., but it was much later when at last I arrived and found my grandmother and Captain Preston extremely anxious on my account.

Within a few days of this a young country girl came and asked to speak to me in the courtyard. She was so mysterious in her manner and evidently so terrified, that at first I took her to be wrong in her head. It seemed to confirm my suspicion when she began to undo her hair, but she took a note from between the coils and I saw it was in English. She told me at the same time that she and her father, who was a keeper, had found a group of English soldiers in the forest and were helping to hide them. The officer had given her this note, saying something about an English officer and Bellignies. She had come to Bellignies, but not knowing who to apply to, had gone to the Mayor's house. Our Mayor at this time was a simple old countryman, who, once the enemy came, was much too frightened to be of use in the village. He had been very thankful when Reginald and our Curé had helped with the billeting, requisitioning, and all other troublesome duties war brings. So when Rosa came in and asked him where the English officer was hidden, the poor Mayor, who knew nothing about it, took her for a spy and turned her roughly out of the house. Tired and frightened, she did not know where to turn, when in passing the gates she saw me and was inspired to apply to me. I did not tell her, of course, where Preston was, but I said I knew someone who might be able to carry the note to him. Rosa also spoke of a mysterious spectacled lady who was enquiring about soldiers hidden in the forest, and said she and her father had no doubt she was a German spy, and it had been discussed whether it would not be better to shoot her quietly. I was able to put her mind at ease, while shuddering at the danger Mademoiselle Thuliez had run.

The Girl Guides, duly informed, set off at once, and finding the men, or what was left of them, as after a raid that the Germans made some had got lost, led them to a part where the undergrowth was very thick, in the vicinity of Obies. Here the first little group joined them, having also been driven by the enemy out of the cottages where they were lodged, and the whole party lived for some time in roughly-made shelters, while Mesdemoiselles Thuliez and Moriamé came forward and back, carrying food and looking after them generally with admirable devotion. I managed on several occasions to send Amand out to the wood with a cart of provisions covered over with faggots, or straw. At this time Amand had been over twenty years in our service, and we had never known him to say an unnecessary word. While waiting on the Germans he did his strict duty, but still eyed them with such visible disfavour that some of them remarked to me how much he hated them. He never put his watch to German time, and this required some calculation when they gave orders for meals, etc., because firstly, the hour of Central Europe was in advance of French time, and secondly, the Germans adopted summer time before it was known in our country, and therefore they were two hours in advance of French legal time. However, Amand's stolid disposition and taciturn countenance allowed him to pass unmolested on his dangerous errand.

The gardener, Dubuisson, too, had been several years in our service, and we knew him to be trustworthy, besides being far too frightened to say a word that could put anyone in danger. We impressed frequently upon the whole household that if discovered everyone would be shot together.

But our poor men in the forest were getting more and more harried, the Germans making regular beats and posting sentries where the green drives which separated the squares of the forest at regular intervals intersected, even bringing police dogs to help them track down the men. At last, one night, in despair, the Girl Guides brought the thirty remaining men with Lieutenant Bushell to Bellignies. The poor young officer was absolutely worn out and suffering from violent neuralgia, so we put him to bed in the tower room where Captain Preston was, but left all the men in the attic of the gardener's house, which, being hidden among bushes near the gate, had so far never been visited by the Germans. Of course they had arrived in the middle of the night, and the gardener's wife, Juliette, looked after the poor fellows in the most maternal way, making soup and coffee for them, the latter beverage being a panacea for all ills in our country.

November 12.—The information that kept arriving got more and more frightening: we heard of German patrols getting closer, and some had been seen examining the footmarks in the road where our men had passed. The English army boot had an iron horseshoe on the heel, easily recognisable by its imprint, and our poor gardener had to go along the road with a rake to obliterate the footprints leading in our direction. But evidently it was only a matter of time before they would be discovered, and on hearing this, Captain Preston said that he considered it to be his duty to order the men to be given up as prisoners of war to the Germans if there were any means of doing so without putting either them or anyone else in danger.

A little before this we had had one day a visit from Monsieur Delame, a manufacturer of Valenciennes, and a member of the Chamber of Commerce in that town. Mademoiselle Thuliez had got into touch with him through the brave young son of a butcher, who, not having been found strong enough to join the army, had given himself up to any and every patriotic work at home. Monsieur Delame had been entrusted with the revictualling of Valenciennes by the German authorities, and for this he had been allowed to retain his motor-car and given passes for the different roads. He had brought us meat and other provisions for our soldiers. He had a long discussion with Captain Preston, and also agreed that if shortly no means were found of getting the men away safely we must try to surrender them through a Red Cross hospital. He on his side promised to make every enquiry, while the two girls started off on a last desperate round to try and find some way in which the men could pass to safety. They walked thirty miles in the direction of Hirson, where rumour had said French troops to be, but they found the canal closely guarded at every bridge. They even discussed the possibility of creeping up in the dark, followed by some of the soldiers, and overcoming the German sentries, who were to be gagged and thrown into the canal. But this plan seemed to hold very few chances of success, and was given up.

In the meantime, food being strictly rationed, I had great difficulty in feeding my troop. Vegetables we had in the garden, and Monsieur Delame had brought us meat, but bread had to be got. Our baker and his help had been in the army from the first, and the work had been carried on by his sister, Maria Sohier, with two young boys of seventeen, who acted as *mitrons* (baker's men). They were obliged to provide great numbers of loaves daily for the German army, after which they were allowed to bake for the village, but flour was rationed, besides which no one in the village must know of the presence of thirty men here. However, I knew Mademoiselle Sohier, and had never appealed to her in vain. So I went to see her and said, looking intently into her face, "Mademoiselle, I want fifteen loaves daily that no one is to know of. Can you provide them?" She reflected a moment and then said, "Could you have them fetched at night?" I answered "Yes", and she said, "They will be ready at eleven o'clock every night." A small side gate opens from the grounds just opposite the bakery, there is only the road to cross, and nightly the loaves were fetched in by this way. The flour, I believe, was purloined from that set aside for the German troops, who thus had the honour of feeding their enemies.

When at last the girls returned again after their fruitless quest, we were obliged to agree with sad hearts to Captain Preston's decision. That evening, in the twilight, he went up to confer with the men. They were lying in the attic of the gardener's cottage, and the scene was lit up under the slanting roof by two or three night-lights only. Captain Preston explained the situation in low tones to the two sergeants, telling them that although at great risk to ourselves we could hide their officer, it was impossible that so many men could remain much longer without detection, in which case both they and all of us were liable to be shot. They agreed not to tell Lieutenant Bushell because of his weak state, and while Captain Preston, leaving the sergeants to talk the matter over with the men, all of whom had not heard his words, returned to the house, I also went up to the cottage. It was a touching scene which I shall never forget. At first they would not hear of giving themselves up, saying that it was against their duty as soldiers. I told them it was the only way to save their lives, adding, "You are many of you married men; think of your wives and families". They answered, "Our families know that we are soldiers and must do our duty". Then, as a last resource, I said, "Think of the countrypeople who have been risking their lives for you. Think of us all, for if you are caught we shall be shot, and the village probably burned to the ground, whereas if we take you to a Red Cross hospital from whence you are given up, no one need know where you come from, and you will be treated as prisoners of war".

I left them then and found later that they had accepted to be given up on condition that we guaranteed to make every effort towards sending their officer out of the country. But even then we had to delay until some of the men who had lost their uniforms while hiding in the forest could be fitted out again, as anyone found in civilian clothing was liable to be shot as a spy. A man from the next village, named Loutre, had frequently helped me to obtain food on the quiet, and I knew that he thought nothing of finding his way about the country at all hours of the day and night and was always ready for an adventure. I therefore applied to him to collect any British uniforms that could be found in the neighbourhood. During the retreat from Mons the men had thrown away their heavy khaki overcoats, and although the Germans had ordered these to be given up, many were still hidden in the cottages. Loutre procured several of them and brought a bundle in at night, and Mademoiselle Thuliez had the bright idea of cutting breeches for the men out of some of them. So the two girls, with the help of my maid and the Curé's housekeeper Louise, went to work, cutting and sewing, and by the next evening all the men were fitted out. Long strips of cloth made puttees, and with the overcoat on top, they looked quite a respectable troop, although I dare say not quite orthodox.

Just as all were ready and we were collecting enough five-franc pieces to give each a little money before leaving, Monsieur Delame arrived from Valenciennes, accompanied by Madame Tavernier. This lady was in business in Paris, but had been staying with her daughter at Valenciennes when war broke out, and, knowing both German and English, had been able to render good service, especially to the ambulances, for which she had made several excursions, at great risk, to Lille, and even to Dunkirk, to obtain serum which was badly needed. She had visited our little troop several times in the forest when they were being hunted from one spot to another, and carried them warm wraps and blankets which were most useful when they were forced to abandon both hut and dug-out. When I told her of the decision that had been taken about the men, she combated it at first, but on hearing the latest report from the neighbourhood, both she and Monsieur Delame agreed that we must obey orders. She accompanied me up to the cottage, where we gave out paper and pencils to the men, that they might all write to their families, and we promised to forward their letters as soon as it should be possible to find a way of smuggling them through. Madame Tavernier had a warm heart and a generous disposition, and while talking to the poor fellows for whom she had done so much she wept, and added all the contents of her pocket to the little store of money I had given them.

At midnight once more our two brave girls started out with the little troop, one going ahead in case they should meet German sentries, the other in the rear with the men, whom she could guide to safety in case her companion were challenged. Creeping through lanes and along hedges in the dark November night, they managed to get into the town in safety. While they waited in a quiet corner near the hospital, Mademoiselle Thuliez went and roused the Mayor, and told him that a group of English soldiers were waiting in the town to be given up through the French Red Cross to the German authorities. Monsieur Dérome's first impulse was to say, "No, we cannot give them up, I will take in some and get other townspeople to hide the rest." But on hearing all that Mademoiselle Thuliez knew of the situation, he at last gave in, and came and led the men into the hospital, where they were given beds until the morning.

At daybreak, poor Monsieur Dérome went himself to the Commandant, and told him that a group of Englishmen had arrived from no one knew where during the night, and that he came to give them up, according to the orders published by the German authorities. At once, there was tremendous excitement; the German officer questioned all the Englishmen, insisting on knowing whence they came and who had been helping them. Everyone remarked that they were far too clean and well fed to have been living for three months in the forest as they pretended, but not one of the men gave us away, and the Germans, unable to obtain any information, seized upon the Mayor, Monsieur Dérome, whom they sent as a prisoner to St. Quentin, where he was told he would be shot. Next day, the Conseiller Général, Monsieur Lescut, and the Mayor of Houdain, came to beg us to intercede on M. Dérome's behalf with the German authorities, not realizing that we were the last people in the world who ought to draw attention to ourselves just then. We were dreadfully distressed on the poor Mayor's account, but felt, nevertheless, that nothing could be proved against him and that he would certainly deny all knowledge of the affair. We heard later that after being treated with the greatest rigour for several days he had suddenly been brought before an officer and spoken to with deference. It seems that the Chanoine Lebrun, convinced that the Mayor could not escape from death, had offered to be shot in his place. This courageous and generous offer had made a great impression on the enemy, and shortly M. Dérome was allowed to go free.

We were much relieved to learn that the soldiers had been correctly treated at Bavay and forwarded to a prisoners' camp in Germany, but we still had the two officers hidden, and it became urgent to find some means of getting them out of the country. Every now and then dreadful stories were brought to us about soldiers who had been discovered and shot after a pretence of a trial, as well as the people who had harboured them. In Lille, several inhabitants were shot at the Citadel for having hidden an English aviator. In Fourmies, four French soldiers, of whom one was a coloured man, a Senegalese, were denounced by a traitor, and all four shot. And at Hiron, eleven Englishmen, together with the miller who had hidden them, were all condemned and executed.

November 1914.—Towards the end of November, shortly after the departure of our little troop, of which he heard with great regret, Reginald returned home, bringing us good news of Leopold. In Brussels he had duly received the long list of the missing, and the extracts from letters for our neighbourhood, which he had entrusted to the army messenger. One of his unknown English correspondents begged him to find her husband whom she had last heard of as wounded and being nursed in an English hospital in Brussels. On enquiry, Reginald learned that no English ambulances were left, but that there was an English matron at the head of Dr. Depage's clinic. However, he did not meet Miss Cavell until later.

A few days after his return we had a visit from Jeanne de Belleville[1] with her nephew Eric, who had managed to get here through fields and lanes without being discovered. Although those who lived in central Belgium were allowed to move about more or less freely, provided they had an identity card with the German official stamp, we who lived across the frontier and in the "Etappen" were not allowed to leave the village without a special pass which was extremely difficult to obtain. Eric was nearly eighteen and was determined to go and enlist in the French Army, and his aunt told us she was starting the next day for Brussels in the hope of finding some way of getting him out of the country. All those who up to now had been helping soldiers to escape told them that it was getting more and more difficult, and refused to help in any way. Directly after the battle of Mons, quantities of British soldiers had been found hidden in the miners' cottages, after having been cut off from their regiments during the hurried retreat. A group of patriots, among whom were Monsieur Capiau, an engineer, Monsieur Libiez, a lawyer, Monsieur Dervau, and others, had helped them. At first, the miners contented themselves with giving a suit of their own clothes to the Tommies, who lived like one of the family. It is the habit of the coal miners to sit after their work on the ground outside their houses and smoke their pipes, and the Tommies did

---

[1] Comtesse Jeanne de Belleville, a French lady living just over the Belgian frontier.

likewise, blackening their faces, wearing sabots, and smoking too; they seemed thoroughly to enjoy the joke, winking at each other across the road while the German troops marched by. But after a time, this got too dangerous. There was always the risk of being betrayed, besides which, food got scarce and bread especially was rationed. It was then that the group of patriots stepped in and organised the departure of these men, first towards Dunkirk, the lines not yet being strongly guarded, and afterwards to Brussels, from whence they were conveyed to Holland. Among others, an English Major had been rescued and taken to Brussels to the Institute of which Nurse Cavell was the head. She had harboured her compatriots willingly and found guides for them. At first the Dutch frontier was only guarded at intervals by sentries, many of whom could be bribed to shut their eyes when necessary.

On hearing all this from Jeanne de Belleville, Preston and Bushell got very excited and begged her, as soon as she discovered a means of escape, to return here and inform them, so that they too might get away. She spent several days in fruitless search in Brussels until at last she met the Abbé de Longueville, a priest who had given himself up to patriotic work. The latter offered at once to take Eric with him on one of his secret passages of the Dutch frontier, and shortly afterwards they escaped safely. When Mademoiselle de Belleville came to tell us this good news, our two officers were delighted, but they still had to wait, as it always took some time for a guide to get back again after leaving the country, and it was not until well on in December that we had news of the Abbé de Longueville's return. In the meanwhile, as Germans came frequently back and forward on various errands, our two officers spent their days quietly in the shuttered tower, only coming out at night after the gates were locked, to dine with us if all were quiet. Young Bushell had been dreadfully distressed after hearing of the surrender of his men, to whom he had grown much attached. It brought on a nervous breakdown, and he needed careful nursing, while showing a resentment which we easily forgave. The day after their departure, I had handed him the letter that they had left for him. I have a copy of what can still be deciphered after having been buried with other compromising documents for four years. The confidence and affection they expressed towards their officer do honour to the British Army.

One Sunday afternoon, a day on which we were rarely disturbed by the enemy, while Preston took tea in the hall with us, and for once our vigilance was at fault, we got a great fright. Suddenly we heard the front door open, and Preston had only just time to hide behind the screen which was at the back of my grandmother's chair, when in came Monsieur de la Grange; it might just as easily have been a German. He had brought over some news, which he had heard at Anzin, of which mines he was one of the directors, and began talking eagerly as soon as he came in. During a lull in the conversation, he was much surprised at hearing a voice coming from behind the screen: "May I come out?" and Captain Preston, who had gathered that it was a friend, got up from his corner on the floor. Baron de la Grange spoke good English, and from now on, although he evidently thought we were playing with fire, every time he visited us he went down to the tower and chatted with our refugees.

On another occasion, on seeing a motor stop in front of the gate, I had just put the two Englishmen in the *cachette* and arranged the shelves as usual, when the local Commandant, Freiherr von Mehring, got out at the door, and told me he was interested in archæology and would like to visit our tower. Without showing an instant's hesitation, I took him to the passage which leads from the drawing-room through the massive wall into the tower. He stopped to remark on the thickness of this wall, leaning his back against it, and, measuring it with his arms outspread, enquired the supposed age and history of the building. I was very uncomfortable, as the two officers were within a yard of him overhead, and an incautious movement on their part might have betrayed them. So I broke my rule of never inviting a German to sit at table with us, and asked him to come and take a cup of tea. Whether this unusual civility on my part destroyed any suspicions he may have had, or whether his visit was really due to interest in archæology as he said, he left the dangerous spot and came and sat in the hall and chatted quite amiably. He told us his wife was a relation of the old Princess de Sayn-Wittgenstein, Ludmilla, whom we had known, and who died aged 105 at her home at Ouchy in 1918. She retained her mental powers until the end, and being allied to people in most countries of Europe, was able to intervene in favour of many war prisoners, of whom I became one later on.

We heard afterwards, through other Germans, that von Mehring had been separated for many years from his wife, but he did not mention this to us, and offered to send any news we might wish to forward to our friends, through relations of his in Switzerland. We thanked him, but did not avail ourselves of his offer. He made several visits after this, bringing with him in the car a fine German wolf-hound, which, however, looked very fierce and used to pursue our peacock and the latter's faithful companion, a tame crane called "Cleopatra", who generally disported themselves on the lawn. Later, after I had been taken away from Bellignies, a dog killed poor Cleopatra, but I do not know if it was this one, or one belonging to another Commandant.

December 1914.—At last, a few days after Christmas, we were able to send our two officers off on their way to Brussels. We dressed them like well-to-do artisans, taking care that none of their clothes bore any mark by which they could be traced if arrested. The first stage of the journey was as far as Montignies, where the Bellevilles offered them hospitality.

During the first phase of the war, when the house had been full of wounded, I had asked for extra help to clean the wards, and a woman called Charlotte Matha offered her services. She was from Paris but had been spending a few days' holiday with relations in the village when war cut her off from returning; her husband, a Territorial, was among the garrison of Maubeuge. Being without means of existence for herself and her two children, she was glad to earn a little money, especially as we allowed her to bring her son and daughter to live in the house too. Charlotte was a good patriot, and was both energetic and discreet, and therefore we accepted her offer to guide, with Mademoiselle Thuliez, Captain Preston and Lieutenant Bushell to Montignies. Reginald went directly to Mons, where he hoped to obtain false identity papers for them. He knew an official at the Bureau de la Population who remained in the office during meal hours, when the German Superintendent left, and during this interval he managed to obtain the forms and stamps used for the passes.

The two officers duly arrived in Mons, convoyed by Mademoiselle Thuliez and Charlotte. Reginald had given them rendezvous in the Church of Ste. Waudru, and as it was too early to take the tram, he invited the whole party to a small and quiet restaurant to have lunch. While they were at table, to their dismay in came two German officers who sat down near them. The conversation became very strained, the Englishmen only daring to say an occasional "Oui", for fear their accent should give them away. When Bushell went to wash his hands in the adjoining toilet-room, one of the Germans followed him and wiped his hands on the same runner-towel as the Englishman, who by this time was extremely nervous! But they got at last safely into the tram, where they were provided with some of those newspapers, censored by the enemy, which no patriotic Belgian cared to read. The passes were duly examined at Enghien, where all passengers were made to get out of the tram, which was then searched, but no suspicion was aroused. In Brussels, Preston and Bushell were lodged in an empty flat belonging to Madame Henderyck de Theulegoët, a cousin of the Bellevilles, who had taken refuge in England. During the few days that they were obliged to spend there, while new false papers were being procured for the further route, they were cared for by Madame Nélis-Calmon, a French lady married to a Belgian (already a prisoner), and by Dr. Bull, an English dentist, who had lived for many years in Belgium, and who rendered great services during the occupation, collecting and transmitting information useful to the Allies. When at last he was arrested, it was thanks to his prudence and that of his housekeeper, Madame Van Horenbeke, who had destroyed all incriminating documents, that he got off with a term of imprisonment, instead of sharing Miss Cavell's fate. Early in the new year, we learned that our two officers had reached Holland safely, but, of course, we could not follow their further progress. However, we have since heard that they were conveyed to the War Office, where an enthusiastic reception was given them. They passed the frontier in the region of Antwerp, dressed as carpenters and carrying tools, and at danger spots they measured stacks of wood, etc. . . . The Abbé de Longueville, shortly after this, was obliged to fly for his life, a price being placed on his head.

Early in the new year the German authorities took away the last of the Allied soldiers from Bavay Hospital, and at the same time fetched the two who had been so long forgotten at Bellignies. We had to deliver these when called upon to do so, and the Germans agreed on this condition to leave them with us until quite cured; the two men, Tom Hogg, R.A.M.C., and George Goodier, Scots Guards, helped to look after other refugees, and could many a time have escaped with them, but, having given our parole, we were obliged to surrender them. They were sent to Germany, but returned safely to England after the Armistice.

Having succeeded so well with the officers, we were all anxious to find any more soldiers left behind the lines, so as to send them away too. Therefore, Reginald, Jeanne de Belleville, Mesdemoiselles Thuliez and Moriamé all began touring the neighbourhood in different directions, bringing in men to rest a few days in the house, before starting on their further journey. At first, Reginald took them on himself to Brussels, where Nurse Cavell, among other people, hid them in her hospital in the disguise of invalids. Reginald had got into touch with Miss Cavell some time before this, when with Jeanne de Belleville he had hunted the Borinage for an English Colonel. At last they traced with much difficulty the officer's whereabouts to a chemist's house at Dour, only to find he had left for Brussels the previous day. On his next visit to Brussels, Reginald heard from Miss Cavell that Colonel Bodgers had left for Holland on the preceding day with guides she had provided. She offered to lodge any men we should send to her on their way to Holland, and arranged a code with Reginald by which she could recognise our refugees. These were to announce themselves as coming from Mr. "Yorc" (our name reversed). But ours was not the only organisation collecting, and it soon became necessary to find other safe lodgings in the town. The lodging-house keepers not only accepted their dangerous mission willingly, but charged merely for the bare keep of the men. It was consoling to see the spirit of patriotic generosity in the nation. We noticed also a chivalrous sentiment among the French country people, which made them especially anxious to help the British first, knowing the latter to run greater risks than their compatriots through their ignorance of the language.

Although Reginald had to give up conducting the men himself, because on two or three occasions he had been recognised and remarked upon, he went continually forward and back to Brussels to consult with the various confederates, and to see that the men kept quiet in their lodgings. Miss Cavell complained to him that many of the Tommies, finding themselves in a town where life appeared to go on normally, did not realise that by going out they put both themselves and her in danger. The sight of several men leaving and entering her house could not fail to draw attention, especially as an English soldier has a very characteristic walk.

Jeanne de Belleville also frequently convoyed men to Brussels, taking them first to safe houses in Mons, and sitting opposite to them in the tram, without, however, appearing to be acquainted with them. Two of the first she convoyed were her cousin, Edward d'Hendecourt, and our neighbour, René de Witte. Here is Baron de Witte's story, told by himself:

Having been dispensed from military service and unable to enlist, after having passed eight months in occupied territory, I left my home at Gussignies, which was separated from Belgian territory by trenches and barbed wire, on May the 6th, 1915.

I start at 3 o'clock on foot for Mons, provided with a false identity card by Princesse Marie de Croÿ. I am now Monsieur Albert Masson, commercial traveller; my photograph is stuck on the card, which bears the stamp of an imaginary official of a small Belgian village, and is signed "Jean Fontaine, commissaire de police".

Under the guidance of Mlle. de Belleville, and accompanied by her cousin, Edward d'Hendecourt, become for the present "Monsieur Bonjean, wine merchant", we reach Brussels. Through the intermediary of Princesse Marie de Croÿ, Miss Cavell has promised to find us guides to the Dutch frontier.

I visit Miss Cavell at her clinic. She receives me coldly at first, very reserved and sure of herself. She is tall and slight, wears her blue nurse's dress, her grey hair gathered under the white cap; her big eyes show sympathy and intelligence. She signs to me to take a chair, and seating herself before me, her arms crossed on her breast, looks at me intently, as if to read my thoughts.

Learning who I am and whence I come, Miss Edith Cavell speaks out. "I am very anxious," she says. "My guides have not yet returned. Can anything have happened to the men? No, no, God forbid," she adds. "Have patience, dear sir, the passages are difficult."

After hiding a few days in a friend's house, we start, six English soldiers, Edward d'Hendecourt and myself, for Antwerp. Our guides precede us in a small carriage, we follow them in a van. The danger spot will be Malines, a town full of spies and strongly guarded. After Brussels our identity cards are useless. Disguised as workmen we leave the van about a mile from Malines, and singly, at a distance from each other, enter the town on foot. Twice I am stopped, twice, thank God, I am able to get free.

That evening we sleep at Vieu-Dieu, and next day reach Cappellen on foot. This evening we shall try to reach Holland, from which we are only separated by five kilometres (3 miles). But our attempt fails lamentably, and we return in haste to Cappellen, having lost our guide, and pass the night cowering under a wall, in pouring rain, and exposed to the danger of being seen by a passing patrol.

The following night, at 10 o'clock, in Indian file, we go in silence through a pine wood of which parts are cut down, and pass near an ancient fortress. Crouching in high grasses, we listen, while near by officers give orders, patrols pass, we crawl, climb through barbed wire en-

entanglements, and crawl again, while twice a searchlight passes over us.

About one o'clock, close to the sentries, we pass through the last barbed wire entanglements which separate Belgium from the Dutch village of Mollenputten. We are saved. Customs men give us hot coffee. We take train to The Hague, to get passports.

In Paris I parted from d'Hendecourt. A few months later near Verdun, I heard he had fallen fighting.

Mademoiselle Thuliez also, when not otherwise engaged, took them to Brussels to their lodgings, and each and all informed Miss Cavell of the arrival of the men, whose subsequent movements she directed. Her guide conveyed the men to Holland, which country they attained in various ways, mostly by creeping at night between the sentries and over the barriers erected along the frontier. When electrified wires replaced these barriers, it only added difficulty and danger to the last step before attaining safety. The first guide, a man named Gilles, got arrested at last, but another, to whom the same name was given, replaced him. At least one of these guides was shot, but others were always found ready to take their place. They made themselves known to the men they were to convoy by passwords which were frequently changed.

Monsieur Capiau, who became our most precious auxiliary, had managed to get some cards printed which were an exact counterpart of the German identity card, and the chemist Derveau of Mons had also procured a stamp, which, though bearing every appearance of being an official one, was engraved "Commune de St. Jean, Hainaut". There is no such commune in Hainaut, of course, but nobody found this out, and the soldiers carrying these passes got safely to Brussels and even as far as that zone, near the Dutch frontier, beyond which it was only possible to travel in the dark, and at the risk of being shot at. Photographing the men and filling in their identity cards became my business. I had a camera of my own, but it required plates, and these could no longer be obtained. However, I found an old box of very large plates, and with the aid of a glazier's diamond cut these into small pieces. I also managed to procure a few films for the little Kodak I had rescued from the Château d'Eth. As it was necessary to photograph the men by daylight, careful watch must be kept while they came out of their hiding-place, as well as while I developed the plates and films. The photos once ready and stuck on the cards, these had to be filled in, an *état civil* (legal status) to be invented, and names which they could pronounce found for the Englishmen. The French kept their own names, but were given a supposed domicile in Belgium. A few of these passes fell into German hands later and were brought forward as evidence against me. The police paid me the compliment of saying they were very good forgeries.

Our life at this time was a very busy and strenuous one. Reginald went forward and back to Brussels, while the Girl Guides continually brought in soldiers, among whom were a number of Frenchmen who had been cut off during the retreat from Charleroi. They would arrive every few days, generally towards morning, often having done an eighteen-mile walk during the night, sometimes Frenchmen, sometimes Englishmen, or sometimes both together. Many came from the district around Maroilles, where Monsieur Maillard, of that place, and his daughter, had concealed them. A group of Englishmen had been hidden in a dug-out in a small wood, and having only been able to creep from their hiding-place by night, looked very miserable after living so long in the dark and damp. There was also the sergeant, Robert Penniket, of the 1st Loyal North Lancashire Regiment, who with a comrade had been cut off in August, and had been hidden by the Legrand family ever since. He told us how since their arrival the Legrands had had to defend them from both friends and enemies. Timid inhabitants fearing reprisals were they discovered had adjured Madame Legrand to send the Englishmen away, and frequent visits from Germans had forced them to take refuge in strange places, sometimes for hours at a time behind clothes in a press, sometimes for days together in a duck-hut near the river, where old Madame Legrand brought them food by night. Only after much persuasion could Mademoiselle Thuliez allay their suspicions, and fetch the men away.

Generally the men were left in a tool-hut in the paddock across the road, while Mademoiselle Thuliez came down to where I was waiting among the bushes near the gate for her signal. Before the Girl Guides left on an expedition, we discussed routes and distances with the aid of some excellent German maps, as well as the phase of the moon, another enemy of ours at this time, so that I had a general idea of when the next arrival could be expected. We had strips of carpet ready in the hut to bind up the men's feet so that they should neither be heard nor leave the tracks of their boots on the soil, on their way in. When, after a long wait in the darkness, during which the dropping of the dew or the cracking of a twig made one jump, I heard the rattle along the railing announcing Mademoiselle Thuliez's presence, I would go with her to the paddock to question the men in English before bringing them down to the house. This was a necessary precaution, as sometimes the country people mistook German deserters for Englishmen, and one was once brought to us. Luckily for us he was a genuine deserter and never betrayed us, but pocketed the five francs I gave him and went on his way.

The immediate neighbourhood having been cleared so far as we knew, the girls then went farther afield, to the region of Cambrai, which is thirty-five miles from us. This necessitated a two nights' march, and they were given a day's rest *en route* by patriots, who ran a great risk in thus harbouring people without permits, who could not avow their occupation if arrested. Indeed, passes were almost impossible to be obtained. A woman in our village, having heard that her daughter, who lived two miles away, was dying, asked for a pass to go and see her, but it was refused. Reginald also, who was getting anxious about our forest property situated at Solre-le-Château, twenty miles away, asked for a permit to go and visit the woods, alleging that our agent and some of the keepers had fled since the beginning of hostilities. But the Commandant who lived at Le Quesnoy (one of the lesser worries of this time was the constant change of Commandants, each of whom altered all the regulations of his predecessor) answered that it was impossible to accord it, with the usual pretext, "C'est la guerre". Of course, Reggie went without a pass and found the head keeper, Legat, at his post, hard put to it to prevent pillaging. He discovered that several French soldiers were hidden in small farms near the woods, and gave them addresses and passwords for our associates in Brussels, who sent them through to Holland. The real reason for the refusal of a passport was that Solre was in a different "Kommandantur", and the Commandants seemed always to be adversaries of each other. Generally speaking, the German military authorities despised the civil, and one General suspected the other and put obstacles in his way, so we were often able to play our enemies off against one another.

Legat told Reginald that he knew of some German deserters, supposed to be a father with his last surviving son, who were hidden in the woods; but although he avoided going near them himself he believed some pitying peasants carried them food. While at Solre, Reginald managed with great difficulty to get as far as Trélon, where he found the château belonging to Count Herman de Mérode occupied by a German Staff. He also went to the Château de Beaurieux, whose owner, the Comte de Robeaux (who was fighting, of course), had sent us letters for his wife.

On Reggie's return he was again entrusted by the local French authorities with various petitions and messages for the Commission for Relief in Belgium. He carried these to Brussels, where the Committee sat, and also to the American Embassy, as several concerned breaches of the rules of war. Of course, it was useless to complain of abuses; the most arbitrary orders were published, and had to be obeyed on pain of dire punishment, the innocent often paying for the guilty. Long proclamations were posted continually on our courtyard doors, the chief point in these being always the necessity for declaring at once any mobilisable Frenchmen or Allied soldiers.[1]

---

[1] The following is the actual text of one of these proclamations.

ORDRE DU COMMANDANT SCABELL
Gouverneur d'Aulnoye

Par la présente, j'ordonne aux Maires et représentants des communes dépendant de la commandanture des Étapes d'Aulnoye-Berlaimont (inclus le canton de Berlaimont) de faire connaître immédiatement aux habitants.

Les Maires de toutes les communes dépendant de la commandanture des Étapes d'Aulnoye-Berlaimont doivent y remettre pour le 3 Novembre à midi (heure allemande) une liste de tous les habitants mâles de leurs communes classés comme suit.

Anyone found harbouring these was liable to be shot, but those who helped them to escape out of occupied territory were to be hanged. Nevertheless,

---

Valides—Invalides, appartenant aux autres pays en guerre avec l'Allemagne, déserteurs ou évadés.

Pour tous les endroits du ressort de la commandanture d'Aulnoye-Berlaimont, les habitants et les arrivants doivent se présenter de suite à la Mairie (X).

Chaque habitant qui quitte un endroit doit demander un laisser-passer à l'autorité militaire avec indication du but et du motif.

Les représentants des communes sont responsables au prix de leur vie et de leur commune avec tous leurs biens du manquement à la liste exigée d'un seul habitant et d'un seul arrivant.

La commandanture se rendra compte de la stricte exécution de l'ordre ci-dessus en ordonnant inopinément un rassemblement général.

Tout qui ne se rendra pas à la Mairie comme il est dit plus haut (X) ou toute personne sans laisser-passer sera immédiatement fusillée comme espion.

A partir de Huit heures du soir (heure allemande) aucun civil ne peut plus circuler dans les rues.

Il est interdit aux civils de circuler en automobile ou en vélo.

Tous les vélos et tous les autos doivent être remis à la commandanture pour le 3 Novembre à midi (heure allemande).

Celui qui sera pris à circuler en vélo ou en auto sera fusillé comme espion.

Les représentants des communes doivent remettre à la commandanture pour le 3 Novembre à midi (heure allemande) le serment écrit qu'il n'y a dans leur commune ni armes, ni munitions, ni pigeons voyageurs.

Celui chez qui il sera trouvé des armes, munitions ou pigeons voyageurs, sera immédiatement fusillé.

Les listes des habitants des communes doivent être remises tous les trois jours à la commandanture d'Aulnoye-Berlaimont.

Aulnoye-Berlaimont, le 31 Octobre 1914,
La COMMANDANTURE des Étapes, SCABELL,
Major et Commandant.

all worked on, and tried not to think of possible consequences. Monsieur Delame having told us of the reported presence at Le Cateau of three English officers, our two girls searched that region, only to find they had been sent to Belgium some time previously, but they brought back some soldiers that they had collected on their way. Among these were two English sergeants whom they had found at a farm. Seeing how much fatter and well cared for the latter appeared than most of the poor refugees who arrived, I questioned them and heard that they had been harboured by a "farm lady". They sang her praises, and one told me that after the war he meant to come back and marry her. Surprised, I asked him how old was the lady. He answered that she was forty-six and that he himself was twenty-eight. Still more surprised, I asked if she understood any English, as he did not know a word of French. He answered, "No, but we understands one another!" However, I heard after the war that the kind farmer had married one of her own compatriots.

We begged our guides never to mention names or places to the soldiers, to prevent any indiscretion after they should leave us. As they frequently saw me in my Red Cross uniform, which I wore when going out to dress Madame Caillaux's wounds or to nurse any sick in the village, the Englishmen called me "Sister". But the Frenchmen, when receiving their orders from me, frequently saluted, and answered, "Oui, mon Commandant". As the two girls had enough to do collecting the men, we had to send them to Belgium with Charlotte Matha, the guide Loutre, or a young man from the village called Dossche. Now and then, when roads and lanes were suddenly found to be barricaded by barbed wire, and the whole country was patrolled at all hours of the day and night, on account, we supposed, of preparations for some military operations, it became impossible to send off the men, and we had to keep them hidden for two or three weeks at a time. They used to sit in their shuttered room, ready to pop into their hiding-place at the least alarm. We had got acquainted with the German routine, and knew that it was rare for any to arrive before seven in the morning, and so the men were able to get up and have a good wash and shave in a little toilet-room downstairs, after which they rolled up their blankets on the hospital beds, and left all tidy for the day. But one morning, while I was keeping watch during the men's dressing hour, my maid came to me looking very pale, and said the back garden was full of Germans. Rushing to the dressing-room, she and I hurried the Tommies who were shaving there quickly off to the *cachette*, where the others had already preceded them. I remember how they ran, covered with lather, while I opened the door on to the terrace at the back, so as to be the first to meet and parley with the enemy. However, I saw only a few "Feldgrau"[1] running along the wall which surrounded the garden, and

[1] German equivalent to "Tommy".

apparently taking no notice of the house. I walked up to one and asked him what he wanted, and he answered, "We are placing a new telephone wire". The trees that bound the garden made handy posts on which to fasten this.

On another occasion, when we had buried a large case full of rifles and ammunition which the men had brought in, and to explain the disturbance of the earth had planted a group of small fir trees over the spot, we were horrified a few days later at seeing a party of Germans arrive, one of whom took the gardener's arm and, crossing the lawn, pointed to the very spot where the firearms were buried. Reginald rushed to the rescue of the gardener, while I watched from the window, fearing to see them begin digging operations. Instead of which I saw the whole group walking away, chatting quite amicably. Some time later my brother returned laughing, and said that the German captain wanted a Christmas tree, and had sent to ask for one from us. On seeing our little fir trees, they had thought them just the thing, but had easily accepted one from another part of the garden.

Early one morning Jeanne de Belleville arrived as usual to see what work she could do, and as we had just been informed of the presence of an English officer somewhere in Feignies, she agreed to go and fetch him. She walked the eight miles there, and, with the help of a man she knew, beat all the likely houses in the village, after which she went on to Maubeuge, where he was said to have been removed.

Here she found that the officer had left on the previous day with a safe guide for Brussels, and she returned, doing the ten miles on foot, to arrive here late in the evening. By this time she must have walked twenty-five miles, and I tried to make her stay the night, especially as it was dangerous to be out after nightfall. But fearing her mother would be anxious on her account, she determined to go home. We waited until all was quiet, and about ten o'clock I went to guide her to a little wood which is between Montignies and us, and well off the high road. Having reached the wood and pointed out the direction as well as I could in the dark, I returned home. Jeanne told me afterwards that she got hopelessly lost in the wood, going round and round among the trees, without being able to find her way out. When at last she managed to get home, happily without meeting anyone, it was towards morning. This frail-looking woman had executed a day's march such as few soldiers could have endured, and to the bodily fatigue was added the mental anxiety and necessity for keeping her wits about her in case she were challenged.

We did not dare to let the country people have their notes that Reginald had brought from France, openly, for fear of gossip, so he copied out each little letter separately and entrusted them all to Monsieur le Curé, who slipped them at night under the doors of their addressees. The poor parents who thus received what was often the first news of their dear ones since war broke out were so delighted that they could not resist sharing their joy with all they knew, and many brought us the mysterious notes they had received, at which we pretended to be very surprised. A few deaths had been announced, but we had not had the heart to send this news, thinking that time would prepare the minds of those who had lost husband or son. Reginald had also brought back from Brussels some of the pamphlets and clandestine newspapers which circulated freely underhand there in order to enlighten the population, whose morale might otherwise have been affected by the mendacious information given in the censored papers which the Germans alone allowed, and which were published, sometimes, alas! with the help of traitors, by the authorities. We distributed the patriotic literature freely in the neighbourhood, and sent it as far afield as St. Quentin. Besides the Girl Guides, we had quite a number of messengers who were only too ready to run the risks of travelling from town to town, and these in their turn brought back information which we forwarded. (Among others, Lamant, father and son, of Houdain, were very active.)

Monsieur Capiau invented a safe means of sending information without the messenger's knowledge. He had boots made with a hollow heel, in which notes could be put. The refugees wearing these boots were unaware that they carried anything special; they were given orders simply to report each to their own military attaché at The Hague. In this way, General Dupré and Colonel Oppenheimer were generally kept well informed as to what was happening. But we ourselves got more and more anxious for reliable news, and it was agreed that Reggie should once more try to obtain a pass for Holland. This had become more and more difficult and was only accorded on condition of promise to return again. Evidently he was getting suspect at headquarters by now, because it took many days and much persuasion on his part before he received his permit from the "Pass-Centrale", the plea being, of course, as usual, the need for money, a very true one by this time. The necessity for obtaining clothes and shoes for so many men had drained our resources. Guides, food, and lodging had to be paid for in ready money, and Reginald determined to try and obtain subsidies from the Army for this, and especially for Miss Cavell, who by now had spent not only her own money but some belonging to the Nursing Home.

Whilst Reggie was away, the work went on regularly and the organisation perfected itself. The girls would do the thirty-five miles separating us from Cambrai in a two-nights' march, resting *en route* at Salesches, and bringing each time several men back with them. The Curé of Salesches, l'Abbé Deschoodt, had hidden from the 25th August until the following April six soldiers of the French and English armies. He had had to beg food to be able to keep them, and often he and his servant, Florence Coffrain, lived on turnips and potatoes. After these men had been sent through our organisation to

Holland, Monsieur le Curé offered his presbytery as a stopping-place for the guides who went forward and back to fetch men from further afield, and Mesdemoiselles Thuliez and Moriamé used it regularly. He continued his brave work after we were arrested, until he got arrested himself and was sent to Germany in his turn.

One night, when they had been away some time, and I was getting the last four men of the previous batch ready to be sent off to Belgium, the guide Loutre, who generally arrived before dark so as to rest and take supper with the men before starting, did not turn up until very late. He looked scared and said that he had examined the roads before coming, and found them quite impassable, as trenches had been dug across them, and patrols were in every direction, and he had been fired at on approaching. Therefore, our four soldiers must settle down until things quieted again. A rumour had been brought to me that day from Maubeuge that the Germans were likely to make a descent on us and search the house. Therefore, I was very worried at not being able to get the men out, and especially anxious that no more should arrive. However, to my dismay the girls turned up with twelve more men, mostly Connaught Rangers, making sixteen in all. We had to impress upon them that a special danger menaced, and they had barely time to take some refreshment when we made them hide in the old staircase, while we obliterated all tracks.

Scarcely was everything in order when a large

party of Germans appeared at the gate, and as soon as it was unlocked forty-four of them, led by an officer, came down to the house. Trying to appear as unconcerned as possible, I sat working at my embroidery frame in the room next to the tower. The officer came in there and told me he had a search order, at which I expressed great indignation, and said I hoped he would be responsible for any depredations. Immediately parties spread themselves about, going from room to room, while the officer went into the library, and began taking books out from here and there on the shelves, opening them and shaking them before putting them back. I heard afterwards that bank-notes had often been found hidden in books, and these were always confiscated, although in some cases German notes were given in exchange. Now and then when the soldiers came to report, I heard them mentioning the tower, and wondered if any indiscretion had made them suspect our hiding-place. Also I was terrified that so many men in such a small space might suffer for want of air, although there was a loop-hole in the staircase hidden by the ivy which covers the wall outside.

When the search had lasted for some hours there was great excitement over the discovery of the wine-cellar, in which a good deal of wine was still left. The officer told me that he would have to confiscate this, and he ordered the cart that they had brought with them to be driven round to the back door. This gave me the opportunity to express more indignation, and say that as all their General Staff had been served to the full of their requirements, which were not small, as well as their sick and wounded, I therefore claimed to reserve what wine was left for our own sick and for my aged grandmother. Evidently being ashamed of his errand, he agreed to leave one hundred bottles. While the rest was being removed, my maid called me to look out of a back window. Two soldiers stood in the cart packing the wine, but one in every few bottles had its neck cut off by a sharp movement with a bayonet, and they drank from it in turn. The clean cut they made showed that this was not their *coup d'essai*.

It was bitterly cold, a strong March wind was blowing, and as fuel was hard to obtain notwithstanding our nearness to the mines, we had only wood fires. Both officer and men soon began to have enough of it, but before leaving, they sounded the walls and floors with iron bars, and I was thankful that the tower walls were so thick that even near the hiding-place they gave out no hollow sound. At last, after one o'clock, hunger and cold proved too much for the search party, and the order was given to retire. When to my relief the cart and its escort left the grounds, I opened the panelling of the staircase, and the sixteen men came out, looking pale and frightened. They had heard the shouting, the guttural orders, the knocking at the walls, and wondered if their last hour had come. It must have been a fortnight before vigilance was relaxed again and the roads free.

Charlotte Matha, the Parisian woman I have mentioned, had a relation who lived a few miles away in the Borinage (mining district). She was the wife of a miner who had gone to fight. This woman, named Angelina, lived in a small cottage outside the village of Faÿt, which was easily accessible in a short night's march, and was a safe hiding-place for the men. If there were no moonlight, the party would start with muffled feet about eleven o'clock, after having slept for a few hours and had some supper. They, of course, were dressed in civilian clothes, from which all marks of origin had been removed. My brother's and the men-servants' wardrobes were soon used up. We bought up all the boots we could find in the country, but, as the stocks in the shops could not be renewed, these also were soon exhausted. Then Monsieur le Curé came to the rescue. He said that the manufacturers, before leaving the village, had left the keys of their houses with him, telling him that any bedding we might require for our ambulance was at our disposal. Therefore, he did not doubt that we might also take any clothing left behind, especially as empty houses were sure, sooner or later, to be looted by the Germans. Indeed, in many cases, vans had come and carted away the whole contents of a house, and this had even been done while the owners were there: on many doors the notice had been chalked up, "Nicht mehr plundern".

Not wishing to draw attention, the Curé and Reginald visited the empty houses at night, and came back with their arms full of men's clothing, and with boots dangling from their shoulders. This amateur burglary amused us all.

The men had to be visited in their lodgings in Brussels and given directions and passwords, and once or twice when Reginald went to do this, I accompanied him, walking up and down to keep watch while he entered the various houses. In one of them we left a band of Frenchmen, some of whom were regular soldiers, and others young men approaching military age and anxious to serve their country. Indeed, once it got known in the villages that the boys could be smuggled away, almost without an exception they applied to the Curé, who was our recruiting agent, for the means of gaining unoccupied territory. Scarcely had I returned home on this first occasion, leaving Reginald in Brussels, when the police made a descent on this particular house. Luckily they were seen coming, and the men rushed out through the backyard, where they jumped over the wall into the street and fled in all directions. Many of them were in shirt-sleeves and slippers. A Belgian, named Heuze, who had indicated this lodging to my brother, heard what had happened and came to inform him, and the two of them started off to try and find the dispersed men. They went from one *estaminet* to another, followed by Monsieur Heuze's wife, who was terrified on her husband's account and kept begging him to go home with her; but they collected most of the men and took them to another lodging. The poor ladies, however, to whom the pension belonged, were arrested and sent to prison.

One of the soldiers who had run away, a little Breton, who was a *fusilier marin* and must have had an extraordinary instinct for direction, found his way back on foot to Bellignies, where he arrived with his feet raw, and worn-out with fatigue and hunger. He told us how, when fleeing, he had met a funeral, and had slipped in among a group of mourners walking behind the hearse, thus getting out of the town in safety. The brave little fellow was got through to France at last, and in 1919, when unfortunately I was lying ill in Brussels, he managed to return to Bellignies again, where he explained to the household that he had been determined to come back and thank us, as he could neither read nor write. He was given Charlotte's address in Paris and went also to see her, after which he disappeared from our ken.

After my return the work went on again, regularly at first, the Girl Guides frequently arriving with men. When a group was ready to start off on their way to Brussels with their guide, they would wait among the bushes by a small gate giving on to the back road, which I patrolled with my little dog to make sure all was quiet. 'Sweep' had a very good nose and barked if he smelt a stranger. When all seemed safe, I took him under my arm and came in, and with a silent handshake the little troup would file out to find their way through fields and lanes to Angelina's house. When possible, two guides went, one walking ahead of the men, the other remaining with them. If the first guide were challenged, the back party were instructed to throw themselves flat in the nearest ditch, while the one in front excused her presence out at night as best she could. One night, the guide we had expected never turned up, and I was much perplexed what to do, when Charlotte suggested taking her daughter Suzanne. The child was only twelve, but a sensible little thing for her age, and not knowing what else to do (I dared not leave the house myself, and Reginald was away), I accepted. Little Suzanne had been in bed and asleep for hours, and we had some difficulty in awakening her. Her mother and I explained, while she sat up and rubbed her eyes, what she was to do, and she dressed without an instant's hesitation. She was so successful as a guide that we used her continually afterwards, sometimes sending her away at twilight with the men following at a certain distance behind, and although she often had to pass patrols, when the men hid behind hedges, she always managed to pick up her charges and take them to Angelina's in safety. Children were less liable to be suspected than women, just as women got about more easily than men; also I found them to be more discreet notwithstanding popular opinion.

Now, to come to my next visit to Brussels. Reginald had obtained with much difficulty a new pass for Holland, on the plea of seeing our agent there and obtaining money. Hearing, after he had left, that he was getting very suspect, I sent a letter in code, by one of our special messengers, begging him to stay away; unfortunately, this never reached him. Since the raid on the boarding-house in Brussels, it was getting more and more difficult to find lodgings and guides for the men. I heard of frequent arrests, and suspicious-looking people came continually to the house. I knew it was useless to ask for a pass, and, therefore, made one out for myself on a form provided for the soldiers, inventing a name and address. Charlotte accompanied me, and we set out on foot before daybreak. I left her in Mons after giving her some money to buy clothes for her boy, who was going shortly to make his First Communion. This was a most providential thing, as events proved. Much to his surprise, I called on my cousin, the Dean of Ste. Waudru, in Mons, who had already been to see us once or twice, when the frontier between Belgium and France was still open, and had visited some of our refugees in their tower. The Irishmen among them especially were delighted to be able to talk to a priest. Then I took the tram for Brussels, stopping at Enghien, where my home-made identity card passed muster. I went to the Hôtel Britannique, fearing to compromise friends by staying with them. It was full of German officers, the only ladies except myself being three Americans, who openly showed their dislike of our neighbours, shrugging their shoulders in disgust when bottle after bottle of champagne was ordered.

Early next morning I went to the Rue de la Culture, where several houses in a row composed the Nursing Home. I was received by Nurse Wilkins, who told me that Miss Cavell was attending to a serious operation upstairs and could not speak to me. I begged her to say I would wait until she was free. I sat in her little sitting-room, whose sole ornament was two shelves containing books of devotion and works on nursing, until Jack, a big shaggy dog of whom she was fond, but who was anything but friendly to strangers, bounded in, followed by his mistress. Nurse Cavell was slight, but very straight, with large earnest grey eyes which seemed to see through one, and a quiet dignified manner which commanded respect. In her gentle voice she said, "I wish you hadn't come; I am evidently suspect. Look at those men cleaning the square in front; they have been there several days and are scarcely working at all. They must be set to watch the house."

I answered, "I came to say that we must stop. I have had search parties and dare have no more men brought to Bellignies."

She replied, "I also had a search party yesterday; I heard their footsteps downstairs and only had time to throw my papers in the grate, pour some alcohol over them and set them alight, when Germans came in and began searching the room. But all my records are gone, and how shall I explain the use of his money to Dr. Depage?"

I answered, "Do not let that worry you. If we all come through this alive I will be your witness as to what you have done. But this shows that we *must* stop now."

I saw an expression of relief which I understood come over her face. We had been living so long with the sense of danger hanging over us, it seemed too good to think of rest. But suddenly she asked, "Are there any more hidden men?" "Yes," I answered, "Mademoiselle Thuliez has found over thirty more in Cambrai." "In that case we cannot stop," she said, "because if one of those men got caught and shot it would be our fault." So there was nothing for it but to continue our work, although we agreed no more refugees should be sent to her. She would content herself with directing the guides and communicating orders as to means of passing into Holland.

It must have been about this time that the electric wires were placed along the frontier. It was impossible any longer to count on bribing the Landsturmen to look another way while the men passed. Several had been detected doing so, and had paid with their lives for what was certainly a military crime.

After concerting measures, as we thought, for every emergency, Miss Cavell told me how to leave her house safely. I was to go to the end of the road where a shop-window reflected the street behind me, and stand looking in this window for a moment. I must then quickly turn down the road on the left to where another shop—if I remember rightly, a pastrycook's this time—was in front of the

MISS EDITH CAVELL

To face p. 128

spot where the tram stopped. I was to stand hesitating, as though I meant to enter this shop, until I heard the bell announcing that a tram was going to start, and turn and jump on to the tram as it was moving off, not minding in which direction it went. These different manœuvres were pretty sure to throw anybody who might have followed me off the track, and I carried them out exactly.

On my previous visit with Reginald, I had lunched with Count and Countess Hippolyte d'Ursel at Boitsfort. Their son-in-law[1] had just left Belgium with great difficulty, and notwithstanding bad health, to go and serve his country. Their two sons, who were officers in the Guides, had been at the front from the first. Jeanne de Belleville was also in Brussels, and we lunched together before I returned home.

Charlotte met me at Mons and we reached Angelina's house without difficulty, where I changed my town clothes for a less noticeable attire. We started off on foot for the most dangerous part of the journey: getting again into the "Etappen" from relatively free Belgium. She carried the clothes she had bought for her boy, and we went through fields and small country lanes, creeping along hedges, until suddenly from behind one a German patrol, consisting of two men, came out, and asked us what business we had to be there, and told us to follow them. One took Charlotte in charge, while the other walked beside me. Before going ahead,

[1] Comte Jacques de Lichtervelde.

Charlotte, who was a little pale, gave me a look which seemed to say, "I'll do the talking".

We were marched in grim silence for several miles until we came to the village of Faÿt, where we were taken before a German officer. I will own that I felt extremely guilty; Miss Cavell's letter, of whose contents I was ignorant, as well as some hundred *Mots du Soldat*, and about fifty pamphlets of Cardinal Mercier's famous Pastoral Letter, *Patriotisme et Endurance*, all distributed about my person, made me wonder what would happen if I were searched. In a whining voice Charlotte said that her child was going to make his First Communion, and as no clothes were to be found in our district, we had been to buy some in Belgium. The elderly officer, a kindly-looking man, said, "Is that true?" upon which Charlotte and I opened the parcels and spread out a boy's suit, cap, and shoes. He looked at them with a softened expression and said, "I have children of my own at home, so I will let you go this time, but don't get caught again". Our relief was so great that we scarcely felt the fatigue of walking the few miles that separated us from Bellignies, where my dear grandmother looked extremely relieved when I arrived. At this time when anyone departed even for a short journey, one wondered if one would ever see them again, and all of us were generally strung up in the expectation of bad news.

Soon after this, when the service had begun again, one morning Reginald walked in, rather to my dismay, I own, and said he had found new lodgings for the men in Brussels, and had made arrangements with our own authorities in regard to their escape. He had seen Leopold, who was now doing liaison work on the Ypres Salient, and on returning through London had called at the War Office. Just as he was about to leave, he met one of the officers whom we had nursed during the retreat from Mons, who said to him, "Would you like news of your home? Twelve men have just come in, who left Bellignies a week ago", and Reginald was taken to the office, where these reports were read to him, and he knew that so far we were safe.

The group in question had arrived here before dawn on a Saturday, and ought to have left us on the following night. But the guides who were to conduct them across the Belgian frontier reported conditions to be impossible, and so they had to wait a few days, to the great disappointment of the men, who were eager after nine months in hiding to get to safety and freedom once more. I never dared to leave the house when there were soldiers hidden in it. Even on Sundays, pretexting indisposition, I stayed at home, although our church is merely across the road. On this particular Sunday morning I went into the shuttered room where the men were sitting, ready at the slightest alarm to disappear behind the panel. Carrying some prayer-books, both Catholic and Church of England, I said to them: "We had hoped to get you far on the way to safety to-day, but once more we must all resign ourselves to have patience. You have got here at the risk of great danger to yourselves and others, and you have still to run a great danger; would you not care to hold a little service among yourselves, as it is Sunday?" Before leaving the room, I stopped to bind up the sore hand and arm of one of the poor fellows (hiding in damp holes underground caused many sores), a boy of about eighteen, who being far the youngest of the troop was the object of special care from all the others.

When I turned to leave the room one of the two sergeants came forward, and, saluting, said, "If you please, will you hold the service?" "I fear I cannot", I answered, "as I am a Catholic, and I daresay you are not of the same faith". Pointing to a group of men, "These are Roman Catholics", said he, "and these are Church of England, while my comrade and myself are Presbyterians, but we are all Christians and would like you to conduct the service". So, taking up one of the missals, I read the Gospel and Epistle for the day, and repeated the Lord's Prayer and the Creed, while all the men knelt round the table, and joined in as simply as children praying at their mother's knee. The little service over, I left them, feeling more moved than I can say. These men departed in groups of three or four, the "boy", as they called him, being got away among the first. Mademoiselle Moriamé had brought some blessed medals for the Catholics, among whom were several Connaught Rangers and Royal Irish Rifles, but all the men insisted upon having a medal, which they fastened inside their clothes.

After calling at the War Office, Reginald took the boat for Flushing, but before getting on board took up a newspaper, in which among other items a sensational paragraph about the escape of twelve British soldiers, "who had lain hidden in a château in the North of France and had just arrived after a dangerous passage through Belgium", caught his eye. Although no names were mentioned, the details given were enough to bring suspicion down on us, and Reginald rushed to the telephone and called up an official at the War Office with whom he had been in touch, begging urgently, that, unless they wished us all to be shot, this sort of publication should cease. From that date the Censor prevented any further dangerous disclosures. But the men themselves frequently forgot that although they were in safety once they got to Holland, we were left behind in the power of the enemy, and several wrote postcards of thanks to Miss Cavell, Madame Bodart, and others who had lodged them. One of these postcards, signed with several names, was brought into court as evidence during the trial.

Once Reginald was at home our Girl Guides took up their work again, traversing the country in every direction, carrying the clandestine *courier* and bringing back men. But we had been instructed to stop sending young boys for the time, and to collect rather iron-workers from the big works around Maubeuge, who were badly wanted in the munition factories of France.[1] The only men left, of course, were fifty years old or more, but of these, in a short time, a great number, nearly two thousand, I believe, were found ready to go. Reginald met the Mayor of Maubeuge, Monsieur Walerand, who was an excellent patriot, and promised to help in the collecting of the workmen. But Mademoiselle Thuliez was very keen to get away first some of the young French soldiers she had seen and talked to in Cambrai. One young fellow, an officer, wrote the most touching letter begging to be taken. Just as all was arranged, we got bad news from Brussels, saying that the passage

[1] The following were the terms of the appeal for workmen of the kind required:

CONDITIONS GÉNÉRALES

POUR LE

RECRUTEMENT D'OUVRIERS POUR LA FRANCE

1° L'appel s'adresse aux ajusteurs et aux monteurs possédant bien leur métier;

2° Avant leur agrégation, les candidats doivent faire une pièce d'épreuve dans un atelier, qui leur est désigné en Hollande; qu'ils soient acceptés ou non, les frais de voyage, à l'aller et au retour, leur sont remboursés;

3° Les salaires de début, en France, sont de Fr. 0.65 à fr. 0.80, et peuvent même atteindre un franc par heure, suivant les localités et les aptitudes de l'ouvrier;

4° Les ouvriers sont transportés et nourris gratuitement, depuis le départ des Pays-Bas jusqu'à l'arrivée en France. La famille des intéressés (femme et enfants) peut les accompagner, si elle n'est pas trop nombreuse, et elle est également transportée et nourrie gratuitement.

5° Une occupation permanente est garantie pour tout le temps de la guerre.

of the frontier was getting more and more difficult. Several young fellows from our village had been arrested and sent as prisoners to Germany, and two of our soldiers had never reported in Holland, and we feared that they had either been made prisoners or shot while escaping.

These were anxious days, and the only moment of rest we accorded ourselves was after luncheon, an hour at which we were rarely disturbed by the enemy. We used to walk in the garden with my grandmother, and sit by a little lily-pond watching the growth of a lotus plant I had acquired the year before. The large flat green leaves rose up out of the water and spread themselves in the sun, and we saw a bud beginning to rise in the same way. Granny, who had many old superstitions, would look at it and shake her head, saying: "It won't live; the lotus only grows where there is happiness". But the bud rose higher and higher, and got larger and larger until each morning we expected to see it open into a flower. Reginald said one day impatiently he believed it never would open. Alas, next morning one of our confederates, a watchmaker from Mons, by name Chaffotte, arrived breathless to say that Monsieur Baucq, Miss Cavell, and Mademoiselle Thuliez had all been arrested in Brussels.

Some time before this, Miss Cavell's guides having been arrested one after the other, and the sending of men from Brussels to Holland having become almost impossible, Reginald had made desperate efforts to find new lodgings and guides. After knocking at many doors in vain, he made the acquaintance, through Marie de Lichtervelde, of the Père Quévit, a Dominican Father, from the Monastery of the Rue Leys, and was put in touch with M. Baucq, who was described as a man of great courage and high mind. Baucq was an architect and one of the most ardent patriots that it was possible to conceive. He had dined with Reginald on one of the latter's last visits to Brussels, and had accompanied him to see the Abbé Delannoy, Professor of Rhetoric at the Collège St. Louis. This priest wished to make arrangements to get all the boys of his class off to Holland clandestinely as soon as the school-term was over, so that they might join the Belgian Army. I had seen Baucq when on our last visit to Brussels with Reginald. He had come to Comtesse de Lichtervelde's house, in the Avenue des Nerviens, to see us, and had explained by which different routes he hoped to get the men away. Just previously he had taken an Englishman, three Frenchmen, and two Russians from Madame Bodart's house, and had successfully got them over the frontier.

The Russians had a curious history. One morning, Charlotte came in to say that an old Belgian woman was asking to speak to us. The latter explained that she had found two soldiers in rags hiding in a hedge of her garden. She had given them some food and came to ask us what to do with them. I instructed her to get the men to write down their names and regiments on a piece of paper, knowing well that I should soon thus be able to judge of their genuineness if they were really English. But the paper brought back was undeniably in Russian, and not being able to read it, we sent it to Monsieur Capiau, who had been to Russia on mining business and spoke a little Russian. He had the two men brought to where he could question them, and discovered that they were prisoners of war who had escaped from a munition factory at Valenciennes, where they had been forced to make and handle bombs. Trains loaded with ammunition left the factory at night, the gates being closed at all other times. The two men managed to conceal themselves on, or, I believe, under the train, and let themselves fall on the line when it slowed up at a curve. They then appealed to the nearest cottage for help. Of all the prisoners of war, undoubtedly the Russians were the most to be pitied. Badly fed and worse treated, their life was an absolute slavery. These two men seemed to have been well educated and gave no one any trouble, and they were got safely through to Holland and later to France.

It was a terrible blow to us to hear of the arrest of our confederates, and Reginald decided to go at once to Brussels. Out of precaution he stopped at Forest, a suburb of the capital, and went in on foot, first to the Hôtel de Ville, where with the aid of an official he tried to organise the defence of our patriots; here unfortunately he heard of other arrests and rumours of search parties being sent in our direction. He visited several lodging-houses to warn our men who were there, and went to see Madame Bodart. He told her how anxious he was to catch the tram at Forest, but must first go to see some young men who were lodged behind the Gare du Midi. Madame Bodart promptly offered to go and warn the latter herself, so that Reginald should not miss his tram. He heard afterwards that when she arrived at the lodging-house the door was opened by the German police, who immediately arrested her. Knowing nothing of this, Reginald arrived here that night to communicate the distressing news, and early next morning Madame Capiau announced that her husband had also been arrested, and begged Reginald to meet her in the tram and travel together as far as Mons, so that they might talk without being observed. She wished him to get certain influential people to intervene on her husband's behalf. One of the first remarks the brave woman made was: "Who will take my husband's place?" showing how much she thought of the patriotic work to which Monsieur Capiau had devoted himself. When war was over and I was received for the first time by our Queen in the Palace, from which traces of the occupation were being hastily removed, I repeated to her Madame Capiau's words, and I saw her eyes fill with tears.

So Reginald returned at once to Brussels, and even discussed giving himself up, if it would disculpate our friends. It was a terrible moment for us to pass. Although we said as little as possible to our grandmother, she seemed to understand, and from that moment her set white face bore an expression of suffering it was never to lose, but she neither complained nor objected to his leaving. He gave me the keys of his desk, with last instructions for every emergency that we could imagine, and started on the 8th of August.

Miss Cavell had been arrested on the 5th, a few days after Monsieur Baucq and Mademoiselle Thuliez. Then Madame Bodart and Monsieur Capiau followed in rapid succession. We could not communicate with Belgium, and were obliged to live in ignorance of all that was happening, which naturally increased our anxiety. Outwardly we continued the same life, receiving the villagers, taking our daily walk, and sitting by the lily-pond, but the day after Reginald left we were astonished to see the beautiful lotus bud which he had so wished to see open, hanging limp and faded on its stem as if it had been touched by frost. Granny said sadly: "I told you it would never flower", but a few days later another bud rose from the water and I watched it daily swelling with what I own was a superstitious feeling, as if my own fate hung on it. I never saw the bloom. . . . When I returned to my devastated and deserted home in 1919, the gardener told me that the second bud had faded after my arrest, just as the first had done, and that from then on the whole plant had withered away.

August 24, 1915.—At the end of the month of August one morning early I saw a car go by our gate, and to my horror thought I recognised Jeanne de Belleville sitting with German soldiers in it. Within a few moments frightened villagers came down to tell me that it was she, and that certainly she had been made prisoner. Granny immediately wished to go to console old Comtesse de Belleville, who was nearly eighty. So we took the horse and cart, which until now had been spared from requisition as being too aged for use. We found Comtesse de Belleville and her daughter Marie in great grief, but brave and trustful, as their deep faith held them up under this terrible anxiety. The two old friends in adversity consoled each other, and we explained how Reginald was in Brussels, and would try to assure a proper defence of all our patriots.

Shortly after we returned home, Charlotte came to where I was sitting in the garden, saying with a white face: "There is a strange man asking to speak to you. He is in plain clothes, but I am sure he is a Boche and a spy." I followed her in, and found a medium-sized man of military appearance waiting, who told me he was an escaped British prisoner and had been hiding for some months in Brussels. He had heard from a priest that I was able to get him to England, where he was anxious to rejoin his regiment. Seeing at once that Charlotte's surmise was correct, I answered: "Unfortunate man, why did you not stay in Brussels, where you were safe? Here in the 'Étapes' you are in great danger, and we cannot even get a letter through, much less a man: the wisest thing for you to do will be to give yourself up to the German authorities. Here you are only putting us all in danger." To gain my confidence, he told me that he had been in the English Army and had served several years in India. He certainly spoke English perfectly and with the intonation of a Tommy, but nevertheless I had not the slightest hesitation in deciding he was a spy. The next time I saw him was at the court-martial, where he wore German uniform, and I learned his name was Otto Meyer. I have since heard that he was instrumental in the arrest of Nurse Cavell, telling her that my brother had been arrested and had said that all the accused had better make a clean breast of it; that Reginald declared he had given Nurse Cavell five thousand francs to pay her guides, so that it was no good her denying any longer. The poor woman was taken in and answered, always scrupulous in money matters: "I assure you it was only two", thus giving herself away entirely.[1]

A day or two after I had got rid of the spy, one morning two cars arrived filled with German soldiers. Guards were posted all around the house outside, and four officers entered, one of them speaking French with the accent of our neighbourhood. They told me they had come to speak to my brother and must see him at once. I answered that he was away, and I did not know where he was. He frequently made absences of a few days and would doubtless be back very shortly. I was cross-questioned very

[1] It is only fair to add that O. Meyer declared subsequently that he was forced against his will to play the part here described.

closely, and had to weigh every word I uttered, before speaking. The most important thing, it seemed to me, was to draw off attention from Brussels. The only way I could think of doing this was by making these officials, whom I discovered to be heads of the police in Brussels, Mons, and Maubeuge, believe that Reginald was still hidden in the neighbourhood. So I pretended to slip out by mistake the word Solre-le-Château, and mention our property there, at once saying that I knew he could not have gone there as he had no passport for that region. I suppose my acting must have convinced these men that Reginald had fled to Solre and was hiding in our woods there, and my protestations must have confirmed them in this belief. They sent a guard to arrest our head keeper Legat, who had been as he said, "born in the family", his father having been keeper in our woods for forty-eight years and being himself the son and grandson of our foresters.

Even had Legat known anything, I am convinced he would not have spoken, but the poor fellow really had not seen Reginald since the latter's flying visit to Solre weeks before. Therefore, when a man in civilian clothes and professing to be a wood merchant arrived, and told him that Reginald had promised to meet him there so as to discuss the sale of some trees, Legat at once protested that he did not know where Reginald was and was not expecting him. However, he consented to accompany this man down to the village, and scarcely had they turned the corner when he was arrested by men in uniform who were hidden there. They took him to the Citadel at Maubeuge and put a *mouton* (spy and informer) in his cell. This man pretended he was from Bellignies, and had been arrested by the Germans on account of his patriotic activity. Legat was submitted to much cross-examination, the "Kriegsgerichtsrat" who questioned him saying that the way his hand trembled proved his guilt, and assuring him that he would be shot. This trembling was the result of a childish illness and persisted until the faithful fellow's death which took place in April this year (1931). The Germans had got wind of men being hidden in the woods (these being evidently the deserters I have mentioned before), and, believing the keeper to be carrying food to Reginald in his hiding-place, they kept Legat a prisoner for three weeks.

This at any rate gained time for Reginald, who, on arrival in Brussels, had gone at once to the Lichterveldes' house in the Avenue des Nerviens, where he heard that a mysterious man had been there that morning asking after him. Marie de Lichtervelde, suspecting this man of being a spy, would not receive him. At last, in despair, he sent in his name, saying he came at the request of Baucq to warn Reginald to disappear at once, and he urgently begged them to forward this message. Poor Marie was very agitated, and implored Reginald to follow Baucq's instructions, and hide immediately. The messenger was a glass-painter who had been acquainted with Baucq, and who, with the complicity of the devoted director of Saint-Gilles, had been able to receive messages from him. The officials and warders of the prison had been left at their posts, but were overlooked and accompanied on their rounds by German soldiers, as by this time half the prisoners were political ones. Notwithstanding the close watch kept, correspondence went on with the outside regularly, and the cleverest means were invented for sending notes under the nose of the Germans. Baucq declared that he knew Reginald was liable to be arrested at any moment, and if so, would most certainly be shot. He therefore implored him to try and reach safety, which was also the best way he could help all.

While they were discussing this news, which Reginald, to Marie's despair, *would* not take sufficiently seriously, he looked out of the window, and to his astonishment saw a man named Quien, whom we suspected of having turned traitor, apparently watching the house. After having been sent to Holland safely once, this Quien had returned and been seen about Brussels in doubtful company. This at last made Reginald hesitate, but even then he asked first that Maître Alexandre Braun[1] should be consulted. The answer received was formal: Reginald must hide at once. So Marie started off to see a French nun who was the Superior of the Clinique of Linthout. She told her the whole story, and the sister at once offered to

---

[1] M. Alexandre Braun was a well-known lawyer and Vice-President of the Senate.

take my brother into the Institute, under a false name. That evening, Reginald, or rather "René Desmet", took up his abode at Linthout, where he stayed for ten or twelve days, until he was told by one of the nuns that the wife of a sick German officer, who was being nursed on the floor above, was getting very curious about the gentleman who spent all his days in the garden. It became urgent for René Desmet to change lodgings. But the difficulty was how to get away. Marie de Lichtervelde made attempt after attempt to try and get into touch with one of the many associations which had been working on the same lines as ours. But frequent arrests had dislocated all the services, and a reinforced watch on the roads, and especially along the frontier, made it more and more difficult to leave Belgium.

Our Curé's housekeeper, Louise, who had helped so much with the wounded, had a married sister (wife of a Belgian officer) living in Brussels, and she had luckily given us her address. This excellent little woman lived with her son and a very young Flemish maid-of-all-work, and at once offered Reginald the spare room in her house, which he accepted gratefully, receiving there the few people who were in the secret. Not only did the little Flemish maid know nothing, but she was a simple child from a very poor family, and passed the time when she was not working in saying her prayers, so there was no fear of indiscretion from her. They did not know it at the time, but Madame Maghe's husband had already found a soldier's death in Flanders. She was a worthy soldier's wife, and accepted bravely the risks she ran, but it became more and more urgent for Reginald to escape. The Germans had seized on all his photographs while at Bellignies, and these had been circulated, while a price was placed on his head. I was afterwards told it was a large one, twenty thousand marks, but I do not know how far this is true.

One of our most useful correspondents in Mons, at whose house both Reginald, Jeanne de Belleville, and Mademoiselle Thuliez, as well as myself, often stayed on our journeys to and from Brussels, was Mademoiselle Dutillœul, who lived alone in the Rue des Clercs, which had the advantage of being quite close to our cousin the Dean's house. The latter had a brother in the Belgian Army. He had had trouble himself for protesting on several occasions against abuses, and especially the desecration of the churches. We therefore avoided compromising him more than necessary. Next door to Mademoiselle Dutillœul lived the watchmaker, Chaffotte, who was always ready to bring us the letters which arrived by German post, open, of course, in Mons. Miss Cavell wrote with certain conventional phrases to let us know when the men she was hiding got through safely, addressing the letters to "Madame" Dutillœul. The latter was the daughter and sister of Belgian officers, and was rather like an old soldier herself. On the day of the descent on Bellignies, the same German officials paid a call on Mademoiselle Dutillœul, whose name I had never mentioned, however, and searched the house very thoroughly. Her account of this perquisition and her interrogatory is very amusing, although at the time I dare say she hardly perceived the fun.

They began by asking her did she know the Prince de Croy? Our cousin Henri, an officer in the Guides, and now at the Front, had stayed long with the Dutillœuls in former years when Col. Dutillœul and his sister had had a large house in the Rue de la Grosse Pomme. Therefore, Henri was certainly the Prince de Croy she knew best, so, without naming the precise person, she answered at once, "Yes, very well". "Where is he now?" was the next question. "At the Front, fighting for his country," was her answer. This probably made them begin to think Reginald was safely away. "Have you his photo?" "Certainly", said she, and took from the mantelpiece an American photograph, showing six times the same person sitting around a table. Handing this to Bergan, she said, "There he is." "Which of them is it?" asked the German. "Whichever you like", said Mademoiselle Dutillœul, amused at their not perceiving that all six photographs were of Henri. They then began a thorough search of the house, but, evidently not realising how clever the old lady was, they left her alone, and she was able to her great relief to snatch several long lists containing names and regiments of the men who had passed there, and pop them into the fire. These lists had been forgotten by

Mademoiselle Thuliez, who had most unfortunately also kept on her both of the two false passports she used, one being for our neighbourhood, and calling her Marie Mouton, the other for use in Brussels in the name of Madame Martin. The police left Mademoiselle Dutillœul's house no wiser than they came, and her acting must have convinced them that she knew nothing, as they left her quiet in future.

But to go back to the search party. I had felt for some time that it would be wiser not to keep any compromising papers about. Some of these I buried, but I had great quantities of letters which the soldiers had written to their families before leaving us; this in case they were taken or killed on the way. These letters I put into long tin boxes and hid in the thick ivy on our tower, showing the spot to Monsieur le Curé, with a request that if ever I were taken he would put them in safety. But certain papers I *had* to keep at hand. These were the cards Monsieur Capiau had provided, which, filled in, and with a photograph stuck on them, and stamped with our cleverly-imitated German stamp, became the false passes with which all the soldiers had to be provided. I generally kept these printed forms between the palette and the cover of my paint-box. The latter was always beside my easel in the window of the hall where we usually sat, and I spent a great deal of time sitting before it, as from there I could keep good watch on the front gate.

But an uneasy feeling made me take these papers out and try to find a safer place for them. On the day the search party came, I had tried various hiding-places—in the grand piano, behind pictures, in the backs of furniture—but, each time dissatisfied, I had taken them out again. Beside the easel were two baskets with red cushions in them, in which my little pom and the fox-terrier Vicky slept. Animals have a strange instinct, and these two, generally of a friendly disposition, evidently felt my uneasiness when the enemy was in the house. Invariably directly a German appeared they got into their baskets and lay quiet. On the day in question, I held the printed forms in my hand, after having for the second time put them back into the paint-box, but something urged me to take them out again, and I was holding them when I saw a car stop before the gate. There was no time to hesitate. Lifting up a little dog, I pushed the papers under its cushion. I think that was the only place left unsearched. The first thing they investigated was my paint-box, even squeezing the tubes of colour.

It was a Sunday, and the women servants had gone for a walk, but Amand was on duty. On seeing the Germans, he retired to his room on the third floor, and later, leaving them time as he thought to be gone, he peeped cautiously out of one of the windows, and was immediately spotted by the man on guard below. This fellow at once rushed in and told the officers, who were now investigating the contents of Reginald's desk (where the letter of thanks from the British Government mentioned before and a sealed envelope inscribed "Mon testament" seemed especially to interest them) that a man was in hiding upstairs, and they at once rushed up to search, and came face to face with Amand. I followed, fearing that under cross-examination he might say something imprudent, but I did not realise the steadfastness of a Flemish head. "Where is the Prince?" they asked. "I do not know, Monsieur." "When was he here last?" "A few days ago, Monsieur." "Where did he go?" "I do not know, Monsieur. The Prince goes and comes and does not tell his servants what he does." This sort of thing went on for some time. The blank expression on the old man's face evidently satisfied them at last that he was too stupid or too stubborn to say anything, and they continued their search, diving in furniture, looking in beds, behind pictures, under carpets, until they *must* have found anything had it been there.

In a Chinese cabinet in the book-room were the engraved metal triggers, all that was left of a fine sporting gun which had been sent back to me by the Mayor after the first passage of von Kluck's army, the rest having been smashed in small pieces by the soldiers. Seizing upon this, von Kirchenheim, chief of the military police of Maubeuge, held it up triumphantly before me, saying, "And what is that?" He was a red-faced, brutal-looking man with protruding eyes and a rasping voice. "That is all that is left of a valuable sporting gun belonging to my brother." "And where is the rest?" asked he. "That you must ask of the Germans who broke it",

I answered. At once he flew into a passion, held his clasped fist in my face, and shouted, "Do you dare accuse our brave soldiers?" Looking him straight in the eyes, I answered quietly, "I accuse no one. I merely answered your question." His gaze dropped, and he lowered his fist, but I heard afterwards that on many occasions he nearly felled with a blow those of our people who said a word to displease him. One railwayman, who was my fellow-witness at the court-martial on a traitor after the war, showed us the scars which still disfigured his face, resulting from blows given by von Kirchenheim with the butt of his revolver.

Leaving the three to continue their search, I returned to the hall, where I found the fourth officer, who spoke French so well, evidently waiting there to see me alone. Putting on the air of a sympathiser and a confederate, he told me that it would be much better for us to avow frankly all that we had been doing, as denial only angered the authorities. Therefore, I should do well to give them Reginald's address at once. I answered that I did not know what he was speaking of, that we had none of us done anything to be ashamed of. Then in a low voice he whispered in Walloon French, "Nevertheless I advise you to disappear too". I kept a contemptuous silence, and considered his words and their motive in my mind, settling that they hoped I would take the same route as Reginald, and would, therefore, lead to his detection.

There was a few days' ominous quiet after this.

We heard that everyone who tried to get into the village was stopped on the road and turned back. I destroyed the last identity cards, feeling it was hopeless to get any more men to escape our way. The sole exception to visits was our doctor. He had received a pass to see some sick people, and came in to us on the way. He remarked that I was looking ill myself, and insisted on sounding my heart, telling me that I required absolute rest and quiet. I mentioned my anxiety about my brother, and gave the doctor the address of friends in Brussels to whom he could carry news of us all if he managed to obtain a passport. Some time previously his young nephew had availed himself of our association to go and volunteer in the French Army, and by a curious coincidence, on one of his trips to Brussels, Reginald had also met the nephew of Dr. Mariage, our consulting physician, from Valenciennes, and had been able to help him also to get away. I spent these days putting papers, etc., in order, burying valuables, and especially trying to reassure my poor grandmother, who kept on saying, "Will they shoot him?" My brother, being the youngest of the family, and resembling a much-loved uncle who had died in early manhood, was the dearest thing that remained to our grandmother. On the last evening we passed together, she asked me to read from the Gospel of the death of Lazarus, but the only word of complaint she uttered was, "Why did God let me live so long to see all this sorrow?"

Next morning, at daybreak, a car arrived in

which were Pinkhoff and Bergan. We came down at once, and they explained that they had come to fetch me as a witness in Brussels. They spoke civilly, and as if the affair were quite simple. I asked, "Witness to what?" In an affair of an aeroplane in which a French officer had come down lately in our neighbourhood. Indeed, I was suspected of hiding both the 'plane and the officer. The story was too stupid, and I answered, "In that case you can easily find them. I have not got them in my pocket." They said their orders were that I must go to Brussels with them at once, but I could return home directly I had given my evidence. I saw it was useless to refuse (they would merely have used force), and so told my maid to get a dressing-bag ready. Wishing evidently to gain time and perhaps to spare a scene, they said, "It is not necessary to take anything; you will come back to-night". My grandmother, standing tall and straight at my side, put her hand on my shoulder, and asked, "Is that true?" Both raised their hands as on taking an oath, and answered, "We give you our word she will return to-night". It was three years and three months later that I returned. So much for the word of honour! My grandmother looked them in the face and said, "If she does not return, I shall die". When I kissed her she was as cold as ice.

I got into the car, the usual long military open one, with the two officers, while an armed man sat by the chauffeur. I saw scared faces at every cottage door and window while going past. We drove to the station for the express. Bergan and Pinkhoff cross-questioned me the whole way in the train, sometimes speaking of things which appeared to me totally irrelevant to the case, and it was often after a thrust and parry on many other subjects, during which I prayed to keep my wits, that I discovered the object of these seemingly useless questions. I remember especially that "Monsieur Henri", as Pinkhoff was generally called, who was a Jew, and boasted he was an atheist, told me sarcastically that as a Catholic I was bound to tell the truth and nothing but the truth. I answered that that was my habit, and I own that it had been terribly repugnant to me to be obliged to make statements the whole of that morning which were all absolutely untrue; but I knew my duty required me to defend not only myself, but all those implicated. He kept assuring me that the others had made a clean breast of it, and many details that he gave could only, unfortunately, have been told him by our confederates. Nevertheless, I continued to deny all acquaintance with them, and when he said that Miss Cavell owned to having received money to pay her guides from me, I indignantly protested, upon which he said to his comrade, "The Princess is one of those good Christians whose right hand doesn't know what the left hand does".

I had had no breakfast, and when we arrived in Brussels they offered me a sandwich in the waiting-room, but I could not eat, of course, and I also found my brain kept clearer when fasting. A car was waiting for us, and we were rapidly driven to the prison of Saint-Gilles, where I was taken to a waiting-room. Although we had all promised each other never to recognise one another in case of arrest, I was dismayed at being greeted at once when confronted. I still, however, continued to deny any complicity, and tried to convey by my answers that my brother was still free, and that I would never acknowledge anything that could not be proved against me. Pinkhoff watched us closely while questioning us. He was an extremely clever detective, who must have had long experience with criminals, and found our brave folks fall easy victims to his cunning. I heard afterwards that he had lived in various frontier towns of France, where he must evidently have been a useful spy. He had been in business in Belfort and other towns, and told me that influential friends in Paris had offered to obtain permission for him to remain on there, even after the outbreak of war. He also said that he had been a member of the Chamber of Commerce of Paris. He did not conceal his German sentiments and the great ambition of his life, which was to obtain the Iron Cross. I believe he got it after the court-martial at which we were all condemned, but if I had been a German soldier wearing this decoration for valour on the field I should not have felt flattered at seeing the same cross on the breast of Pinkhoff.

Then Jeanne de Belleville was brought in. She was anxious about her mother, and I told her all I knew. During our morning's cross-examination, Pinkhoff had spoken rather contemptuously of the "Comtesse", as he always called her, but Jeanne's quiet courage impressed me. After she had been taken back to her cell I was left for a few moments alone, while evidently my jailors made their report and telephoned to headquarters. By now it was six in the evening and I kept saying that I must return home at once. At last they came back, and, throwing off the mask, said that they had orders to convey me to the Kommandantur, that I was implicated in far too grave an affair to be allowed to go home. Of course, I demanded the means of writing at once to the Governor-General. I was conducted to No. 6 Rue de la Loi. The whole of this street and the park in front of it was reserved entirely for the use of the "occupant," civilians only being allowed into it on official business, and with a pass. No. 6 had been our Ministry of the Interior or Home Office. The ground floor was now Police Headquarters, and I was taken before an official where my *mandat d'écrou* was made out.[1] Then I was taken upstairs and shown

---

[1] The German documents are as follows:

KOMMANDANTUR BRÜSSEL,
    Gefängniswesen,
        Eingang am 6.9.15., No. N 1.

Brüssel, d. 6 Sept. 1915.

Die Prinzessin Marie de Croÿ, geb. 26.11.75, in London, wohnhaft Schloss Bellignies bei Bavay, wird heute, am 6 Sept. 1915 um 8 Uhr nachm., wegen Beihilfe zum Kriegsverrat (Zuführung von Mannschaften an den Feind) zur Verfügung der Polizeistelle B. eingeliefert.

BERGAN, Leutnant.

to a room on the second floor looking on to the courtyard at the back. Immediately a sentry was

POLIZEISTELLE B., BRÜSSEL,
   des Generalgouvernments in Belgien,
   TAGEB. No. . 1 . 1 . . . .
                              Brüssel, am 7 September 1915.
   BETRIFFT
Festnahme der Prinzessin   (1) Am 6 September 1915 8
Marie de CROŸ in BELLIGNIES. Uhr nachm. wurde die Prinzessin Marie Elisabeth de CROŸ, geboren am 26 November 1875 IN LONDON, wohnhaft auf Schloss BELLIGNIES bei BAVAY, wegen Beihilfe zur Zuführung von Mannschaften an den Feind festgenommen und der Kaiserlichen Kommandantur-Abtlg. Gefängniswesen BRÜSSEL zugeführt.

Sofort.   (2) dem POLIZEI-ABSCHNITT IV. z. Hd. des Herrn Oberleutnant EBERLIN
                                 MONS
   mit der Bitte um Kenntnisnahme und Weiterleitung an den zuständigen Herrn Ortskommandanten überreicht. Auf die telephonische Mitteilung wird Bezug genommen.

                              (s) BERGAN, Leutnant.

         Mons, 8 ix. 15
POLIZEIABSCHNITT IV.
   des Generalgouvernments in Belgien,
   TAGEB. No. 1925.
         U. der Ortskommandantur
              Bavay
         zur Kenntnisnahme mitzuteilen
              (s) EBERLIN
                 Oberleutnant
                 Abschnittsführer.

placed at my door, another stood opposite it, and a third at the end of the passage. Here I was left alone, feeling terribly distressed about my poor grandmother. I was given some paper and pencils and wrote in the most urgent way I was able. These letters were carried to the police office downstairs, where most of them remained, or at any rate were never delivered. I was waited on by the orderlies of the Kommandantur, the Officers' Mess was beneath my bedroom, and my supper was brought up after they were served. I could hear them singing and cheering, while they bumped their glasses against the table when news of some special "victory" was announced to them. The waiters, Karl and Fritz, were easy-going fellows, who were thankful to have a "soft" place and good food instead of being sent to the Front. They wondered at my want of appetite, and recommended favourite dishes, among which I remember was that German delicacy "Carpfen".

It was lucky that I had insisted upon taking a change of linen. The bed was made and the room kept by two "Landsturmen", evidently simple peasants who had not learned to wash much. Every time they left my room I was obliged to throw the window wide open to air it. I had forgotten most of the German learned in childhood, but, in any case, could not understand the guttural patois these men spoke, and evidently they had received orders not to speak to me. The watch outside the door was changed daily. At night one lay across my door-sill, while the other stood further down the passage. One of them (he seemed a decent fellow) once dared to have a conversation in perfect English with me, saying he had been in business in England and America, but he did not dare take the open letter I asked him to deliver for me to Prince Saxe-Meiningen at Government House. However, one of the policemen took it next day, and delivered it, for I got an answer. Prince Georg told me that he had appealed in vain on my behalf. I heard afterwards that the Military Governor, General von Sauberzweig, had rudely refused to receive him.

The first night after my arrest, what with anxiety over my grandmother and fear for Reginald, I was unable to sleep, also the very loud noise that the sentry made walking up and down before my door, of which I was not allowed to keep the key inside, disturbed me. Motor-cars and police vans kept bringing in people who had been arrested, and discharging them in the courtyard beneath my windows. I saw ladies, priests, people both old and young, and once a Belgian soldier, being taken into the police office on the ground floor opposite. The upper stories were evidently used as prisons, for all the windows were barred. On one floor were women, and above them, men, several in a room together. I watched carefully as the newly arrested prisoners passed in front of the motor-lights in the courtyard below, terrified lest among them I might recognise my brother. On the next day, Lieutenant

Bergan came to say that, notwithstanding the solemn promise he had given to me that I should return at once to my grandmother, he was obliged, by order, to keep me prisoner. He said he had got into trouble for letting my brother escape, that they had heard that he had arrived in Holland, but that if I knew of his whereabouts and would tell them, they would immediately order my release. My heart jumped with joy on hearing that Reginald was supposed to be in Holland, although I was not sure if it were true. But it was wiser to pretend to be certain of the fact, and, however much contempt I felt for those who dared to make such an offer, I endeavoured to answer calmly that Reginald was safe and could never return.

Judging from what the police told me, the watch along the frontier must have been a very close one, and therefore I knew that the journey had been both difficult and dangerous. On my return to Brussels after the Armistice, I heard the whole story from the man who had saved my brother, the *passeur*, Henri Beyns. This Flemish working-man, living on the outskirts of Brussels, father of several small children, was a devoted patriot. He acted as guide or *passeur* to a nun, who, under the name of Mademoiselle Joséphine, helped to repatriate soldiers and send young men to fight for king and country. Another who worked with Mademoiselle Joséphine was an electrician, called Michel Richard, who collected letters and sent them by secret means to the Belgian Army. Doctor Van Swieten, on hearing from Marie de Lichtervelde the danger that threatened Reginald, urged her to trust Richard and Mademoiselle Joséphine to find a guide. Marie had already been in touch with Richard, who, having once fetched letters from her house, had been arrested on leaving it, and while waiting to be questioned at the Kommandantur had eaten the letters, thus destroying all evidence. He had since received from Marie a letter destined for Reginald, sent from The Hague, and giving directions as to sending on workmen for munitions, with the password by which they were to make themselves known to the authorities. As Reginald had not returned from Bellignies just then, and Miss Cavell and Baucq had been arrested two days previously, the possession of this letter was a danger in itself, but Richard kept it until Reginald arrived, and was able to learn it by heart before destroying it.

As it was evident that Reginald could not use the German pass given him on previous occasions, the first thing necessary was to get identity papers of some sort. It was found that his appearance was sufficiently like that of a Belgian who had died lately for an impersonation to be possible. To obtain an identity card, a witness ready to answer for you must accompany you in person to the local town hall, and a brave young lady was soon found ready to run this risk. She went with Reggie to the "maison communale", where he duly received papers in the name of René Desmet. This allowed him to travel by tram as far as Vilvorde, after which town Beyns considered it safer to continue on foot. At Waechter, all the bridges being guarded, they took refuge in a wood, until, under cover of darkness, a friend of the guide's ferried them across the Dyle. The rest of the night was passed at the cottage of Beyns' friend, and next morning they were joined by Monsieur van Maldeghem of Brussels, who also desired to leave Belgium, although, not having a price placed on his head, he was freer to move about the country.

The three continued on foot, passing through the Mérodes' woods at Westerloo, where they nearly met our cousins face to face, and went on to the Abbey of Tongerloo, where the monks hid them. Here, having waited several days in vain for the special guides who made it a business of getting men across the danger zone, they decided to go on to more friends of Beyns who were ready to run the risk of harbouring fugitives. Living in woods by day, travelling by night, sleeping in haystacks, they arrived at last near Baelen, where they spent five days. The good folks who hid them were miserably poor; the husband, burned by molten lead in a factory accident, was nearly blind, while a child was dumb and paralysed. But, without asking for any remuneration, they took in those whom they knew to be in danger, and shared their potatoes, black bread, and chicory with them.

At last a guide who knew the region was found, and he promised to get them across the canal by night. The rendezvous was to be at a hut in the wood, not far from the canal, but when M. van Maldeghem, Reginald, and Beyns reached this hut in the darkness, they were suddenly faced by several people who held them up at the point of a revolver, and searched them. Finding no fire-arms, and having examined their papers, they at last appeared satisfied, and explained that they, too, had been given a rendezvous at this hut by the guide. Our travellers' fears that they had fallen into a trap began to abate, and at last the guide turned up. Beyns had provided himself with a long rope and a canvas bag for their clothes, and he also carried two packets of letters and military documents. Monsieur van Maldeghem and Reginald, being the only two able to swim, agreed to cross the canal and tie the cord to a tree on the other side, so that the others could pull themselves across. Reginald swam first, pulling his guide with him, Beyns bringing the bags of clothes and letters. Still several miles from the Dutch frontier, they crept into some brushwood to dress while some of the strangers followed, but when about half of them had crossed, the cord broke, and with a great splash a man fell in the canal. Immediately the German watch, which was only about two hundred yards distant, turned the searchlight in their direction, and the party on the far side were obliged to lie low, fearing all the while that a man might be struggling in the water, and knowing that the six who still remained on the other side were without clothes. Beyns crawled to the bank and waited some time hidden in the rushes, but neither seeing nor hearing anything, and fearful of being surprised by daylight before reaching Holland, they decided to leave the clothes at a cottage, and continued their way through the marshes.

The guide went ahead, feeling rather than seeing the track between dykes and undergrowth. Beyns missed the plank bridge over one of these dykes, and tumbled in the water, without, however, losing hold of his bag of papers, and Reginald fished him out. Wet and draggled they hurried on to do the seven kilometres which separated them still from safety. It was not until day was breaking that they saw a fire among the trees, which the guide surmised rightly was that of the Dutch soldiers on watch there. The whole population in this part of Holland felt sympathy with Belgium, and showed much kindness to the refugees, and the soldiers gave our party coffee and a guide to the nearest village, twelve kilometres off. Here, at last able to breathe freely, they dried their clothes, and hired a cart to take them to the nearest station, still some miles distant. But after lying for three weeks in woods, haystacks, and peasants' cottages, without means of shaving, their appearance drew the attention of the Dutch police, when they got into a first-class carriage for The Hague. However, when Beyns whispered Reginald's name to the gendarmes, the latter bowed politely and gave all information for the further journey. Our cousin, Ligne, Minister at The Hague, had taken measures for Reginald's safety, on hearing of his possible arrival.

A touching incident, showing the delicacy of the guide's mind, is the fact that Henri Beyns kept to himself the knowledge of my arrest. He had learnt it on one of his many journeys to find a new route, but guessing that this might induce Reginald to return and give himself up, he said nothing, and it was only when safely in our cousin's hands at the Legation that my brother heard the truth. His surrender at that time would have certainly meant his own death, and would have made no difference to me, or rather it would have made it harder for me to defend myself; so I could not be too grateful to the guide for showing so much discretion. It was openly said that Reginald would be shot, and the following letter which Governor-General von Bissing wrote to a cousin of his is significant.

BRUSSELS, 23 *October* 1915.

DEAR COUSIN,

In answer to yours of the 16th I send you back Countess d'Ursel's letter, and communicate the following about Princess de Croÿ's affair:

The Princess was condemned a few days ago to ten years' penal servitude for treason. She was obliged to own to having taken in a great number of enemy soldiers, sent them through the frontier, and helped them to re-enter the enemies' armies. In the same case five people were condemned to death; the brother of the Princess was the leader of the organisation, and, if arrested, would doubtless have been condemned to death.

After such a grave misdemeanour, it is quite impossible for me, now after the announcement of the verdict, to take an appeal for mercy into consideration. The Princess acted, as she herself declares, in full knowledge of the penalty she incurred, in the gravest way against the laws of war, and through her action presumably brought many of our brave soldiers to their death. In such cases indulgence would be a crime against one's own Fatherland. Consideration as to position or sex is the less to be used, because our enemies, in an objectionable manner, prefer the help of women for espionage, knowing that in case of condemnation they can always count on the sentimentality of the masses.

Please convey my best regards to your parents. Cordial greetings, always your cousin,   MORITZ BISSING.

(I add a translation of the letter received by my brother from Henri Beyns early in 1916, which gives some idea of the Belgian patriot's mentality at the time. It loses much in translation.)

FLUSHING, 7.3.16.

HIS EXCELLENCY THE PRINCE DE CROŸ,

Already many times have I wished to write, but not knowing your address, it was impossible. Now, by the help of my Chief in the service, the Rev. Abbé de Moor, who promises to forward this letter, I take the respectful liberty, dear Prince, to write these few words. I remember always the days and nights we passed together hidden in hay or straw in many different places. Since that time the passages become more and more difficult, and I find myself in the same situation as with you of not being able to pass. Since 28 days I am in Holland, unable to get back, although at present my journeys are most useful, because for some time I have worked for the Rev. Abbé de Moor and other gentlemen on most important business. I go forward and back to Brussels every ten days or so, carrying each time 14 or 15 kilos of letters, also I am entrusted with the *Mot du Soldat*, which is well organised, once more thanks to the energy of the convents. For I can truly say that if every one did their duty like the religious and the clergy, who work night and day for our dear country, things would go ten times better. Unfortunately, it is just the contrary with a few bourgeois and bad women, who betray the Belgians who do their duty. But courage, their turn will come. Now for a year I have worked for XX in Flushing, and since you passed, I have been denounced three times, and each time I got a new identity card, with the help of the convents. Since you left I went once to see my dear wife, now and then I see her in Brussels, but go home and see my children I dare not. It is hard, for I love my children, but I fear their seeing me, because several times they have been asked, "Where is your father?" and they answer that I am in England. But courage, I will not abandon my service, especially now that hardly anyone can get through. I have a duty towards my country, and will do it; my country above everything.

My son of 16, poor boy, was condemned to three weeks' imprisonment because a letter from a soldier at the front was found on him. He was beaten and got three weeks. I am proud of him, because he got out of it so well, and on his release he said to me, "If they had killed me I would not have denounced you." He asked me to take him with me so that he might join the army. I took him, and he volunteered for the artillery; now he is 16½. Here is his address: Jacques Beyns, 1st Battery Artillery, A. B. Instruction Camp at Eu, Seine Inf. He is very contented, and has asked three times to be sent to the front. I am not surprised, he is furious against the Germans. My poor wife was arrested too, and kept five days at the Commandanture through the fault of an idiot who came to me several times to ask me to take his son through the lines. I did so, but when later the young man did not present himself to the German control, they enquired of his father where he was, and the fool answered,

"My neighbour, Henri Beyns, took him to Holland." Naturally they came to my wife to get news of me. She answered, "Don't ask me about my husband. He has left me with five children, that's all I know." The fool continued saying she knew where I was as she had had letters from me, and she was kept five days at the Commandanture, where she always denied, until they released her. But the neighbour is ill at ease, as all are furious against him.

With the help of the convents I have organised a good service for getting young men away, but unfortunately the watch on the frontier is very strict. However, I shall not lose courage; I have worked since the first day of the war.

Hoping, Monsieur le Prince, that this terrible war will end soon, I present to you my best salutations—Thy servant, H. BEYNS.

September 9.—At last, after several days of solitude, I had a visit on Thursday the 9th from Marie de Lichtervelde. She said she had only just heard of my arrest, and had obtained with difficulty the permission to bring me some linen. She was accompanied by Bergan and another policeman, who watched us closely, but she managed to whisper the one word "passé" as she kissed me, and I knew my brother was in safety. She said that Maître Alexandre Braun would undertake my defence, but that both he and she wished to know of what I was accused. Before bringing her in, Bergan had told me that the visit was allowed on condition we spoke only of family affairs, and that I did not say one word about the case. I told her of this, and then we talked about my grandmother, whom she promised to look after if she could get a permit to go to Bellignies. She gave me the linen she had brought, which the two officers minutely examined before letting me have it, and then left, promising to return in a few days if possible. I asked Bergan for permission to attend Mass on Sunday, and to take a walk in the park. He answered that the Mass was impossible, but that I should be allowed half an hour's walk every two days, accompanied by my guard, and in a spot indicated. This spot was the *Quinconce*[1] just opposite the Kommandantur. I was allowed to walk between two rows of tall trees, while further down in the same square an elderly gentleman in plain clothes was also walking up and down, followed by two soldiers. Every time we passed between the same row of trees and, therefore, caught sight of one another, my fellow-prisoner made me a deep bow. My guards told me that he was a Belgian General, but I did not learn his name. He was imprisoned in a room not far from mine, but I never met him in the house.

Across the courtyard, opposite my windows, the rooms got fuller and fuller. Most of their occupants looked to me like soldiers, or young men of military age, whom the enemy were collecting to send to Germany. At meal-times, when the watch was relaxed, they used to crowd around the window and sing patriotic and national airs in subdued tones. Seeing how much pleasure the *Brabançonne, Flanderland, Vers l'Avenir, Sambre et Meuse*, etc., gave me, after a while they did this regularly twice daily,

[1] Square planted with trees at right angles.

while the Germans beneath my room were shouting and singing too. One day my young compatriots held up a large sheet of paper behind their bars, on which in very large black letters they had written my name followed by a note of interrogation. When I nodded my head they all clapped their hands noiselessly and began to hum the *Brabançonne*. I was infinitely touched at this patriotic manifestation of sympathy.

An insufferable personage seemed to rule all at the Kommandantur. I saw him in the courtyard strutting about like a turkey-cock, snapping out orders to the soldiers, who seemed terrified of him, and generally poking his nose in everywhere. A more ridiculous figure could not be conceived; as he bulged out his chest while strutting up and down, he was a regular caricature. This was the Feldwebel (sergeant-major), in his own estimation at any rate the most important person, and in that of others the most insufferable, in the German Army. One day, when I had had bad palpitation and the sentry had found me fainting, he had fetched this pompous *sous-officier*, who promised to send a doctor. Shortly afterwards a young medical man arrived from Government House, who, after sounding my heart and looking perplexed, asked me why I was there. Suspecting an impertinence, I answered, "Because I am a patriot." He looked confused and said, "But have you no one, not even a *femme-de-chambre*?" I answered, "No, only an orderly." The next day, a German woman arrived, saying she had been sent by order of the doctor to look after me, and from now on she did the service of my room.

A few days later I had at last got news from home. Mademoiselle Louise arrived with Marie de Lichtervelde, of course accompanied as usual by policemen. They told me that the letter I had written and confided to Bergan on that first evening had been delivered to my grandmother, who had had a fainting fit after reading it. She had herself written to the Kommandantur authorities when I did not return. This made me more and more anxious, and I sent urgent letters asking that I might be permitted to return home until the trial, offering to give my word of honour not to escape, and saying that perhaps my grandmother's life depended on her seeing me. But these letters remained without any answer. A few days later, on the 19th of September, our Curé arrived, looking very serious, to tell me that my poor grandmother had had a seizure the day before, and was unable to speak or move. He had brought with him a letter she had written before falling ill, addressed to Prince Saxe-Meiningen. Monsieur le Curé told me he had visited my friends in Brussels, as well as Maître Braun, and that all were interceding on my behalf. He would return home next day and hoped to reassure my grandmother. The doctor came after he had left, and gave me a tonic for my heart, which was feeling the strain and anxiety.

On Saturday the 25th a military *auditeur*, called

Lukas, arrived to tell me that permission had been accorded for me to return home for a few hours on the following Monday, on condition that I gave my word of honour to return immediately, adding, "because it would be awkward to have to use force towards a lady". He said that two policemen would accompany me with the order not to leave me out of their sight even by the sick-bed, and that I must not mention the affair; also that Maître Braun had offered me the use of his car and to accompany me on this sad journey. All this was told in a harsh, almost insulting, tone of voice. I naturally accepted the conditions, caring only to be able to console my poor grandmother. They left me quiet for a few hours, but about seven in the evening, when I was lying on my bed, the door opened suddenly, and in came Lukas again, saying in a hard voice, "The permission that I told you had been accorded you for Monday has been withdrawn by order of his Excellency the Governor-General." Seeing by my blank look that I did not understand, he repeated the same phrase, and went out and shut the door.

Three days passed without news, days of mortal anxiety for me. At last Maître Braun, accompanied of course, came to see me and broke the sad news. Even had we gone home on Monday I should have been too late; my grandmother had died on the Sunday night without regaining consciousness. Charlotte, seeing that the case was getting graver, had managed to reach Brussels on Saturday, and my brave, devoted friend Marie de Lichtervelde had returned with her and remained several days at Bellignies. They had both written to me at once, but the letters had not been delivered. Maître Braun told me that the whole village had shown their sympathy by taking it in turns to watch and pray until the funeral. The Mayor and Municipal Council had attended the funeral, and some had even been allowed to follow the hearse as far as Solre, to our family vault, where Marie de Lichtervelde had thanked all in my name.

It seems that after I left home, on two occasions Germans arrived to search the house, taking away the last bottles of wine which had been left before by permission, as well as the little carriage which was the only means of fetching a doctor, as the telephone was long gone, and not even a bicycle was left in the country. The old mare had been requisitioned, too, but after a few miles the Germans had found out that they had been told the truth when assured that she was over thirty years old, and let her go again, but they had kept the dog-cart. The soldiers who came down in my absence, unable to speak French, still frightened the household by pretending to hold a gun and aim at someone, saying at the same time, "The Prince", upon which all imagined that my brother had been caught and would be shot. After a few days of this anxiety, one day my grandmother had fallen senseless on the floor, and it was the little dogs that by their barking, and rushing forward and back to her, called the servants' attention. The Curé had been fetched, and the two doctors from Bavay had been allowed to come, but she never spoke again, and lay watching the door through which she doubtless hoped to see me arrive, until mercifully she died.

Nothing could exceed the kindness and sympathy Maître Braun showed me when breaking the sad news, and even the official interpreter, present, of course, at our interview, appeared to feel the poignancy of the situation. I heard that the trial was fixed for the following week, and it was rather a relief if anything. That evening I fainted while undressing, and the sentry outside the door, hearing me fall, picked me up, laid me on my bed, and called out of the window for a doctor, as my woman attendant was absent at the time. I had once or twice lately had a slight haemorrhage of the lungs, and when the doctor arrived, seeing blood on my pillow, I believe he suspected at first an attempted suicide, a thing much commoner in Germany than with us. Indeed, before my grandmother's death it was this thought or fear that it might appear like suicide which had prevented my making an attempt at escape by means of a fire-ladder which passed not far from my window, and by which I believed I could reach the roof, and from thence over other roofs find my way to some house inhabited by Belgians. But in jumping to reach the fire-escape I ran a great risk of falling two stories, when I should inevitably have been killed.

October 7.—At last on Thursday the 7th October the trial began. With my woman attendant and a soldier, I was conducted before nine o' clock (German time) to the Senate. As I entered the Parliament, I saw before me on my left a row of gentlemen in civilian clothes, who bowed deeply as I passed; among them was Maître Braun, and I understood these were counsel for the defence. As I was conducted across the floor, one of many German officers grouped there came forward, and, bowing politely, told me in case I felt unwell to apply to him; it was the doctor, and this public act of respect on his part showed great courage. A few days before, after my grandmother's death, when he had found my heart in a bad condition, and had also been hearing evidently ominous predictions as to my fate, on leaving the room he had suddenly turned and said, "Was haben Sie doch getan?" "Nothing but my duty, doctor", I answered: "You would have done the same thing in my place." "No," said he almost violently, "women should have nothing to do with war, women should remain in their own homes." "I *was* in my own home looking after my own people. It was your people who tore me away." By the expression which came into his eyes, and by what he next said, I realised that he expected me to be condemned to death.

I was conducted to one of the Senators' seats; a soldier sat on either side of me. It was the first time I had been inside our Government House, and the sight of the enemy's uniforms filling all the galleries was a very displeasing one. All these officers had come to look on as at some entertainment; some even had field-glasses with which they fixed the members of our association spread about the room in the different Senators' chairs, separated from each other by soldiers. Even in the royal box I saw officers, one or two of whom kept more or less out of sight behind the curtains. I supposed the Governor-General von Bissing to be one of these, but later it was announced that he was out of Brussels at the time. When we were all in our places, five judges, elderly men, in various uniforms, but, I believe, all decorated with the Iron Cross, took their places at right angles to the bench where our defenders were sitting, and then the *Auditeur militaire*, Kriegsgerichtsrat Stoeber, young, tall, very elegant, and with a glass in his eye, opened the proceedings. I heard afterwards that he had been brought to Brussels especially for this case, as he was known to be what in England would be called "a hanging judge". He evidently thoroughly enjoyed his rôle, speaking in an authoritative voice which he modulated as an actor does, using occasionally low persuasive tones, but more often sharp incisive expressions. Then Bergan, the police officer, who took credit to himself for the whole affair, forgetting his brilliant second Pinkhoff, to whose ruse most of the success was really due, made a long deposition.

After this, which was entirely in German, and which, with one or two exceptions, none of the accused understood, we were all removed from the

Court for the cross-examination to begin. Among those whom I had recognised, and who sat at short distances from me, was Miss Cavell, whom I regretted to see in civilian clothes, a simple blue dress and sailor hat. It was the first time I had seen her out of nurse's costume, and I think it a great pity she had not worn it during the trial, as, apart from its charitable significance in all eyes, anything in the way of a uniform imposed on the German mind. Jeanne de Belleville sat looking collected and firm. Further on were Mademoiselle Thuliez, Capiau, and Baucq, and other gentlemen whom I did not know, but have learned since were Messieurs Desmoustier, Libiez, Severin, and Hostelet. Still further off was Madame Bodart, Irish by birth, whom I had never seen, but knew from those who had taken men to her house to have been an active confederate. Indeed, it was her having kindly offered to warn one of our groups of young men, so that Reginald might not miss his tram, that had led to her arrest in his place. She was a widow with two young children, one of whom, notwithstanding his young age, twelve or thirteen, I believe, was to be used as a witness against his mother. Taking advantage of the innocence and inexperience of a child did not seem to strike our jailers as being a shameful thing.

I was conducted to a room set aside for the medical staff of the General Government, in which several officers were working at statistics. Here I was offered some refreshment which I refused, although I had taken nothing but some water that morning, fearing to be drugged, as I knew had been done in other cases. Indeed, I fear that some of our prisoners in this case had been given something which excited them and made them unfit to reflect calmly. More than one medical man has shared this surmise.

After some hours I was taken back to the Senate, where I found five or six of our confederates sitting in their places, by which I judged that they had already been examined. To my great relief an oath was not asked of me. Although I had been assured on various occasions that even an oath was not binding in these circumstances, I felt I could not give it when I was determined to go on denying everything that could not be proved against me. Indeed, each time that I had been questioned up to now (and the police had frequently come to my room and startled me with suggestions which showed that someone must have spoken), I had contented myself with saying that I knew nothing. This had made them say to me one day that by continuing to deny I was only making my case worse, as they all respected those who took the responsibility of their acts upon themselves, whereas those who denied them were incurring the utmost rigours of the law. "Look at *die Cavell*, and one or two others, they are admirable women, they cannot tell a lie. . . ." But I had decided to refuse the oath if required of me. At the beginning of the proceedings Bergan and Pinkhoff had taken a solemn oath, holding their hands up and repeating the words after the judge while the whole assembly stood. It made me think of the word of honour given with raised hands to my grandmother, and I wondered if the good faith in this case would be equal to what it had been then. On my left were the Belgian lawyers, whom I was not allowed to face.

I was given a chair in the centre of the Court, facing the five judges, in front of whom was seated the Court interpreter. The usual questions as to name, age, nationality, and religion having been answered, I am asked if it is true that I am the sister of the Prince de Croÿ. I answer that I am the sister of two Princes de Croÿ, one a Belgian officer at present at the Front, and the other of whose actual whereabouts I am unaware. Then I am asked if it is true that I have housed, between March and June, French and English soldiers who had been hidden in the country. Knowing that this can be proved, I answered, "Yes." Do I own to having photographed these men when they were with me? Yes. Why? Here I had to be careful because I had denied all knowledge of the false papers, so I answered that the men required photos to obtain their identity card, so as to be able to travel to Brussels.

The next question was, did I not know that it was to enable them to leave occupied territory as I had said during the instruction of the case? I answered, "Ainsi qu'on m'a fait dire." ("As I was made to say.") This angered the police because it showed, what was a fact, that they had turned our words and often changed their significance by the interpretation of them. I said that my aim in helping these men was to get them out of the "Étapes", where their life was in danger, as we were continually hearing of men being taken and shot, notably at Hiron, where eleven soldiers, as well as the miller who was hiding them, had been shot together; that I believed by putting them in Belgium, where there was a responsible Government, I was saving their lives. Why in this case, if I only wished to save their lives, did I not give them up to the German authorities? I answered, firstly, because they would have refused, and, secondly, when in the beginning with great difficulty I had prevailed on some English soldiers to give themselves up, grave trouble had been brought on to the district, our Mayor had been arrested, threatened with death, and at last condemned to a big fine, and, finally, all who knew of what had been done had blamed the surrender of the men.

Where did these soldiers go?—To Brussels.

Who took care of them there?—I did not know.

How could an intelligent person like myself let men go away without knowing where they were going?—I never wished for information which might bring danger to others.

Who conducted them?—My brother and Mademoiselle Thuliez (she had avowed before me).

Why had I done this?—Because my brother had asked it of me. (By a secret sign on which we had agreed I knew that Maître Braun wished me to put all the culpability on my brother, and, indeed, I had hoped, by letting them know he was not arrested as they had been told, that all the accused could have exculpated themselves by accusing him.

But here Stoeber leaned forward and said in a low sarcastic tone of voice, "Then it is only to obey your brother that you have acted as you have done." On hearing this, and seeing the malicious flash in his eye, my pride revolted, and throwing prudence to the winds, I answered, "Oui, mais je ne demandais pas mieux." A look of satisfaction spread over his face, while I heard a movement on the bench of the defence, but he continued, "Did you not know what danger you ran in acting so?" Without hesitation I answered in the first words that came into my mind, "One must do one's duty without thinking of the consequences." Maître Alexandre Braun told me later that this answer had been quoted in a sermon at Maredsous, but after all I only stated a fact that was patent to us all, however disagreeable it was to the enemy. I was next asked if it were true that I had given Mademoiselle Thuliez money, and I answered, "Yes, for her personal use." There were a few other futile questions, such as whether I had photographed one or two men on each plate, but the above is the most important. At the instruction of the case, seeing it was useless to deny having taken in English soldiers, I had, nevertheless, denied all knowledge of the French, notwithstanding that they had been quite as numerous as the British, if not more so, and Bergan had said sneeringly, "You are not more culpable because some were French, on the contrary." At this time hatred of England was at its height. I had heard officers greet each other with the exclamation, "Gott strafe England", and on every occasion something insulting was said against our Allies.

After I was conducted back to my place, more prisoners were brought in one after the other, and questioned. Among these was a chemist who owned to having received several English soldiers from Reginald. Various other people also inculpated him, which was their surest mode of defence. With an interval for lunch, during which some of our prisoners ate provisions they had brought, and others shared the soup of the soldiers, and which I passed in a room set aside for the medical staff, the trial went on until six at night. Before leaving the Court, the judge called up Lieutenant Bergan and questioned him about certain discrepancies between his depositions and the evidence, among others about my remark, "On m'a fait dire". He fell at once into a passion, accusing me and others violently to justify himself. I was too weary to answer, as well as knowing it useless.

On the next day, Friday, the trial began again at nine o'clock (German time—eight o'clock Belgian time). The various subordinates were examined in turn. Many of our simple folk, who had either helped to guide soldiers from place to place, or had been found hiding them in their poor little cottages, were far too bewildered at finding themselves in a Court of Justice, if so it can be called, to be able to defend themselves. In the heavy dragging *patois* of the Borinage they answered the insidious questions put to them. But, with few exceptions, among these that of a woman who had already been imprisoned for crime, and had by an error of judgment been used as a guide, no one said a word that a patriot could regret hearing in the presence of our enemies. One poor fellow, a miner, when asked how he fed the English soldiers he had hidden after the battle of Mons, answered, "We gave them our portion of bread, and lived on potatoes ourselves, and these were often rotten ones." Attempts were made to prove that the poorer confederates had acted from interested motives; insinuations as to sums of money having been promised by the British Government were made, but the poor fellows could only say that if they had been paid it was merely a pittance they had received to be able to live.

A little in front of me, below, sat Baucq. I saw him feverishly taking notes, and frequently he interrupted the proceedings to mark a point which he considered in his favour. The permission to speak was always accorded to him grudgingly, first Stoeber, then the interpreter, addressing him rudely. The Court interpreter repeated in French the whole of the interrogatory, but although, as far as I could judge, it was an exact translation, he managed to put so much hatred into his voice that the whole sense seemed perverted. Later, when the advocate asked for the death penalty, I remember especially the vindictive tone in which he rolled out the words, "la morrrt". One witness, in his inexperience, gave evidence which was incriminating to poor Monsieur Baucq. Until then the latter had contested point by point. When he heard the fatal "Yes", his head fell between his hands, and his shaking shoulders betrayed his emotion. It was a terrible sight to look on helpless at the despair of this brave father of a family, young, and with a smiling future before him, realising that his life was in jeopardy.

From the beginning a special vindictiveness had been displayed towards this unfortunate man. He had been active in helping with patriotic propaganda, had distributed the *Mots du Soldat*, and especially the *Libre Belgique*, the small clandestine news-sheet which told impertinent truths to our persecutors, and helped to maintain a good morale in the population. Various organisers and producers of this little paper had been arrested from time to time, but someone was always found to continue the publication, and the seeming impossibility of suppressing it exasperated the German authorities. I think one may attribute the rigorous sentence pronounced eventually on Baucq quite as much to this, as to their desire not to let the Englishwoman stand alone as their victim. It would appear that Miss Cavell had admitted in her evidence having received money from another witness. This money had in reality come from a different source, and the witness had only been the go-between in handing it to Nurse Cavell. Therefore, he strenuously denied having given her money, whereupon the judge turned to her and roughly demanded if she had lied. She stood up in her place, two chairs distant from mine, and said quietly, "I made a mistake before, I have reflected since, it was not Mr. X. who gave me money." The rudeness, the brutality even, which a magistrate used towards this brave lady were unworthy of any civilised nation.

Then Stoeber stood up briskly, and, feeling the eyes of all present fixed upon him, showed that he meant to exploit the situation to the utmost. Smart, tightly buttoned in his uniform, with high collar and shining hair, he looked triumphantly around him, and began the speech for the prosecution, and a terrible accusation it was. He said that they were in presence of a great organisation, whose aim was to help the evasion of soldiers and young men of military age from occupied territory, and to send them to the Allied armies; that they knew that by this means more than 250 soldiers had passed. Therefore, all the accused were guilty of high treason, and he asked for the sentence of death for many of them, and hard labour for the rest. This was said in a theatrical voice, and whenever allusion was made to the "brave" German soldiers who fell as a consequence of our plot, he turned towards the judges to receive from them an approving nod.[1]

When he sat down, our defenders began to plead.

[1] A translation of the summing-up will be found in the Appendix.

First, Maître Thomas Braun,[1] speaking also, of course, in German, made a fine appeal, saying that all Germans to whom he had spoken of the case agreed that they would have acted in the same way. He said that we had none of us gone out of our way to hurt the German Army, but had found ourselves placed before a fact, and had only the choice between helping our people and denouncing them. When Maître Kirschen in turn spoke he said something which put Stoeber into a violent temper. To calm this irascible judge, he had to explain that he was speaking a foreign language and might occasionally use a wrong expression.

When Maître Braun at last took my defence and that of Jeanne de Belleville, he called the attention of the judges to the fact that I had acted under the influence of my brother, and that my aim through all had been to save human life. He touched on my care of the German wounded, and of how I had already suffered through the death of my grandmother, and read to them the letter I had addressed to him during her last illness, in my anguish. But as he had never seen the act of accusation any more than the other counsel for the defence, and had, of course, never been allowed to confer with the accused, he did not know the true facts, and showed that he believed me to have helped the wounded I had nursed to escape. So after he had finished I asked to be allowed to explain. I tried as far as possible to disculpate my

[1] The son of Alexandre.

companions, especially Nurse Cavell, whom I said to have been brought into danger by having the men sent to her, and I formally denied the existence of any organisation. But one saw perfectly that nothing any of us said would have an effect on our judges, as their minds were clearly made up, and, in any case, they would not have dared to show leniency. Indeed, the fanaticism of German patriotism at this time would have made them rejoice if we had all been condemned to be shot there and then, and I appreciated all the more the courtesy and courage of the doctor, who again bowed as I was leaving the Court, and said he was at my service if I required him. Herr Behrens permitted me to shake hands with Maître Braun as I passed, and all the Belgian lawyers bowed deeply. At the door was Otto Meyer, in German uniform, who a fortnight before had pretended to me he was an English Tommy wishing to escape, but, of course, I did not deign to recognise him.

This second day's sitting had lasted from nine in the morning until five in the afternoon without any break, a very exhausting ordeal. The next two days seemed interminable. I had a visit from the German chaplain, Herr Leyendecker, whose demeanour showed me that he thought very seriously of my situation. He promised to bring me Holy Communion on the Tuesday, and I wondered as he said so if he thought it would be for the last time. On the Monday afternoon, suddenly my room was invaded by several officers, among whom was Stoeber.

In an official voice he said that he had come to announce the sentences, whereupon he began reading a long list, headed, if I can remember rightly, by the name of Baucq, after which the word "Todesstrafe" (*la mort*) followed, as well as for Miss Cavell, Comtesse de Belleville, Mademoiselle Thuliez, and others. Then various sentences of penal servitude with hard labour, among which mine was for ten years.

While the long list droned on I was thinking rapidly if it were possible to obtain a commutation of the death sentences, and before they left, asked to be allowed to see my lawyer. I remarked that Stoeber's manner had considerably softened since his speech in Court, and he listened civilly while I told him that the police had given a false impression during the whole affair, at least in as far as those whom I knew were concerned, especially Miss Cavell, Jeanne de Belleville, and Mademoiselle Thuliez. He said that I might make an appeal in their favour, that I had better write at once as briefly as possible and he would have my letter sent to the Governor-General. He said I could not be allowed to confer with my lawyer, but must do it entirely alone, and he reiterated, "Do it at once." He asked me if I would not also appeal for myself, but I answered impatiently that all that mattered just then were the lives that were in danger. On his way down he met my German attendant to whom he again expressed his desire that I should send in the appeal *at once*.

Weak and bewildered I wrote, divided between the desire to save the lives of my friends at any cost, and repugnance at asking a favour, or making excuses to our persecutors. Again long hours of anxiety, and at last the chaplain came and brought me Holy Communion. He began talking almost at once about Miss Cavell and Monsieur Baucq, and to my dismay I discovered that they had both been shot within twelve hours of having heard their sentence. He believed me to know it, but I explained that I had heard nothing and seen no one, and then he told me that he had been present at the execution, although Miss Cavell had been assisted by a Protestant clergyman. He said our heroic ally had remained dignified and calm until the end, that her courage had been so great that she had slept quietly until morning. As to Baucq, he appears to have met his fate as a man and a Christian, and I heard afterwards that he had had the courage to pretend to his wife, at their last interview, that he was only going as a prisoner to Germany. Herr Leyendecker showed himself to have been deeply moved by this execution, and I could feel that he regretted it, and considered it to have been wrong.[1] He listened

---

[1] The following is a translation of the letter he wrote to the victim's family:

Brussels, 19 Rue Plétincx.

DEAR BAUCQ FAMILY,

I wish, after having assisted your well-beloved husband, father, and son in his last moments, and having taken your place at his side, to make a little report to you, which will, I know, be a small consolation. I saw M. Baucq yesterday often, both before and

patiently to my expressions of horror, and my prediction that Germany would pay dearly for such a crime.

---

after the sentence. I found him always brave and calm, but more especially at the very last moment. When the sentence of death was pronounced, I did all in my power to obtain a reprieve, but all was useless, and at midday yesterday I had the sad mission to announce that the execution would take place this morning. He confessed with deep piety, knowing the execution would take place. I would have warned you, but he preferred not to let you know; especially that the sentence was to be carried out at once.

He had the courage to keep the secret, and I beg you not to find this decision hard; he did it for love of you. Last evening I talked long with him. He begged me to transmit his last wishes and recommendations, which will reach you at the same time as this little report, which I make to you with my door besieged by people who are asking to speak to me. As he had more writing to do in his last hours, I left him to come back early this morning to bring him Communion, which he received with touching piety. We recited the prayer of Pius X., which bears an indulgence at the hour of death. He spent the greater part of the night with soldiers and prisoners, which will have kept his mind from too sad thoughts. Soon after we left the prison, and I remained at his side, until the supreme moment. We prayed together until the end.

M. Baucq took leave of the soldiers in the prison in the most touching way, thanking them for their services, and saying that he died without feeling of rancour against anyone. He also said goodbye to the soldiers on the field of execution. Again and again he asked me to say farewell to his family, and at the time of death his thoughts would be with them. I embraced him a last time for you all, we recited the act of contrition, a last word of farewell, and in an instant his soul was before his Judge, Who will have welcomed it, resigned and purified, with the smile of a Father receiving a child in the Eternal Home. I immediately administered the Extreme Unction, although it is usual only to do so when a little life remains, but in this case at any rate there was no consciousness Then after death had been certified, his body was placed in a coffin, and buried with the ceremonies of the Church.

Dear Baucq Family, your husband, father, and son died the

After this visit I received one from my kind defender, Maître Braun, who told me that there was great hope that the appeal for the rest of our condemned friends would be successful, as the King of Spain had intervened personally. Also that our protecting Ministers[1] had spent two nights with the Government, pleading for all the condemned, and that he considered I could be reassured as to the fates of Jeanne de Belleville, Mademoiselle Thuliez, etc. Then I had a visit from Marie de Lichtervelde, who told me how anxious everyone was on our account, that the Spanish Ambassador (or rather Minister, as the Legation was only raised to an Embassy after the war in recognition of the great services rendered by King Alfonso and his representative) had spent the whole night disputing the lives of the condemned with our judges. Unfortunately, Governor-General von Bissing was absent at the time, and all power was in the hands of the military Governor, General von Sauberzweig. The latter had recently been nominated, and I remember how, on the evening of his first appearance at the Kommandantur, when he had dined with the Staff in the mess below my room, I had heard the guttural voices of the speech-makers, and the

---

death of the Just, and his soul will soon be in heaven, if it is not already there. He does not regret now that he is dead. He awaits you, and tells you by my voice, "Farewell, until we meet in Heaven, in eternal Peace."

P S LEYENDECKER, D M.P.,
Rector of the German Catholic Mission in Brussels.

[1] The Ministers of Spain, Holland, and the United States.

thumping on the table with the "Hoch, Hoch," of the applause which followed. That night my supper was brought up very late, and the orderly explained that he had not been able to leave the banquet sooner. While waiting on me he said, "The new Military Governor is a fine soldier and very *nett*. When the Herren cheered him for his great victory in Roumania, he answered, 'Gentlemen, it is not *I* who conquered, it is the German Landsturmmann,' and taking my arm he said to me, 'Friend, art thou not a Landsturmmann?' and when I answered, saluting, 'Jawohl, Excellenz!' he said to all the gentlemen present, 'These are the men who won the battle, German Landsturmmanner, cheer them.' Oh, he is a fine officer, our new Governor!"

But this wily General seems to have been the most perfect brute it was possible to conceive, not only in the opinion of those of our countrymen who came in contact with him, but in that of many Germans, who dared to express their disgust at having such a ruffian put in command in Belgium.

Music and singing went on late that night. They had found a gramophone in the house, which, as I have said before, was our Home Office (Ministère de l'Intérieur), and it was curious to hear English light operas, among which the most popular seemed to be the *Geisha*, being sung by the Germans, who shouted out, "Jack's the boy for work," etc., in chorus.

Miss Cavell, of course, being a British subject, came under the protection of the American Legation, and unfortunately the kind and excellent Minister, Mr. Brand Whitlock, was ill in bed at this time. But he was well seconded by the First Secretary, the present American Ambassador in Brussels, Mr. Hugh Gibson. However, as purposely the information had been spread that the sentences would not be carried out for several days, nobody at first understood the urgency of an immediate intervention. Through, I believe, the instrumentality of the Belgian director of St. Gilles prison, Mr. Gibson, the Marquis de Villalobar, Maître de Leval, Belgian Legal Counsellor of the American Legation, etc., were only informed secretly that the execution was ordered immediately. The Marquis de Villalobar told me afterwards how, hearing that the execution was imminent, he had endeavoured to get into contact with von Sauberzweig. He first addressed himself to the Political Director, the Baron von der Lancken, who, being a diplomat by profession and a gentleman, was easily persuaded to try and intervene, and understood that the crime contemplated was not only inhuman, but stupid. The Spanish Minister had run the Baron von der Lancken to earth at the theatre, and it was past eleven at night when they reached the residence of von Sauberzweig. I heard at the time that this worthy representative of militarism was in a towering rage, and would not listen to any appeal for mercy or even for delay in the execution of the sentence. Thumping the table with his fist and saying, "We *will* have these lives," he would not deign to read the moving appeal of the American Minister, but threw it to the ground. Baron von der Lancken tells the story of this tragic night in his recently published memoirs, adding that, as he left the infuriated General, he said, "Then her blood be on your head and that of your children". Von der Lancken admitted to the Marquis his regret at the rigour of the sentence, but said he was powerless. On the Minister's asking him why he did not himself telephone immediately to the Emperor, he answered that he had not the honour, like the Marquis, of being a personal friend of his Sovereign. The Ambassador added, when telling me this, that he considered the Baron von der Lancken to have missed a good occasion of becoming a personal friend of his Sovereign.

I have heard since that the other accused, who were all lodged at St. Gilles, had been collected together to hear the sentence read. Immediately one or two of them had said to Miss Cavell, "I shall make an appeal, won't you?" "It is useless", she answered, "I am English," thus showing that she knew herself to be primarily the victim of the German hatred of England.

The next few days the courtyard was continually full of Belgian soldiers who had been ordered to report and were being sent to Germany. This measure was taken, I am sorry to say, as a result of our affair, and the poor fellows had only twenty-four hours given them before leaving their homes. In the cold and the wet they stood there in long rows for hours at a time. So far I had not heard when I was going or where, but one day the C.O. Oberleutnant Behrens told me that I should be sent to Germany the following week. I received a letter from Madame von Hartmann, the aunt of the officer I had nursed, who was a nun in Belgium, and who had tried in vain to plead for me. I heard afterwards that her nephew had recovered, except for the loss of an eye, from his wounds. He had written to the judges of the court-martial himself, asking to be heard as a witness in my defence, but this, of course, had been refused. Nevertheless, his intervention and that of other Germans had undoubtedly helped to save my life. Already during the war I was able to hear this affirmed by German officers, but since the peace it has been confirmed to me that for a week it was thought I could not escape being shot. My stubborn denial of all that could not be proved, notwithstanding the assurance the police gave me that a full confession assured the leniency of the judges, the personal intervention of the King of Spain, and that of those Germans who had either been cared for by me, or had seen me nursing their compatriots, are the chief factors of my escape from death.

Still, I could not understand how so much information had got into the hands of the police. I had absolutely confided in my confederates and we all promised each other never on any account to admit anything. Afterwards I learned that Baucq had had what in Belgium is called a *mouton* put in his cell, a young fellow of mixed parentage and light morals who had sold himself to the German police. Pretending he had been arrested while trying to cross the frontier, and to be extremely afraid as he had been helping to collect military information, etc., he won the confidence of our brave compatriot, too loyal to understand treachery, and heard from him the whole story. This traitor became suspect to a clever and courageous Belgian, called Louis Bril, who, having followed him and seen him entering the German police headquarters in the Rue de Berlaimont at night, knew that his suspicions were correct. Feeling the harm that could be done by the spy, and the impossibility of putting his compatriots on their guard in a town occupied by the enemy, he took the law into his own hands and shot the traitor dead. But the latter's friends were on the watch and arrested Bril, who was shot in turn, thus becoming a martyr to patriotism.

Two or three times since I had been at the Kommandantur, Allied aviators had flown over Brussels, causing a tremendous excitement. Directly the syrens announced them, the roofs, on many of which some sort of gun was hoisted, were covered with soldiers. One never realised danger to one's self on these occasions. My one hope was that they would throw a well-placed bomb, and I heard afterwards that in many parts of Brussels the whole population came out and cheered the aviator. This angered the "occupant", and notices were put up all over Brussels telling the townspeople that they would be punished by having to lodge soldiers in their houses the next time the town was flown over. Articles were put in the papers about our trial, and on all the corners of the roads the big posters told of the condemnation and the executions. Evidently the Belgian soldiers from their prison across the court had knowledge of these, because when I approached my window they made signs of silent applause.

One day I was conducted downstairs to the office of the Kommandantur, where I found the Spanish Minister. This devoted friend of Belgium was a worthy representative of his King, and his manners of *grand seigneur* imposed respect on our enemies. With the perfect courtesy of the Spanish he gave me news of my home, and told me that my two brothers were safe and well so far. He assured me that the fate of my compatriots was the object of his constant solicitude, and that I could be assured their sentences would be commuted. He had brought a letter addressed to me by an old friend, a Benedictine Father of Maredsous. Immediately the German witness to our interview stretched out a hand, saying, "I must see that letter". Looking him *de haut en bas* with supreme scorn, the Marquis answered, "Sir, *I* have read the letter, that suffices", and gave it to me. The other did not dare insist. The address on the open envelope, which neither of us tried to conceal, bore after my name the words, "glorieusement prisonnière". The Benedictine Fathers worked by every means in their power for their country, and several of them, among them the Prior and my correspondent, Dom Idesbald, were shortly afterwards to be arrested and sent to Germany, where they spent months or years in the men's prison at Siegburg. There were few religious orders in Belgium which did not do active patriotic work. Many of the convents took in soldiers, and I was told that one of the French black troops was concealed in a Carmelite cloister.

Volumes could be written relating the adventures of all the soldiers who were hidden in occupied territory. One case that came to my knowledge was that of a wounded Frenchman taken into a house in the Ardennes and nursed devotedly by the Belgian family who harboured him. Sometimes when the Germans made a sudden raid, while the others parleyed, one of the women carried the wounded man on her back out to an empty cistern, where he was sometimes obliged to stay day and night to escape detection. This life went on for four years!! One Belgian lady, the daughter of a professor of Louvain, who lived in a cottage near Namur, gave her whole life up to finding dispersed French soldiers in the forests and conducting them to safety in Holland. The long marches by night, the still longer bicycle rides by day, the constant alarms, wrecked her health, and it was with shattered nerves that she arrived at last as a prisoner in Siegburg. After the Armistice, badly hit both in health and fortune, she managed to get in touch with some of those whose sons she had saved. One of these, a French officer, had given her his seal-ring on attaining safety. He had fallen later fighting, but his parents thanked the brave girl for bringing their son out of that most dangerous of all situations for a soldier, being lost behind the lines.

The German chaplain, who visited all the political prisoners at St. Gilles (no Belgian priest being allowed to go near other than criminals), brought me word that Jeanne de Belleville and Mademoiselle Thuliez would like to see me. I asked permission to visit them, and after much delay obtained it, as well as the authorisation at last to attend Mass. So I was driven with my usual guard to the prison, where I saw my two associates, who occupied the same cell. On the night of the condemnation no one had been allowed to put out their light, so that the occupants of each cell could be watched from the outside. This order, it seems, was given in consequence of the suicide of one of our band, a poor fellow whose nerves gave out and who hanged himself, for fear of being condemned to death. This did not prevent the Germans, who have little sense of humour, condemning him on the following day. Mademoiselle Thuliez's sentence also bore the enigmatic mention, "condemned to be shot and to one year and one week's imprisonment". They told me how they had asked Miss Cavell why she also did not appeal, as they meant to do, and repeated her answer, "Je suis Anglaise, c'est inutile". They had heard a visitor being conducted to her cell late that evening, who had remained for some time with her. We knew afterwards this to have been Mr. Gahan, the British chaplain, a good man, whose kindness and prayers had undoubtedly helped to strengthen the brave and deeply Christian woman. She had been allowed to write to the nurses of her institute and to her family. There was no sign of faltering in her clear handwriting, and the sentiments she expressed could be taken as a lesson for all peoples and for all times. "I know that Patriotism alone is not enough; one must also have no feeling of hatred against anyone." Mademoiselle Thuliez told me that she had to be tried again in another affair, and that, therefore, she would be retained for the present in Brussels, but Jeanne had heard that she would be sent to Germany at the same time as myself, in the following week.

Then I was conducted to the chapel, going down interminable corridors, where every now and then the iron gates had to be opened to admit us, and one met non-political prisoners wearing the grey *cagoule* which strikes one with horror at first, until one realises that it is a merciful means of preventing a criminal being recognised after he has expiated his crime. German soldiers shadowed the Belgian warders who had been left at their posts, but this did not prevent the latter bowing deeply and with every sign of respect to me. I was taken up a spiral staircase which, in my weak state, was difficult to climb, but the two German guards came to my aid, and between them almost carried me up, trying in a way to show that they too shared in the sympathy shown me by the Belgian warders. The prison chapel, like all prison chapels, I suppose, is partitioned off into small wooden cells, whose occupants can see the altar but cannot see each other. Mass was said by Herr Leyendecker, who preached in French, which he knew perfectly, having been for twelve years chaplain in Brussels. It was All Souls' Day, and my recent mourning made it a doubly sad one. I thought of the grave where my grandmother had been laid in the peaceful little churchyard surrounded by our woods, and where, so far, no one belonging to her had been able to kneel and pray. This was the only religious service at which I was allowed to attend during the seven weeks I was a captive in Brussels.

Having obtained permission to buy some books, I gave the address of a bookshop to the German orderly, and asked him to get the shopman to recommend some, forgetting stupidly to tell him to say they were for a lady and a prisoner. On seeing his uniform, evidently the bookseller thought he had been sent by a German officer, and sent the sort of literature that is most popular with these gentlemen. Notwithstanding my desire for something to read, I could do nothing but burn it.

One day I had a farewell visit from Maître Braun, who told me that Reginald's will was in his possession, and brought me a formula to make mine. Life in these times was so precarious that it was always wiser to settle all business matters in case of one's death. I had made a provisional will before the trial, but now made another according to the instructions Maître Braun gave me. It was no wonder that the police had shown such anger on opening Reginald's will, as I heard that, although made in 1910, he had excluded any member of the family who should be of German nationality from ever inheriting our family property.

I had asked the Marquis de Villalobar to arrange for the return to France (as we alone called the unoccupied territory) of Charlotte and her two children, fearing that should the part she and her daughter had played ever become known, they also would be thrown into prison. Happily they were never denounced, and were repatriated through Holland and England, and were able to give Reginald details of all that had occurred since his departure from Bellignies. A few other visitors were allowed at this time, accompanied of course by the usual interpreter, and one day my Cousin Ferdinand, Dean of Ste. Waudru in Mons, came to see me. His perfect German seemed to allay the suspicions that the sight of a priest's costume invariably roused.

November 5, 1915.—On the 5th November I was taken down to a waiting car with my woman attendant and the usual guard. I heard that an officer was to travel with me. While waiting for him the orderlies crowded around and said goodbye in the friendliest way. It amused me, but a few moments later a tall, stiff, young Lieutenant, with the inevitable eyeglass in his eye, came out, and studiously avoiding looking at me or addressing me, got into the car, and we were driven rapidly to the Gare du Nord, not stopping outside but driving right into the hall of the station. It was in this hall that in 1919 a memorial service in honour of Nurse Cavell was held in the presence of all our authorities and of the heads of the Allied armies, while the train which was to carry her remains to England, draped in black and filled with beautiful flowers, stood waiting to start. The contrast between these two days on which I was to stand there has made a very vivid mark in my memory.

On this first occasion the car drew up to the platform where a train was ready to start for Germany. In a row before it were a number of *chasseurs* from the various hotels, and as we passed them I was touched to see the respect with which these men saluted me, after having curtly saluted my escort. One woman, unknown to me, but likewise a prisoner, got into the same carriage, a second-class one, with myself, and there were also the officer and a sergeant. The air and movement after being shut up so long alone, and after suffering from insomnia, had a strong effect on me and I fell asleep almost immediately. I only remember waking as the train stopped at Louvain, and for the first time since my brothers had been students at the university there I saw the poor town, now hardly recognisable. It had been burned during the early days of war, evidently as part of the plot for terrorising Belgium, and striking the world with a sense of German ruthlessness and power. In 1919 I travelled with the Professor of International Law, Baron Descamps, who told me how his wife's father and brother had been shot at Louvain in the street, on the day of terror in which the town had been burnt. The soldiers had gone from house to house, throwing small incendiary discs into the houses, which set them on fire, and nobody was allowed to extinguish it.

Not until late in the afternoon (trains went very slowly in those days) did we arrive at Aix-la-Chapelle, where we had a half an hour's stop, and were taken into a canteen kept by the German Red Cross, where we were given some refreshment. The ladies of the Red Cross received us very suspiciously at first, and looked at us askance, but after I had seen them conferring in undertones with the sergeant and woman attendant, they became much more civil and kind. Then we started again in the dusk, and arrived at Cologne, where we had to change trains. Here there was a violent discussion between the members of my escort and an officer in charge on the station. Tempers were short, and on the smallest provocation our enemies quarrelled among themselves. Evidently all were extremely nervous, and the station struck me as being very dark. I heard later that a few days previously it had been attacked by aviators, and bombs had fallen very near. Being by this time too weak and weary to stand, I sat on my portmanteau on the platform and let my jailors fight it out. Eventually, I was put into another train with only the sergeant, the wardress, and my fellow-prisoner. The sergeant told me he was going on a holiday, and, like all the German soldiers whom I saw travelling, he was loaded with provisions to take home. Although a promise had been made to America that food should not be taken out of Belgium, which was the condition the United States had made for provisioning the population, this was continually done.

At last the train stopped at Siegburg, and we got down in the dark and bitter cold, and heard that there was a half-hour's walk to the prison. Perceiving it was useless to think of asking this of me in my state of health, as by now I could scarcely stand, the greater part of the escort marched off with other prisoners who had travelled in the train, leaving the sergeant and the wardress with me until a late tram should pass. The station was closed, and so I sat on the ground with my back against the wall in the rain until the tram came by. It was ten o'clock at night and the car was nearly empty except for one lady, who sat opposite to me. The latter, seeing a soldier, got into conversation with my guardians, and told them she was the Directress, "Frau Oberin", of the prison. When we stopped I was conducted up to a high dark gateway, where we had to stand in bitter wind and pouring rain until several pulls at the bell brought at last the night-watch to open it. Entering under a covered archway with heavy iron gates at either end, I was conducted across a paved courtyard to the prison building itself. Here, the outer door being opened by means of two long iron keys, one of which was used to lever the other, the sergeant handed over my papers to the Directress and demanded in return a receipt for my person. Having received this, and evidently much relieved at being now free to seek his home, he unloaded his rifle, and, saying "Auf Wiedersehen" cheerfully, was again conducted to the door.

I had to stand in the dark passage while he was let out, but at last the Oberin and night-watch returned. Having had nothing that day except the sandwich at Aix, and being cold and worn out, I would have given anything for a warm drink, but evidently it was useless to think of such a thing. I was conducted practically in the dark, the Directress holding a small scrap of candle in the hollow of her hand by which she guided me down shadowy passages and up a skeleton staircase to a cell door. Opening this she said, "Your bed is on the left", and, shutting the door behind me, left me to darkness.

I threw myself dressed as I was on to a narrow pallet bed, and lay there listening to the rare sounds which indicated that other living creatures were near. Notwithstanding the great care which had been taken when locking my door not to make too much noise, the key had nevertheless turned heavily in the massive lock, and I had heard an enormous steel bolt shot home. From my sensations on hearing this I can imagine those of a trapped animal. On one side of me I heard coughing, the hollow weak cough of great exhaustion, followed by a whimpering groan, and a voice in German asked for air. Every now and then from the other side of me came stifled sobs, and a childish voice cried in French, "Maman, Maman". Once every hour padded footsteps went by the door, stopping occasionally to listen at one or other of the cells, and I heard a stop-clock being wound up at the end of the passage. This was a precaution to make sure that the night-watch did their duty. Before daylight, a bell was rung, and one heard the prison waking up. A wardress accompanied by two prisoners came from door to door, unlocking them, and receiving from the inmates a pail which they emptied into a large tin receptacle carried by prisoners, after which she locked up again. This was done once daily, and constituted the whole sanitary installation of the prison. The atmosphere about this hour in the morning was extremely unpleasant, and later, when dysentery reigned, it became unspeakable.

At about seven o'clock, the doors were opened again, and each prisoner was required to hand out an earthenware mug from a small hanging cupboard, which, with the bed, pail, and a chair, constituted the whole furniture of the cells. In this cupboard were on one side a mug, plate, and bowl, and on the other a brush, blacking, and floor polish for cleaning purposes. Above it was a small enamel pan, which I found was the only washing convenience accorded. This had to suffice both for the toilet and for washing up our plates and bowls. The mug was filled with a hot black drink, surnamed coffee, without, of course, either sugar or milk, but it was certainly warm and, therefore, comforting, after one had been shivering all night. I discovered that nothing solid was given until the midday meal, and even this later on could scarcely be called solid inasmuch as it consisted entirely of soup. But in 1915 a slice of bread was still given daily, and although this was brown and sticky, and extremely bitter in flavour, it was the most welcome thing one received.

When daylight began to appear through the thick striped glass of the window, I was able to see that my cell was about four and a half yards long by barely two wide. The floor was of wood, the walls of whitewashed stone, the door of iron, and the window thickly barred. I discovered afterwards that I was in one of the six Lazaretten or hospital cells, and it was owing to this that I had a window at all, the others being lit by a skylight near the ceiling, opening downwards and inwards, which prevented even when open its inmates obtaining a glimpse of the sky. On the wall, for sole ornament, was a printed card containing a notice which I did not read at first. By the bed was a book of rules for prisoners, and I only regret I could not keep it or a copy of the ridiculous regulations which the official has devised for rendering life as unbearable as possible to the prisoners. Of course, I know that these rules were devised for criminals, but still the latter are human beings, and I cannot think that arbitrary regulations can help to reform the character. I looked at the bed upon which I had been lying. A blue and white bag containing two grey blankets served as a coverlet, two extremely rough and much mended sheets appeared clean, until on turning them down I discovered that the pillow and one of the three square cushions which constituted a mattress were stained with what was evidently blood. It looked as if a previous inhabitant of the cell had cut her throat there. I heard later that suicide, notwithstanding the precautions taken (one's knife and fork, as well as scissors, were removed every evening from the cell), were extremely frequent among the criminals.

During the morning I was taken to the doctor's room in the same corridor as my cell, where I was weighed and examined, and my papers (Akten) were filled out for the medical statistics. As the functionary who accomplished this knew no word of French, I wondered how she got on with those of our prisoners, the great majority, who knew no word of German. The doctor sounded my heart and lungs, and gave orders that I was to be kept in observation in the Lazarett, and have "zweite Kost". I did not realise at the time that this meant I was to have a special diet reserved for the sick instead of living on the bean and pea soup which was the ordinary prison fare. Later on, when food was getting scarce, I demanded and received the same meals as the bulk of the prisoners. But in 1915 not much fault could be found with the quality of this food, consisting of two meals a day. A bowl of soup at midday, in which were vegetables and a very small quantity of meat, and in the evening another soup of either oatmeal or pearl barley. If a slice of bread had been added in the evening, it would have been sufficient, but the one slice allowed daily was given in the morning, and this got smaller and nastier as time went on, until in 1917 I was unable to eat it without being violently ill. But others were less sensitive, and I found that the scrap of bread which I saved to give to any prisoners whom I met was eagerly and gratefully received. For the first few weeks I never left my cell, even to go to the chapel, which was in the top story. Twice a week, on Sundays and Wednesdays, I heard the singing at the two services, one for the Evangelical religion, and one for the Catholics.

On that first day the Directress came back accompanied by the Inspector. The door was always thrown open without a preliminary knock, a proceeding to which never, in the two years I was there, did I get used, and the Herr Inspektor marched in with his hat well down on his head and began questioning me, while the Directress stood in the doorway, only answering when questioned by her chief. I replied to the questions, keeping my eyes fixed on the "gentleman's" hat. When being questioned as to what had brought me there, a low murmur came from the doorway, "Affäre Cavell". After they had been gone a few moments, the lady returned alone on some slight pretext, and before leaving said to me, "You must not take it wrongly ("übel nehmen") if the Herr Inspektor keeps his hat on when visiting you; it is . . . it is. . . ." Seeing her at a loss for a word, I interpolated, "Deutsche Sitten (German manners)". "Oh, no," answered she hastily, "it is the Rule (Vorschriften)." "Then if it is the rule, it is the manners", I answered, upon which she reddened and went away.

It surprised me to find somebody who evidently understood what good manners were in such a position, but I heard afterwards that the Oberin, having been left a widow in tragic circumstances, had been named through the influence of family friends to the post. She must have told her chief of my remark, because the next time he came to see me he ostentatiously removed his hat directly he entered the cell. This did not prevent him crying, on seeing my window open, "You have opened your window, which is forbidden". Notwithstanding the cold, the atmosphere was such that I could not have borne it without letting in air, and I told him so. Tapping the before-mentioned card on the wall he said, "Have you read that?" I had only just done so, and the memory of the wording was rankling in my mind, so, my anger rising, I answered sharply, "Yes, I have, and I won't forget it". Here is, as far as I can remember, the text of this precious notice:

Thou art now a prisoner; thy barred window, thy bolted door, the colour of thy clothes, all tell thee that thou hast lost thy freedom. God has not willed it that thou shouldst abuse longer the freedom He gave thee to sin against His laws and against the laws of man. Therefore He has brought thee here that thou mayest atone for the crimes of thy life. Therefore bow thyself down under the mighty hand of God, bow thyself down under the iron laws of this house. If thou dost not obey freely, thy bad will shall be broken, but if thou receivest with a humble heart the punishment meted out to thee, the fruit of it shall be a humble heart and a peaceful conscience. "God will it so."

This pharisaical lucubration made me very angry. Happily most of our prisoners mistook it for a prayer, and so it didn't worry them. But the Inspector's reference to it made me "see red", and from that time on, our rare meetings were far from pleasant ones. However, he was soon replaced by a Superior or Herr Direktor with whom I lived on no better terms. I probably did these gentlemen an injustice in resenting their treatment of the prisoners; they were mere functionaries carrying out orders, and according to Herr Direktor Dürr, the stringency of the orders was greatly mitigated under his rule. But in my eyes he represented an unjust and arbitrary authority and I therefore combated him.

I was conducted to the accountant's office, and this white-haired little person tried to impress me. After reading over my sentence aloud she observed, "You are here for ten years, but by good conduct you may deserve the clemency of our Emperor and see this sentence curtailed". I answered shortly that somebody else other than her Emperor would have a word to say in the matter. So far I had worn my own clothes, but that evening the Hausmutter, a stout becapped subordinate, came and made a list of my property, and carried it off, including my money, leaving behind her an extraordinary-looking striped cotton garment with a brown cloth jacket. First of all a struggle went on in my mind as to whether I would put on prison clothes or not. Feeling that it would be better not to differentiate myself from the rest of my compatriots, I decided to put on the dress, but to claim the right to wear my own underclothes. So when the Directress again came back I told her of my decision, saying that unless they allowed me to retain my linen I would not dress at all. She promised to ask for orders at headquarters, and in the meanwhile left me my linen. The dress that had been brought to me consisted of a skirt and jacket in a sort of twill, made evidently for a German figure, although it was new and therefore clean. But they had given me, as by this time I had got very thin, the smallest stock size, and it was short in proportion. The short skirts since worn were then unknown, and so in the full petticoat, which scarcely came beneath my knees, I felt rather ridiculous.

On the second night the moans of the sick woman next door were more and more frequent, although her voice got weaker. When the nightwatch passed, I heard her begging them to open the door, to give her air, not to let her die alone. The next day when the doctor made his round, I said to him, "There is someone very ill next door; may I not watch by them at night?" He answered, surprised, "She is a German and a great criminal". "If she were a dog I would nurse her", I answered. "There is nothing to be done; she is in the last stage of tuberculosis", said he, and went away without any further remark. An hour or two later, I heard men's footsteps passing the door and a stretcher being carried by. My neighbour was removed, but I heard that she died a few hours later. Her empty cell was scrubbed out and left open for twenty-four hours, after which I was placed in it. Traces of the former inmate were obvious on bedding and wall: she had evidently coughed her lungs out. Later, when my own cough got chronic, and I broke a blood-vessel, it was natural that they should think at first that I had contracted the same disease as the former inmate of my cell, and, indeed, it seems to me a miracle that I did not do so.

The poor child on my other side was, I heard, a little French prisoner of only seventeen, who had been arrested for concealing her fiancé, a French soldier. She was expecting daily to become a mother, and in her youth and inexperience was crying for her own mother, left so far away. Hers was only one of many babies born in these cells; generally a certificated nurse came for these cases, but sometimes the child was born before they arrived, and in one case it was my knocking at the door which brought the attention of the night-watch to my neighbour. The mothers were allowed to keep their babies with them for nine months, and were given one litre of milk daily, and an hour's walk in the courtyard. After this lapse of time the children were put out to nurse in the town, and the parting of the babies from their mothers was always a tragic moment. The foster-mothers brought them back once a month on a Sunday afternoon for an hour. Each of these visits renewed the sorrow of parting for the poor mothers, as gradually they saw that their infants forgot them.

At first I was given no work or occupation, and the days and especially nights seemed interminably long. There was a gas bracket in my cell, but this was never lit, and darkness came down at four o'clock and lasted until half-past eight in the morning.

The prison was the usual long building in the shape of a "T", with the central hall commanding all parts of it. The six Lazarett cells were on the first floor over the entrance and offices, on the north end facing the building which served as kitchens and wash-houses, and, therefore, received no ray of sunlight, and very little light at all. A thin iron pipe running around the wall was supposed to warm the cell. It kept off extreme cold, if one could have borne the window shut. As it was, I managed to keep the temperature of my cell in winter somewhere about 9° centigrade as a rule (41° Fahrenheit), but on Sundays and feast days this went down, as the offices, being uninhabited, were not heated, and so, in consequence, neither were the cells above them. But curiously enough I noticed that remaining motionless, and always in a low temperature without ever approaching a fire, one got used to the cold and scarcely felt it. It was the same with hunger. Preoccupation of mind prevented one feeling it, except in the case of the uneducated and simple peasants, who thought of nothing else. One poor old creature, who must have lived not far from me in 1917, used to moan a good part of the night, "Oh, mon Dieu, que j'ai faim, que j'ai faim", repeating it again and again in a rising tone until it became like a dirge. The boiled barley at night also disgusted many of those who, unlike the Germans, thought it only fit to be given to poultry. Among these, I remember, was Madame François, the wife of a Belgian Senator, whose anxiety also on account of the little daughter she had left behind was so great that I had fears for her health, and tried whenever I could approach her door to whisper a few cheering words.

Twice or three times a week, when at four o'clock we all received a second instalment of the morning's hot drink, the workers were given a scrap of something solid, generally a bit of cheese or half a red herring. Not being a worker I did not get this, but I heard it being distributed and eagerly received in the cells. However, as the "Besteck", as they called the little case containing our knife and fork, had been previously removed, the prisoners had to eat their herrings with their fingers. In 1915 a slight portion of meat was brought to the prison two or three times a week and cooked in the soup, while on other days salt cod or sauerkraut composed the dinner. Twice a week some dried fruits, figs, or plums were given. But in the winter of 1916 to 1917 food had got very scarce, and neither dried fruit nor meat was available, the soup was composed mainly of beetroot and swedes, cooked without peeling, but with stems and leaves. Indeed, often the evening soup was made of a brownish evil-smelling powder, which they named "Dürrgemüse", and which we heard was composed of the dried scrapings of the vegetables reserved for the soldiers. The prisoners called it "soupe à la souris (mouse soup)". Many of them, hungry as they were, could not swallow the "soupe à la souris", and it was thrown into a receptacle for waste matter which was daily fetched by a farmer for his pigs. But we heard one day that the farmer requested that the evening soup should not be put with the other refuse, as the pigs refused to eat it.

Potatoes had got very scarce, and various reasons were given for this, one of the chief being that they were needed to manufacture alcohol for munitions. But also the regulations requiring all foodstuffs to be collected at central places and rationed out caused much loss, as the potatoes rotted and fermented in the large heaps where they were collected.

At half-past seven the cells were opened one after the other, and the prisoners came out in a long procession, keeping the distance of four paces between each, for their walk around the squares of the courtyard. They were neither allowed to turn nor to speak, but were obliged to follow each the one in front of them in silence for half an hour. In the cold weather they walked at a smart pace to warm themselves, but some of the women being unable to follow, the old and infirm walked around the inner squares only. For the first two weeks I never left my cell, but at last one day the Directress told me that the doctor wished me to have some air, and that, therefore, I was to be given a walk in the middle of the day, and a prisoner whom she had chosen especially would support me on her arm. She said that this young German girl had been condemned to a few months' imprisonment for what was more a fault of inexperience than a crime. The young creature helped me with much gentleness, and tried by her manner, as, of course, she must not speak, to show me sympathy. For two or three days I was able to take a little walk, leaning on her arm, and occasionally sitting on a camp-stool. Later, as I got stronger, I took my exercise alone, except for the two wardresses, who, holding their keys in their hands, watched me from the ends of the court. Sometimes another solitary prisoner was taking her daily exercise at the same hour, and if the paths converged and we managed to reach the same spot, we were able to exchange a whispered word without being observed.

One of these prisoners looked a mere child. She

crept up and down the path dragging her feet and looking at the ground, but when she got within hearing of me I heard a soft whisper, "Are you French?" To my answer, "No, Belgian", she replied, "I'm from Lorraine. I was arrested for carrying arms and powder across the frontier for the French. My father has gone to join the French Army. We were all French at heart." This was said a few words at a time without changing her pace or raising her head, so that the suspicions of our wardresses were not aroused. Another time it was a little Flemish prisoner who, kneeling in the path to do some gardening, whispered without turning as I passed her, "Madame, priez pour Papa".

"Why?" I asked as I next went by.

"Because he is condemned to death", she said. "My mother and I are here and he is lying under sentence in Louvain prison. Pray that he may be reprieved." This child was only fifteen, but she was a brave and sensible little patriot, and must have been a fine example to the other young creatures who kept arriving, and who, being under eighteen, were allowed to work together in the courtyard. Some weeks later, the fatal news arrived that the father had been shot, and she sent me a copy of his last letter to his family.

Last Letter of Joseph Kerf to his daughter Victoire:

MY VERY DEAR DAUGHTER,

I must tell you, my poor child, that to-morrow morning, the 29th of August, I shall make the great journey that you know of, to see God, who, my dear, waits my coming. He knows that for six months I have prayed to be spared the death penalty, or to be taken to Heaven. He says, "Now he is converted, he is prepared; perhaps later he would forget God again".

You must not weep too much for me, my dear child. God wills it so, He wills my happiness. But you must pray for me, say daily a prayer all your life, devoutly; you can do nothing else, my little one. I do not order it, because I know you; I only express the wish, with my whole heart.

Now, my very dear Victoire, think all your life long of your father, and of what I write, then you will keep good. Pray for your poor Mother, who must remain twelve years in prison, that God may preserve her in health, help her to bear her trouble, cure her of her ills, and send her back to you well again.

When you return home, take care of all, and watch over everything like a true mother with economy; say to yourself, "I am now the mother of Xavier and Lucien". Be kind and gentle with them; if they misbehave, say that their father, who sees them from Heaven, will grieve.

Do as you have done up till now; be helpful with others, be just, without deception; do not listen to light talk; be industrious and clean, and keep good account of everything. Watch well over your brothers, so that they shall not be spoilt; tell them what I require of them, that they go to church and the Sacraments, and to vespers on Sundays.

When you return home, Xavier will have left school; take good care of Lucien for his schooling and his First Communion. So that I may firmly hope to see you all again one day in Heaven, and that none will have taken the wrong road. So, my brave little one, have great care of all, especially of your own soul and of those of your little brothers; pray for all, especially for your poor father.

For the last time, my dearest little one, I salute you and embrace you with all my heart.

As a souvenir I leave you my ring, my dear child; there is nothing else that I can leave you.

Farewell, my dear little Victoire, till we meet in Heaven.
Your father who loves you.

As I got stronger the want of occupation became terribly irksome. I asked in vain for work, as the tapestry I had brought with me had been removed with the other contents of my portmanteau. But I was told that the only personal needlework allowed to prisoners was crochet lace, which I had never done. The Directress told me that materials for light work were scarce, and that I should not be strong enough to do the weaving and button-making which were the usual occupations of the prisoners. The buttons manufactured were of metal, and a small hand-press was used. They were evidently destined for the English market, as those I saw were inscribed, "For Gentlemen", in English. I heard that others bore the mention, "Made in Paris". At this time the greater part of the prisoners were German criminals, and from what I heard from the various officials and wardresses they must have come from the dregs of the population. There were several murderesses among them, and some had already done many years' penal servitude. One, so I heard, had been there for thirty years. The result was no recommendation for the system, for certainly it is hard to conceive anything more depraved than this old creature. Sometimes in the night I would hear the gates being thrown open, and a screaming and struggling going on in the entrance beneath me, while someone was thrust into the punishment cell or *cachot*. When the police retired, often for several hours one could hear howls, imprecations, and banging on the iron door of this *cachot*. These were criminals who appeared scarcely to be human at times, and who were left in this dark cell with a slanting board for bed, and bread and water for food, until their rage abated. Some of them had filthy diseases, and as soon as I heard this I determined to make complaint.

One evening when I had been lying, still dressed, on my bed in the dark for some time, suddenly the door was opened and several people stood in what seemed to me like a glare of light from the passage. One tall, nice-looking man came forward, and speaking in French presented himself as the Minister of the Interior, saying that one of his duties was to visit all the prisons and to interview some prisoners in each. He did not say if it was by chance or on purpose that he had come to my cell, but he asked me very politely if I had any complaints to make. I answered, "We are here, a certain number of political prisoners, both French and Belgian, who as you know are all honourable women, and you have put us with the dregs of your population. Do you consider that right?" I saw very clearly by his embarrassed manner that he did not, and he tried to explain that we had been sent there by the military authorities for a political crime. I agreed, and said that, therefore, we should be treated as political prisoners. I then told him how for weeks I had been without any occupation and deprived of light. Turning quickly to the Director, he carried on a conversation in low tones, after which he turned and said that my own work would be returned to me until such time as official work could be found, and that I was to be allowed light for an hour or an hour and a half in the evenings.

This was the greatest boon. My gas was lit about half-past five, and, according to the mood of the wardress, was turned out between half-past six and seven. After seven all lights were out, and the wardresses went home, except for the watch. Hoping, as turned out to be the case, that I might not be searched, I had secreted on my person two night-lights, a small box of wax matches, a pencil, and a notebook. I wrote down the small happenings of our daily life in the latter, which was a great comfort, as paper and writing material were strictly forbidden in the cells. On Sundays, twice a month, a sheet of paper or a post card, with pen and ink, was brought to us, and we were allowed to write to our families, on the condition that nothing was mentioned except personal and private news. If rules, regulations, or especially the shortness of food were mentioned, the letters were suppressed, and of those that passed the censor's office at last, several had parts obliterated or cut out. When parcels from Switzerland began arriving for prisoners, and the bread that these parcels contained was confiscated, a notice was put on the chapel door that any prisoner mentioning the bread in her letters could be certain that these would never reach their destination.

At first the number of parcels was not limited, and those who received many shared the contents with those who got none, a wardress or the chaplain serving as intermediary. Later on a rule was made that only two parcels of five kilos net monthly were allowed, and in consequence many of the extra parcels were returned to their senders. A very aged friend of mine, who had been used regularly to send me a weekly parcel, on receiving back her carefully chosen cakes, biscuits, and potted meats, became ill with grief. Of course, all did not return, and evidently a big traffic was done at one time in prisoners' parcels. Those sent through a prisoners' agency in Switzerland were chosen for soldiers who lived in camps, and were able to cook their food. Therefore, when I received a packet of macaroni, rice, or beans, and tobacco, they were absolutely useless to me, and the remainder of the parcel constituted but a small addition to my rations.

It was impossible to give our families any idea of the conditions in which we lived, and the letters I received showed me that no one understood them. In one I was asked if the fortress was comfortable, and if I had a nice apartment! One dear English lady, who had often helped to look after me in childhood, begged me to allow her to come and be my maid, not explaining how she expected to get there.

She sent me a box of water-colours, a puzzle, and a birthday book, at a time when I was hoping for a box of biscuits and some condensed milk; but seeing the intention I put up with a supperless fortnight, and found a use for the little book, which now is a precious possession. One of the German officials, whom I will not give away, passed it from cell to cell and got my compatriots each to write a few lines about themselves in it. I give some of these extracts to show what were the "crimes" we were condemned for:

Marie Guéant, condemned on the 19th September 1916 to three years' imprisonment at Hirson for having fed a French aviator. Had left three small children and an aged mother behind her. Her husband was at the Front.

Marthe Flavigny, condemned on the 1st July 1915 to three years' prison for having hidden her son, aged eighteen.

Marguerite Bertholet, arrested at Verviers the 28th November 1916, condemned by Court Martial at Liège to six months for having fed a Belgian soldier. Had left five small children at home; her husband was dead.

Flamant, Emilie, schoolmistress at Laon, condemned to two years' imprisonment for not having denounced a neighbour whom she knew to have hidden a bicycle, and accused, without proof, of being animated with "hostile sentiments" towards Germany! Her husband was in prison at Wittlich for the same reason, and they had left two young children to the care of strangers.

Sœur Victoire (de la Doctrine Chrétienne), condemned to three months for having said, firstly, "I smell a German," and, secondly, "The Germans are bad-mannered," before her school children.

Marie Linthout, condemned at Liège on the 23rd November 1916 to eight months for having said, "sales Boches."

Louise Paroche, condemned in 1916 at Montcornet to five years' prison for having given food to two Russian prisoners.

Germaine Bael, condemned at Trélon to nine months' prison for not having declared her husband, who had refused to report himself to the German authorities.

Lhotellier, Anne-Marie, condemned to ten years' hard labour for having provided food for soldiers hidden behind the lines. The twenty-two soldiers she had helped, who had been wounded at the battle of Cambrai, were condemned to death, but their sentence was commuted also to ten years' penal servitude.

Marie Wauters, condemned to death at Hasselt, sentence commuted to hard labour for life (1916). Her husband had been executed on the 20th November for having served in a military intelligence organisation, and while he was ill she had carried it on in his place.

Pauline Deguelte, of St. Michael, condemned in 1916 to four years' hard labour for not having told the Germans that a French officer, who had come down in an aeroplane, was hidden in the village. She did not hide him, but she knew of him, and was condemned because she had not betrayed her compatriot.

A whole family of six people and two friends, condemned for having hidden *one* Englishman, among them Madame Lemaire-Lerche, aged seventy-five, and her daughter, to fifteen years' penal servitude.

Jeanne Merckx, condemned to death in 1916, at Hasselt, for espionage; sentence commuted to hard labour for life. Her brother shot, and her husband and sister condemned to ten years each. The other two brothers were in the Belgian Army.

Madame Quennesson, condemned to ten years' hard labour for hiding an Englishman.

Madame and Mademoiselle Aubry, condemned to three years for having hidden the arms of the husband and father, a colonel, who had fallen fighting in 1914.

Madame de Laminne, condemned to five years and 10,000 marks fine, accused of having helped in the escape of young men out of Belgium.

Rose Boisard, from Aouste (Ardennes), arrested 1916 for having carried food during eighteen months to four French soldiers who were hidden there. Ten years' penal servitude; husband and son condemned to death, husband shot, son's sentence commuted to penal servitude, a second son to three years, and a third son was a prisoner of war.

The cases which are named espionage are chiefly those where information about passing trains had been collected to be sent to the Allies. The above are only a very small number chosen among hundreds to show what were the crimes most common in occupied territory.

Our correspondence arrived very irregularly, of course, open, and smelling vilely of chemicals, but in whatever state it came it was the most welcome thing that we received. Allusions to happenings that I was supposed to know, and which had evidently been told me in letters that I had not received, used to worry me, but certain information conveyed by a code which we had arranged among ourselves reached me without arousing the suspicions of the censor. A Christian name represented Germany, the father of this mythical person was Belgium, the mother France, and the grandmother England. By this means I always knew when a successful offensive had taken place, and about in which direction. As the sheet of paper provided was not large, we had to weigh each word before writing a letter, and, having nothing on which to make a rough copy, it meant quite an effort for the memory. Although the letters had been passed through the military censor's office at Wahn, they had to be again examined by the direction of the prison. This meant that time had to be found by an already overworked head to decipher correspondence in a tongue she knew very slightly. Frequently I heard that a letter was waiting for me in the office downstairs, and sometimes daily for a week or more I hoped for it in vain. Often at last it was pushed under my door in the evening, and this meant a long wait until daylight, or risking detection by lighting my precious little night-light by which to read it. At certain times the correspondence stopped entirely; once I was five months without news of my family, and I heard afterwards through an official that special orders had been given to forward my letters to Berlin for a second examination, as I was particularly suspect.

Some weeks after I arrived, I heard that Jeanne de Belleville and Mademoiselle Thuliez, who had both had their sentence commuted to penal servitude for life through the intervention of the Pope and of the King of Spain, had also arrived in the prison, but I never caught sight of them. I saw many prisoners together for the first time when at last I was allowed to go to Mass, but here also the cell doors were opened one after the other, and the long procession, with an interval between each, wound its way upstairs to the chapel, where small partitions isolated them from each other. The want of air in the wooden box, and in the overcrowded chapel, which had been built for criminals, of whom I am happy to say the Christian population of Germany provided but a small number, was too much for me, and I fainted towards the end of Mass, and had to be carried to my cell. The next Sunday I was allowed to kneel in the aisle where the surplus of prisoners had to stay for want of room in the partitions. All wore prison dress; those condemned to hard labour had snuff-coloured garments with a blue and white checked fichu, the others wore grey dresses instead of brown. All had to do their hair according to regulation: two plaits bound around the head in the German style, which is neat and clean. Notwithstanding the uniformity in the clothes, it was easy to distinguish the criminals from our people. During Mass I noticed that the kneeling figure just in front of me was fidgeting and putting her hand back towards me. I found in it a tiny note, or rather religious picture torn from her prayer-book, on which were written her name and address. She was from Mons, and I was pleased at having someone from our neighbourhood near me, so as we rose to take our ranks again before descending I pressed her hand. The movement was detected by a wardress, who reported us, and poor Victoria Debock was chosen to be one of those sent to a distant prison a few days later. Notwithstanding the hardships she endured at Delitzsch, she returned at the Armistice, and became a nun after she had been nursed back to health. But alas! I hear now that her health has again broken down.

I had been carried back to my cell when I fainted by a prisoner whose face I saw leaning over mine as I came to, and a feeling of horror went through me which must have been instinctive. I heard later that this woman was a murderess and was even suspected of having killed her own mother. The chaplain, an old man who had spent thirty years ministering to criminals, paid me several visits. At first he evidently felt an aversion for us all, as being the enemies of his country, but when, bit by bit, he began to find out for what we had been condemned, and by what underhand means many had been convicted, he forgot his aversion and acted with truly Christian charity. Later, when the number of political prisoners got too great for one man's ministrations, after the removal of all criminals, which took place some weeks subsequently to the Minister's visit, a second chaplain was nominated. The latter was a Benedictine monk from the Siegburg Monastery, the old building which crowns the hill at the top of the town, and which had been fortress and convent in turn since the Middle Ages. Various monks came at times to say Mass at the prison and to visit the sick, and we soon found out that several of these were Christians before being Germans, and disapproved of the treatment their military party inflicted on our helpless population. One of them, when informing me that some more French and Belgian prisoners had just arrived, among whom often some were very old women or mere children, would exclaim, "They've saved the Fatherland once more".

Anyone falling ill had to report, and request to see the doctor, who called every morning and spent some time in his office near the Lazarett, where he also interviewed all newcomers. While waiting for him the sick were made to stand in the corridor, at two paces' distance from each other, facing the wall. No one must say a word or turn their head. This long wait must have been very irksome to those who were weak and feverish. Often the doctor contented himself with sending the prisoner away, merely saying the curt word "Sortez", and from this he became known to all by the name of "Dr. Sortez". He had evidently received orders to be sparing of medicines, and to refrain when possible from ordering a more strengthening diet, but in the cases of dysentery and allied ailments, which got very common, he generally prescribed a few days on oatmeal soup with "rote Tropfen", a decoction of opium, I imagine. Some of the sick either did not report or got tired of doing so, and more than one was found dead in her bed. I remember being much worried by a poor creature who was brought to the cell near mine. She was an old woman from Hainaut, who had managed to call the attention of the night-watch, and had evidently been found dying. I heard them asking her name, which she could scarcely pronounce. As they knew no French she tried to spell it, and I heard her gasp out, "H-o-u-r-i". She got no further, and died without ending what I supposed was Houriez, a common name in our parts.

From my previous experience I could imagine the sequel to this tragic little story. Often during the year I had spent at home under German occupation, I had been called in as interpreter for official documents sent to the Mayor. These were frequently to announce the death of one of the villagers, prisoner of war or civilian prisoner. The curt notice, "Please announce to the family X that X X died on the —— at ——", was generally all that these unfortunate people heard when they lost a relation. In one case where a young girl fell ill just as she, with her mother and sister, was to be sent to a far distant prison to make room she was found to be too ill to be moved. Although she was evidently dying, the mother and sister were sent away, and the poor child died alone on Easter Eve 1916. In another case an old woman, evidently very ill, obtained the permission to receive a visit from her husband, who was a prisoner at Rheinbach, a few miles distant. It would have been very simple to allow the old man to stay in the men's house at Siegburg, but he was sent back to Rheinbach, and never saw his wife again, for she died three weeks later.

These cases were only a few of those causing unnecessary suffering, but such cruelty seemed quite natural to our temporary rulers. Also the separation of families could surely have been avoided. There were many mothers who had one or more daughters in the prison with them, but they were only allowed to meet for an hour on Sunday afternoons. However, when later the great number of political prisoners made space precious, I believe several were put together in the same cell. The solitary confinement was found terribly trying to nervous or simple natures, and after a while several women began to lose their reason. Sometimes when the first signs of this were observed, I was taken to visit the prisoner with a request that I should try to "remonter le moral", and in time I got quite experienced in the symptoms. The first I visited in this way was a poor woman whose husband had been shot on the day after she had come to Germany. They had both been condemned to death for espionage, but she was told that both sentences had been commuted. She had seen her husband in the distance at Mons prison before starting for Germany, and had asked to be allowed to say goodbye to him, receiving the answer that it was not necessary, as he would follow in a day or two. Next day they shot him, and she received the announcement of his death three weeks later. It is not astonishing that her poor mind could not bear the shock.

Another little patient in whom I felt great interest had come from a caravan, where she had been an actress and dancing girl visiting village fairs. I think she must always have been simple-minded, and she could not help dancing and jumping about when let out of her cell, as a performing dog might do. She was punished for this by being thrown into the *cachot*, and kept on bread and water until the doctor ordered her to the Lazarett, where she became my neighbour. For days and nights I used to hear her pacing up and down reciting her parts in old plays. Then they told me that she refused to eat, and I was taken to see her. She was sitting up in bed, looking pale and haggard, with her untouched bowl of soup by her side. When I asked why she did not eat, she answered in a frightened whisper, "Because it's poisoned". "Then I will give you mine", said I, "and we will throw yours away". I merely exchanged the two bowls, and at first she ate my soup after I had tasted it before her. But a little later she refused even this, and after she had been fasting for many days she was removed to an asylum. I heard that she was an orphan, and that the only person who had shown any interest in her, and sent her parcels, probably without knowing her, was the Bishop of Liège. As far as I know she is insane to the present day.

After a time I was allowed to attend Mass from the sacristy, from which one could see the altar.

Mass was served by one of the younger prisoners from the men's house, in this case a French boy from Cambrai, who had been inculpated in a case of what the Germans called "espionnage". Our contention always was that one had a perfect right to try and obtain, for the use of one's own countrymen, any item of military intelligence that it was possible to get. Only those who do this in a foreign country are spies. Young Lestoquoy was a thorough patriot, and by some of the occult means known to every prisoner he was able to communicate with many of those in the neighbouring house. Among these were two friends of mine, the one a Benedictine Father, while the other was the young François d'Ursel. By the help of our sacristan I carried on a clandestine and consoling correspondence with the men's house, after a while, even with some whom I had never met. Of course, a wardress kept an eye on the sacristy from her corner of the chapel by the altar, one of four who were on duty during Mass. But my young postman used to deposit the letters for me in a spot that I could reach without being observed, and as he never appeared to take any notice of me our little stratagem was not discovered.

One day when I had been sent for to the Directress's office to receive one of my parcels, she pointed to the long procession of prisoners who were taking their walk outside her window, and said, "There is a new arrival who is surely a friend of yours, Mademoiselle de Bettignies". I did not know her, and said so, but saw I was not believed. I heard that this "great spy", as they called her, had been condemned to death, a sentence commuted to penal servitude for life, and had just arrived. She was pointed out to me, a short upright figure, the two long plaits of hair making a crown around her head. But after a time the severe strain she had been under while awaiting trial (every means had been used in vain to make her speak), followed by solitary confinement, began to tell on her nervous system. One day I was told that she would share my walk, so that I might try to exercise a calming influence on her if possible. The poor girl was exasperated at being inactive after having played a useful and important part for so long. She had been a regular member of the British Intelligence Service and knew that she was very hard to replace. She frequently got punished for insubordination.

Bit by bit in the men's house many priests and members of religious orders had arrived from France and Belgium. They all wore prison clothes, a dirty-looking linen suit, and at first were not allowed to say Mass, but in 1916, through the intervention of the Pope, permission was given for them to say Mass twice a week. Among them was a delicate old man, the Chanoine Brincourt, Grand Almoner of Rheims. I don't know what his crime was, but believe he had been taken as hostage, as he was the Mayor of his village. I heard through the chaplain that he was unable to eat the food provided and received no parcels from home. I was able to send him certain provisions from my parcels, and from this a correspondence sprang up between us. When it was seen that his health would not bear the confinement in such circumstances any longer, he was reprieved and sent home, but he died on arriving. His patience and gentle dignity impressed all who saw him, and he was respected by friends and enemies.

Some of the prisoners from either house were sent daily in groups to work in the fields. One day several men escaped from one of these groups and tried to reach Holland, but they were retaken after a day or two and brought back to be severely punished. One of them, a Dutchman by birth, and the father of a numerous family, was tied to a chair in a passage of the prison where he could move neither hand nor foot all day. The official who told me of it evidently felt the tragedy of this poor man, whom he had seen with the tears, which he was unable to wipe away, running down his cheeks. But a group of the women prisoners managed their escape better, having collected provisions which they hid about their person when going to work in the fields, and one of them who was from near the German frontier knowing how to read and speak German. They hid in woods by day and directed themselves by the railroads and signposts, marching all night until they knew themselves to be somewhere near the Dutch frontier. Early one morning they were discovered, and some men ran after them, on which they plunged into a stream and crossed to the other side, when to their surprise the soldiers desisted from their pursuit. They had reached Holland without knowing it; the stream marked the frontier. They wrote a collective post card to the Director to say that they had had a good journey, which he must have received with anything but pleasure. An escape meant trouble all round, as, of course, those in authority were blamed, and consequently the rules were made stricter for those left behind.

When the criminals had been removed, permission had been given for the prisoners to take a walk twice daily, going two by two, talking. This was a great joy to them, and it was much missed when in punishment the walk was suppressed. However, I continued to take my exercise alone, except when for a week I had been allowed to walk with the nuns, of whom five from different convents had arrived. Two of these nuns belonged to the teaching order of St. André, where I had been to school as a child. At first, like ourselves, they wore prison clothes, to which was added a grey cloth hood, but in June 1916, when we were allowed to wear our own clothes again, chiefly, I believe, because material was running short and they could not provide so many uniforms, the nuns were allowed to wear their own dress once more. These walks taken with cultured, highly educated, and deeply patriotic women were a great consolation to me, but suddenly one morning they were stopped without any explanation, and again I was condemned to solitude.

These sudden changes, for which no reason or

explanation was given, were very trying. The officials were ruled by iron regulations, and evidently dared not to tell us the why and wherefore of things. One of the worst characteristics which strikes all foreigners is the secretiveness in the German official character. Whatever one said to them they seemed to be seeking an ulterior motive for one's words, and evidently were suspicious of the most innocent declarations. One day while taking exercise I saw some heavy cases carried to the prison, and through the bars of the crate perceived round pieces of brass or copper. Unthinkingly, I asked the wardress who was conducting me back to my cell what these crates contained, and it was only her confused look and evasive answer, something about lamps to be made in the prison, that gave me the suspicion that this was war work. That afternoon a note was passed under my door telling me that the writer had been given some new work which she suspected was for an engine of war. Would I please at once ask the direction for an explanation, and protest against the fabrication of bombs, shells, etc., by our prisoners? I sent a note asking for the Oberin or the Director to come and see me, and was answered that they were away. This confirmed my suspicion, and I sent demand after demand for an interview with the Chief. At last he came to see me, and I at once charged him with the fact that war work was being done in the prison, saying that it was against all laws, and especially contrary to The Hague Convention. I am afraid I knew very little about the latter, and luckily neither did he. He asked quickly how I came to know about the making of these shells, thus confirming my suspicions, and he evidently imagined that some of the officials had told me. By this time the chaplain, who had shown humanity and Christian charity towards the prisoners, had become very suspect. The Prussian party looked down on the Catholic population of the Rhineland as being less good Germans than themselves. Unfortunately the so-called Catholic paper, published in Cologne, perhaps to try and correct this opinion, wrote in a hateful and jingo spirit, and when I was allowed to take in newspapers I preferred to read any paper rather than the *Kölnische Volkszeitung*.

In the meantime others had been aroused in the prison, and a regular mutiny was preparing. Louise de Bettignies, although like myself she had not been given any of the new work to do, fomented the spirit of disobedience, and when at last a young girl from the north of France, called Fernande Mazurelle, refused to make munitions and was thrown in the punishment cell, the fault of this was charged on Louise de Bettignies, who was had up for judgment before the authorities, and condemned to bread and water and solitude again. I had demanded a sheet of paper on which to write to the Spanish Ambassador at Berlin, and I saw that this demand worried the Director, who tried to make me desist, saying that if I complained all my advantages would be suppressed: books, work, and light taken away.

Of course, I persisted in my demand and wrote a letter which was submitted to the weekly council downstairs. It must have proved an uncomfortable subject to them, because the Director at last brought it back to me, saying triumphantly that, according to the rules, I was not allowed to complain on behalf of others, that as I did not make munitions myself I had no say in the matter. I got very angry and told him what I thought of a country which allowed of such inhumanity, and warned him that I would find some other way to have it stopped. I knew that in their secret hearts all the officials agreed with me, but they were bound to carry out orders and wished at all costs to stamp out insurrection.

The place was seething with revolt by this time, clandestine notes were pushed under doors, and some of us agreed on trying a hunger strike. This had only lasted two or three days, when on Sunday after Mass one of the most determined of our patriots made a demonstration in chapel. Jumping upon her seat so as to command the other cubicles, she made an impassioned appeal to all the prisoners to refuse to work against their countries, ending by saying, "Let us all rather be punished together than do anything that may harm our soldiers". The officials, taken aback at first, roughly seized Mademoiselle Blankaert as soon as they could get at her, having to pull the prisoners out of the nearest partitions first. At last the orator was bundled into a punishment cell until judgment should be pronounced. As she had been condemned to death and later to penal servitude for life, it was not very easy to find an adequate punishment, and the affair made a great sensation both inside and outside our walls. Inside we were all condemned to solitude and silence again; outside the Centrum party took it up, and questions were asked in the Government, I believe. At any rate, shortly orders came that war material was not to be made in the prison.

Mademoiselle de Bettignies fell ill, and had to be removed from the punishment cell to the Lazarett. But from this time on her health declined, and later an operation was found to be necessary. Some time before this, Jeanne de Belleville also had observed a growth which the doctor declared must be removed at once. Since she fell ill we had been allowed to take our walks together, and we agreed that it would be fatal to be operated on in the prison, where the conditions were too insanitary. All the cells, notwithstanding the cleaning they got, were necessarily infected by the sick cases that passed through them. Nevertheless, the Director announced that, having been condemned to penal servitude for life, Jeanne would never obtain the permission to leave the prison and go to hospital. She, however, demanded this permission, and I backed her up, as did also, I am glad to say, the Directress and chaplain. At last the surgeon who had been applied to had the humanity to declare he would not undertake to operate in a prison cell, and after three precious weeks had been lost, Jeanne was conducted to Bonn, where the operation took place in a clinic. But even here she was subjected to the strictest supervision; an armed soldier never left her door, and the wardress had to keep the key in her pocket and sleep before the window. She told me, however, that the doctor had been both skilful and kind, and the nursing all that could be desired. When at last she had been allowed to lie in the clinic garden to get back her strength before returning to prison, the other convalescents had looked at her with great curiosity, evidently wondering why this quiet, grey-haired woman should be considered so dangerous.

When Mademoiselle de Bettignies demanded also the right to go to hospital, objections were again made, and although we passed notes to her begging her to remain firm, one day, evidently worn out with weakness and anxiety lest the delay should render her case hopeless, she signed the paper agreeing to be operated on in the prison. What we had foreseen came to pass. The wound did not heal, and when she was seen to be in a critical state she was removed to a hospital in Cologne, where she died in the summer of 1918. I am convinced that if she had been sent to a clinic in time this young and strong girl would have recovered. When she was dying some Christian ladies and some priests of Cologne visited her regularly, and her funeral was followed by a large number of people in mourning, thus showing that many Germans were able to feel for and respect a valiant enemy.

Early in December 1916 there was great excitement one morning when the cells were opened, the wardress announcing that there would shortly be peace. On my enquiring what made them think so, they answered that the two Emperors had written a joint letter proposing peace to the world. On hearing this, I understood, or rather felt, that this feeler would be ignored by the Allies, but some of our prisoners were worried by it, as an incident that happened a little later showed me. An invalid, named Madame Ramet, had been brought to the next cell. Two of her children had been condemned to death, and the son shot, while the daughter with a younger sister were both doing penal servitude here at Siegburg. On Christmas Eve, we were allowed as a treat to have all the cell doors opened, and to stand in the doorway to listen to the singing of carols by the choir, who stood round a green tree decorated with a few candles and paper flowers in the central hall. Madame Ramet and I were the only two inmates just then of the invalid cells, and we were each allowed to sit on a stool outside the door, within a few yards of each other. After a while I heard a whisper from my neighbour, unperceived by the wardresses who were keeping watch on each of the different platforms. "Will there be peace?" asked Madame Ramet. "A little more patience, Madame", I answered. "We can't have peace yet." "But there *mustn't* be peace", she retorted almost fiercely. I was delighted to hear her, and said, "I feared that being ill you were in a hurry to be released". "I don't mind being ill, I wouldn't mind dying here", she said. "But there mustn't be peace before victory". This brave woman died a few weeks later, and the elder daughter, Augustine, returned after the Armistice to Belgium with her health shattered, and died after much suffering, so that one alone remains of this valiant family. The elder daughter, having been condemned to penal servitude, was not allowed to follow her mother's body to the grave, but we heard that a group of townspeople had attended the funeral. What curious contradictions one finds in the German mind!

The bitterly cold winter of 1916 and 1917 caused much sickness, and I for my part caught bronchitis, and a troublesome cough left me no peace, or my neighbours either. The snow lay on the ground for weeks together, food got so scarce and so bad in quality that hunger became chronic. Very few understand the real meaning of the word hunger. Most people imagine they are hungry when they have merely acquired a good appetite for the next meal. But the chronic hunger which reigned at this period in Germany had nothing in common with the other sensation. A feeling of exhaustion, of irritation, accompanied by violent headache and nausea, persisted night and day, often making sleep impossible. The officials also suffered, although in a lesser degree of course than we did, and I heard that many of them obtained a ration of our soup daily. In consequence tempers got short and regulations arbitrary. They all began to dislike each other, and were ready at any moment to criticise the higher officials and the Government. Everything civilian hated everything military, and I gathered that this feeling had become deep-rooted in the population. But fear reigned everywhere, and no one dared, however they might suffer, to criticise the Army or its chiefs. The whole nation was under the despotic power of militarism, and no one dared to call their soul their own. Even the birds suffered, and the high walls which surrounded us were continually covered by bands of crows waiting in the hopes of discovering something to eat in the courtyard.

I rarely went out this winter, my cough and general weakness making me prefer spending weeks on end between four walls. But one day, when the weather was a little finer, I took my exercise as usual, walking up and down between the porch and an angle in the wall. Through this porch the carts bringing fuel and food came daily, dragged by men prisoners who were harnessed to the pole like beasts of burden. Ten or twelve men generally pulled the heavy load, and one of them helped to open and shut the massive inner gates, while an armed warder kept watch. The men looked terribly miserable with unkempt beards, soiled clothing, and protruding bones. Although their rations were slightly bigger than those of the women, they seemed to feel hunger still worse than we did, and, except for those who did manual labour, they also felt the inaction and solitude more. On the day I speak of I was leaning to rest against the wall when the cart came in. A very small Frenchman, having pulled the pole around to allow of turning the cart, then came behind it to close the gate, and this brought him near me and out of sight of the warder. The little fellow turned and said my name interrogatively, and when I nodded confirmation he whispered cheerfully, "Allez, Madame, ne vous en faites pas! On les aura!!"[1] It was the first time I had heard this military slang, but I understood it, and it cheered me. My kind little friend was a French prisoner of war, who had been retaken when trying to escape and sent here in punishment.

The spring came very late, and I got no better, notwithstanding that the doctor had ordered me a portion of milk daily. At last I refused to leave my cell when the wardress threw the door open and proposed "Promenate!" One day after the monthly weighing, when the scales had turned at forty-one kilos, the doctor came to my cell and looking at me said, "You want fresh air; you must go out". It was no use arguing that the air that circulated in the courtyard was hardly what one would recommend to an invalid, as sometimes a blighting blast made an intolerable draught, and at others a hot wind stirred up a filthy dust. So that afternoon I followed the wardress and crept up and down outside for half an hour. When I returned to my cell it was dusk and my supper had arrived, or rather the pint of hot water which, at my request, was provided for me instead of the soup, and with which, from my box of condensed milk and cocoa, I made a palatable drink, eating at the same time two biscuits from my

[1] "Stick it, Madame, don't you worry! We'll get 'em yet!!"

fortnightly parcel. These boxes of oatmeal biscuits contained from twenty-eight to thirty. When there were only twenty-eight, and the month had thirty-one days, I had a supperless night. I had scarcely drunk my cocoa and was undoing my hair, when I began to cough and choke. I felt something warm running down my arms, but it was too dark to see, and during my struggles I heard my neighbour, Jeanne de Belleville, banging violently at her door and telling the night-watch to come to me. As the light fell through the open door, I realised that I was covered with blood and had evidently broken a blood-vessel while coughing. The wardresses were frightened, and one of them fetched Mademoiselle Lhotellier, a French nurse, who had been at the head of the Hospice Civil at Cambrai, and was imprisoned for having concealed soldiers in her hospital. This experienced and devoted woman took charge of me, and asked for a doctor and ice to be fetched at once. But it was a Saturday night, the prison was closed, and they did not dare to break rules, and told Mademoiselle Lhotellier she must wait until morning. Seeing that there was nothing to be done, she demanded that my door should be left open, so that at least she could get to a tap of icy-cold water, and so be able to change the compresses she put on me frequently.

All night she nursed me devotedly, and at last when morning broke, someone told the chaplain after Mass what had happened. None of the upper officials came, as a rule, to the prison on Sundays.

The chaplain looked in at my cell on the way down, and promptly telephoned to the doctor, who came immediately. Directly the doctor saw the crimson arterial blood he said kindly, "I am going to telegraph at once to the War Office, and I think you may count on being out of here very soon". But I knew the nature of those in power better than he did, and being unable to speak, shook my head in sign of incredulity. Mademoiselle Lhotellier was allowed to remain with me for several days, and everything was done that was possible in the circumstances, but no answer arrived from the War Office. One of the officials, whom I will not particularise for their own sake, when paying me a visit, used to ask, "Any news from Berlin yet?" and on my shaking my head, would exclaim, "These Prussians wish to give you time to die here; don't die to please them". One day I was asked to write the names and addresses of relations to whom to announce my death if necessary. Instead of frightening me, it amused me, and I wrote down, "I am not going to die". I told this to the doctor one day, saying that I *would* not die, and I can see his puzzled face when he answered, "But it doesn't depend on the will".

The Archbishop of Cologne, Cardinal von Hartmann, uncle of the officer I had nursed in 1914, was one of the many who intervened on my behalf at this time. Afterwards I found out that the Pope and the King of Spain had both been most active in interceding for me, and it is undoubtedly due to their intervention that at last, after three weeks' severe illness, the order was given for me to be sent to a hospital in Germany. Although the doctor had recommended my being sent to Switzerland, no notice was taken of this. I don't know if it was at this time, or later, that our Government, too, started negotiations for my exchange, but the conditions offered by Germany were absolutely unacceptable, as they required six men of military age in exchange for my person. Later, in September 1918, this was reduced to five. These negotiations having lasted over several months, it is obvious that I was given plenty of time to die.

It was decided that I should go to a hospital at Münster in Westphalia, and one of the chaplains, the Benedictine Father Busch, was designated to accompany me, as well as the Lazarett wardress. Before leaving, the Herr Direktor, with whom my relations had been anything but cordial, told me amiably one day that he would accord any wish within reason. I immediately asked for permission to receive a visit from Dom Idesbald, a Benedictine Father, who was a prisoner in the other house. This request was accorded, and a message sent to fetch Dom Idesbald. I waited in the office, as, of course, the visit could only be paid in the presence of the Director. Shortly afterwards a warder brought in a stranger to me, but who, nevertheless, rushed forward and shook my hand, saying low, "I am the Père de Pierrepont". I knew him to be a Jesuit Father, one of many who had been arrested, and of many more who had done patriotic work, and we had twenty minutes' pleasant conversation, talking too rapidly to be followed by our overhearer.

When my compatriot, whom no one would have taken for a priest in his rough prison clothes and black beard, had been conducted back to the men's house, the Director asked me if that were all I wished. Thanking him, I said that I was delighted to have seen the Père de Pierrepont, but it was not that one whom I had asked for, that evidently a mistake had been made in the number of the cell. We were always all designated by numbers, and I was known as "Lazarett Zwei", the number of my cell. The Director, evidently wishing to be amiable, at once gave orders for a second visit, and I had the great joy of seeing a childhood's friend and comrade of my brothers, whom I should have had difficulty in recognising in his emaciated state were it not for the intelligent eyes and kind voice I remembered. Several Benedictine Fathers had been made prisoners from the Abbaye of Maredsous, and the Germans were highly incensed against them because the Emperor had always posed as the friend of the order, and the Grand Abbot, Freiherr von Stotzingen, was a German. But they had hidden soldiers in the Abbey, and helped in every patriotic work, and so several of the fathers had been sent either here or to Rheinbach.

When my friend had gone again I was allowed to say goodbye to Jeanne de Belleville and Mademoiselle Thuliez, and told that I should be conducted to the Clemens Hospital at Münster. I can't say I was at all elated at the idea of leaving the prison. I had got used to my cell, and knew myself to be surrounded by compatriots and friends, who all tried in the kindest way to show me their sympathy. When they knew I was leaving, many whose faces I had scarcely seen sent me little gifts, trifles made out of the poor materials that they alone possessed. I have some of these still. One gift particularly was made by the united efforts of several prisoners who worked together in a room where the clothes were made. They manufactured a doll, and with scraps of uniforms dressed her in the prison costume, marking it with my number. One of them cut off her own hair to make a wig for the doll, whose plaits are correctly twisted round her head in the regulation fashion. In one hand a cardboard mug, and in the other a scrap of the black Kriegsbrot, made my little effigy more realistic. All was perfect down to the nails in the shoes, for by this time footgear had become hard to get. Indeed, most of the prisoners wore either wooden shoes or, at any rate, wooden soles, as leather could no longer be bought. At first I had received a pair of shoes, sent separately in parcels from Switzerland, but later the Allies forbade the sending of anything made of leather. When my shoes wore out I sent them to be soled, and received them back mended with some sort of cardboard. As this fell to pieces at once in the damp court, I was much worried as to how to manage, until one day I had a happy idea. The preserves and biscuits we received arrived in tin boxes, and I was able to cut soles for my shoes out of this tin, which I fastened on with the bit of brass wire which held the corner of the cardboard boxes together. These tin soles kept the damp out, but rang noisily on the hard passages and stairs. When one's linen and stockings wore out, one garment was made out of the best parts of two, and no scrap of anything was thrown away.

At last the morning came when, accompanied by Father Busch and the wardress, I started for hospital. By this time I was sufficiently recovered to walk a few paces, but when I got into the train I was quite exhausted, as well as being bewildered at seeing movement around me. We had to change trains at Cologne, where there was an hour's wait, which I asked to pass in the Cathedral instead of sitting in the busy and noisy station. But we were held up on crossing the road to the Cathedral, while a long procession of young men, many of whom looked mere children, passed by. One of the soldiers on duty in the road told us that these were the young fellows who had been to take the oath of loyalty (" Eid leisten ") before joining the army. They looked so thin and miserable and so young that I could not help feeling for them and for the mothers whose sons were being sent to the great butchery, and I expressed this pity and indignation to my two guardians, speaking incautiously loud enough to be heard by the soldier in front of us. Just then down the road came one of those queer open German carriages, drawn by a skeleton horse, in which four officers were sitting. They evidently had not yet felt the pangs of hunger; they were stout and bloated and purple in the face, and the sentry, pointing with his thumb as they passed slowly by, whispered to us over his shoulder, "Diese mahnen zum Durchhalten (These are the ones who tell us to hold out)."

At Münster I found a room prepared for me, and filled with flowers and fruit by my cousins from Dülmen, whose children came to see me the next day. This Clemens hospital is an old foundation in the town, and was then full of wounded soldiers. I heard from the sister who nursed me that an old friend of mine, a friend of the happy peace times, Countess Hedwig Nesselrode, was nursing there among the Red Cross ladies. Forgetting all except our old friendship, when she heard I had arrived, she came to see me, and was shocked at my changed appearance. I had not seen her since a happy winter passed in Rome, where, with her mother and sisters, she helped to receive in their flat on the beautiful Piazza di Spagna.

The nuns told me so far no special orders had been received at the hospital concerning me, and I was, of course, the only foreigner there. Luckily for me the official papers announcing my transfer from one army district to another did not reach the General under whose jurisdiction I had now come at once. But a night or two later when reaction caused by the difference in my surroundings, and kind treatment, had brought on a nervous breakdown, and I had collapsed and wept night and day, orders came to remove me again to a prison. The Feldwebel and a guard who came with the order were received by the Superior and doctor, who at once protested that I was unfit to be moved. They telephoned to my German relations,[1] and to the Cardinal, and immediately many people were intervening in my favour, while I lay all unconscious of the excitement my presence had stirred up. I cannot be too grateful to the nuns and the doctor who took my defence against their own officials, doing it simply in the name of humanity. At Münster also dysentery raged and caused many deaths, and I became once more a victim to this exhausting disease. At last the Governor, who feared that I might escape, although how I could have done so in my weak state is a mystery to me, agreed that I should be left where I was until out of danger, after which Cardinal von Hartmann had found an asylum for me in a hospital at Bonn. During this time I received visits from my relations, from the Nessel-

[1] The Duke and Duchess de Croÿ-Dülmen. Twice, during my stay in Siegburg, I had been allowed to receive a visit from the Dowager-Duchess de Croÿ, who was untiring during the whole war in visiting prisoners in camps and fortresses in Germany, and who undoubtedly was instrumental in obtaining commutation of sentence or more lenient treatment for many Allied prisoners. Being by birth a Princesse d'Arenberg, she was able to demand exceptional favours as to visiting prisoners, but, of course, a witness was present at our interviews. However, at Bonn she was allowed to come to see me alone at the hospital, where she spent several hours.

rodes, and also one day from the mother of the officer I had nursed. I woke up from a state of half-consciousness to find Frau von Hartmann standing by me and holding a bouquet of lovely flowers, and saying, "You saved the life of my only son".

At last I was pronounced fit to be moved, and one of the police was ordered to take me to Bonn, but my kind friend Countess Rési Nesselrode obtained permission to accompany me also. It took long hours in the slow war-time trains, where all the travellers continually had their papers examined, for us to get to Bonn. Here I tried to walk up the hill to the hospital, which is on the Venusberg, but my strength failed, and I had to lie down in the wood, with my friend sitting by me, while the policeman went ahead and fetched a litter used for the soldiers. So it was carried by two ambulance men that I arrived at the Marien Hospital, and here, too, I found a cheerful, clean room waiting for me. Rési interviewed the nuns before returning home, and in consequence I was treated with the greatest kindness.

Three doctors were in charge at the hospital. They belonged, one to the Catholic, one to the Evangelical, and one to the Jewish religion. I had to do with each in turn, although the last was my usual physician, and I found them all kind. The hospital, a large and modern one, was filled with soldiers, with the exception of one ward and a few rooms which took private cases. In the grounds was a large building filled with convalescent officers.

At first the authorities wished to keep a guard at my door again, but I offered to give my word of honour not to escape, and the Superior said she would be responsible for me. Orders were given, however, that my door must be kept locked, and that when I went into the garden I must always be accompanied. Although the nuns were numerous, the hospital was so full, generally containing over four hundred wounded men, the poor sisters were much overworked, and bit by bit the rules became relaxed. For weeks on end at first I scarcely left my bed or invalid chair. Later I managed to creep to the chapel, sitting among the sisters rather than with all the soldiers. The Franciscan Fathers from the neighbouring Kreutzberg ministered to the hospital, and I occasionally met one of them and found them always polite.

When I was well enough to lie in the garden, often one or other of the invalid officers would try and get into conversation with me, but I did not encourage this. However, I remember in the spring of 1918, when they appeared much less gloomy than usual, and one announced that the taking of the Mont Kemmel in Flanders meant a speedy victory, I answered that this would change very little, adding, "There are still the Mont Noir, the Mont Rouge, and the Mont Cassel to take". The Germans had been told that the Kemmel was the only obstacle to their advance, and on hearing what I said, the officer looked extremely depressed, and answered, "We have been lied to again as usual".

He had come from the Verdun Front and said that conditions there were "Hell".

I was lying in my room one day when the door opened and an elderly priest came in, introducing himself as Professor Felten. He was a Canon of the Cathedral, and had been asked by the Papal Nuncio, on behalf of the Pope, to visit me. Having been exiled in Belgium and England during the *Kulturkampf*, he spoke both French and English well. At first we kept the conversation strictly to literary subjects, but one day on leaving, Monsignor Felten said, "I hope my visits are agreeable to you?"

Some time previously a group of intellectuals had issued a proclamation, or rather it had been issued in their name, which roused universal indignation. The memory of this outrageous document, which was known as the Manifesto of the Ninety-Three, was rankling in my mind, and I said to my visitor, "Tell me first, are you one of the signatories to the Manifesto, 'Es ist nicht wahr'?" He answered quickly and decidedly, "Certainly not, and some of those whose names it contains did not know what they were signing. For instance, Professor Foerster, absent in Switzerland, received a telegram asking him to lend his name to a patriotic manifesto. He would never have consented had he known what it was." This satisfied me, and, shaking hands, I said, "Now we can be friends. I can understand anyone loving their country as I know you do, but also loving it in honesty and truth." From that time until the day of his death, Monsignor Felten remained my faithful and honoured friend. He was one of the many Germans from whom I had acts of kindness, and if I do not mention them more particularly, it is because, with the spirit of hatred and revenge still reigning in a part of the population, I do not want to draw down trouble and suspicion on their heads.

By this time I was allowed to buy any German newspapers I cared to. At Siegburg prison the *Gazette des Ardennes* had been distributed, and was read because it gave lists of names and addresses of our war prisoners; otherwise people would have refused it, so depressing was a paper which depended for its subject-matter on the pen of traitors or pacifists.[1] Later I had been allowed to subscribe to some German papers, but these appeared in several editions daily, and had first to go through the censor's office at Wahn, which meant that after receiving nothing for five or six days, ten or fifteen large newspapers arrived together. Here at Bonn, however, my *Kölnische Zeitung* and *Berliner Tageblatt* arrived regularly, and now and then I also took the Catholic *Volkszeitung*, which, being printed in Latin type, was easier to read. But I was exasperated by the lies it propagated. The usual stories about Belgian "franc-tireurs", the dum-dum bullets, and the hateful terms in which it spoke of my unfortunate companion, Nurse Cavell, whom it dared to assimilate to the

[1] Not to be confused with those who are genuinely seeking for pacification among nations.

condemned spy, Mata Hari, made me so indignant that on one occasion I wrote a sharp answer. This letter I confided to Monsignor Felten, who was acquainted with the Bachem family, who owned the *Volkszeitung*. Whether he delivered my note or not I do not know, but I noticed a slight difference in the tone of its articles subsequently.

When an offensive was taking place, the wounded arrived in great numbers, and I heard litters being carried to the operating room below, where the surgeons worked night and day. Everything was done that was possible to maintain a good morale in the population, and every success was greeted as a great victory with the ringing of bells and flying of flags. Judging from its effect on those I saw, all this was useless. If I said to anyone, "It seems you have won another victory", they merely answered, "Give us peace; that is what we want". Frequently I saw soldiers sobbing alone in the chapel. They were sent back to their regiments as soon as they were fit to travel, and before they could be said to be well.

At the end of 1917 I saw great preparations being made for Christmas; trees were set up in all the wards, while relations kept arriving with presents for their sick, and entertainments were arranged for the soldiers. Feast-days were the most trying to pass in exile. Even if correspondence arrived it was so censored as to lose all interest, and so late that I got my Christmas letters at the end of March. The Mother Superior, whose kind heart taught her what I was feeling, asked me on Christmas Eve if I would not like to attend the children's Christmas tree, adding tactfully that except for the doctor and herself I should be the only guest. I accepted, and was taken to a ward full of little patients, chiefly surgical cases. Many lay in bed with bandaged heads or limbs, but those who could walk stood around a Christmas tree and a *crèche*, all the boys wearing toy uniforms. Like little soldiers they saluted and marched in military step around the room, and the sight of these sick and crippled infants playing at war depressed me. I said to the Reverend Mother, "Could they not give other presents on this feast of Peace and Goodwill towards men?" but she answered sadly, "It is the only thing they care for".

As I returned to my room after midnight Mass in the chapel, where the beautiful *crèche* with life-size wax figures surrounded by green fir-trees had drawn the eyes of all the soldiers, whose singing had been very beautiful, I found a small decorated tree on my table, surrounded with little presents. Some were from the nuns, some came from Dülmen, and some from the Princess Josephine of Hohenzollern, the King's sister. I sat beside the little tree in the loneliness and silence of the night, remembering old Christmasses passed in the happy family circle at home, and felt sadder than at any time yet.

A few days later I received another present which gave me great pleasure. Madame Boël, who had been my fellow-prisoner at Siegburg, was now interned in Switzerland. Remembering how I had told her, when she was allowed to come and say good-bye in my cell where I lay ill in bed, before she left the prison, that the presence of an animal, even if it were only a bird, would have been a comfort to me, she had written to Frau Manser, one of the higher officials, asking her to buy me a canary and bring it to me. Frau Manser had lived in France, and had acquired by her sensitive compassion for the prisoners the regard of most of them. She had taken advantage of a day's holiday to come the thirty miles which separated Siegburg from Bonn, and one afternoon, when I was lying as usual on the couch near my window, I was surprised to see the door open and Frau Manser enter with a parcel. She looked frightened because she had not dared ask for a permit to visit me, but she undid the parcel she had brought and showed me a canary bird in a cage. "Madame Boël commissioned me to get it for you, and here is some seed for Hänschen" (every self-respecting German canary is called Hänschen), "while here is a little packet of hemp-seed which you can give him on your fingers to tame him."

I did not dare retain Frau Manser for fear she should get into trouble for her kindness. The bird ate from my hand within a day or two; one morning he flew from his cage, which I had left open, to my shoulder, and from that time he was free of the room. He chirped in answer whenever I spoke to him, and having no one else to speak to, I talked to him often. Even in the night, if sleepless, I called his name, Hänschen would answer with a few sleepy little notes from his musical trill. One day when going to sit in the garden, I forgot to put my bird back in his cage before leaving the room, of which the window was always open, and it was only when lying under a tree at a little distance from the window that I thought of this, and looking up saw Hänschen sitting in the open window watching me from a distance. He never tried to fly away, and seemed perfectly happy as long as he was with me, sitting on the table while I took my meals, flying around the heads of the sisters who brought them in, and nestling against my cheek when I took my siesta afterwards.

The affection this little bird showed me was extraordinary, and he seemed almost to think. Daily after my dinner I would give him two or three hemp-seeds from the little parcel which lay near his cage on the window-sill, often cracking them between my teeth if they were very hard. One day, feeling very weak and weary, I had lain down forgetting Hänschen's seeds. He hopped forward and back between his cage and my shoulder chirping; I knew what he wanted, but had not the courage to get up. At last he brought the empty husk of a seed he found in the cage, and pushed it between my lips as a gentle hint, upon which naturally I gave him what he begged for. At last, as the seed was getting scarce, I asked the nuns to order some more, only to find to my dismay that none was to be had in the town. I wrote to Switzerland begging that some might be sent. Three weeks later I received an answer saying that no grain might be exported. By this time my little stock was nearly exhausted, and I tried to eke it out by giving something from my meals to my little companion. But I wrote to my cousin Ligne at the Belgian Legation in Holland, begging him to try by every means to send me a small parcel of seed. Hänschen did not seem to mind the change of food; he ate crumbs or pudding or salad very willingly, but I noticed his song got rarer until it stopped altogether, and I could feel his little heart beating as he sat on my hand. At last, his breathing became more and more difficult, and on the day when a parcel arrived from The Hague, bringing the seeds that would have saved his life a few weeks earlier, he jumped for the last time from his cage to say good-morning as usual, and died in my hand. At a moment when the whole world was grieving for those it loved, and we were surrounded with human tragedy, the loss of a little bird ought not to have affected me as it did, but he was my only friend and companion at that time.

There were funerals almost daily, and those of the soldiers were very impressive. As the coffin was carried through the grounds to the little cemetery on the hillside, the band played the tune that became so familiar to us all during the war, "Ich hatt' einen Kameraden". Then later I heard the sound of the salute which was fired over the grave before the escort left. Some of the nuns also died at their post, from overwork and insufficient food, and children wearing long white veils carried lilies beside their coffins. I wondered sometimes if I, too, should be buried there; but it did not worry me much, as I do not think it matters where one is buried. In another world there will be no nationalities. "God made mankind, and the devil made the nations", as somebody said.

When I wandered into the wood which surrounded the hospital grounds, as I often did when the surveillance got lax, I used to meet little children from the town who came there to play. One day five or six little girls were dancing and singing on the bench I sat on, while another child was weeping. I asked them, "What is the matter with your comrade?" and they answered, "She is crying because her father is *gefallen* (killed), and her mother is ill at home and crying too". "So is my father *gefallen*" cried one after the other, and nearly all these children seemed to have been rendered fatherless by the war. They were barefoot and thin, but clean, and I found that none of them knew the taste of chocolate or sweets. I fetched them a little chocolate that had remained from my last parcel (lately I had directed these to be distributed among our prisoners), and these poor underfed children hardly knew what to think of it.

At intervals the syrens would announce an air-raid by the Allies, and at once all the inmates of the hospital took refuge in the cellars. But I preferred to take my chance upstairs, where I often stayed quite alone. The building is situated at the top of a hill overlooking the town, and it was interesting to watch from a high window the planes appearing from behind the clouds, being followed by little puffs of smoke, and darting out of sight again. But the syrens made such an unearthly noise that it caused a nervous breakdown to many of the sick, and at last orders were given to sound them only at the beginning and at the end of a raid. One of these took place in daylight, and a tram-car in which a sister from our hospital was taking a relation to the station was hit by a bomb and several people were killed, among them being the nun's relation. If any military aim was attained I do not know; nobody was allowed to speak of these events, and the papers did not mention them. But one night the bombardment was so violent, and I heard such a loud explosion, that I fancied that our building had been hit. In the morning we heard that the bomb had fallen between the hospital and the neighbouring monastery of the Kreutzberg.

With one exception the sermons could have been heard by the people of any nation, but in March 1918 a military chaplain came to preach a mission to the soldiers. He had evidently been told to work on their patriotic feelings, and so stir them up to a supreme effort. I had accepted permission to attend this retreat, but the first sermon was enough for me. My indignation rose as it proceeded, and, had it not been for the Reverend Mother's restraining hand on my arm, I think I should have protested publicly. As it was, when the tall preacher walked down towards the door from the middle of the aisle where he had spoken, I sprang after him, and reaching him just outside the chapel door, told him what I thought of his teaching, saying that, instead of Christian doctrine, it was merely one of hate, "Kriegshetzung". Most especially I took up with energy some remarks he had made against King Albert, and he answered, looking rather confused, "It does you honour to defend your King". "My King does not need to be defended by me", I retorted. "He is himself the summit of honour (Er steht auf der Spitze der Ehre)." By this time the rest of the congregation were leaving the chapel, and several officers stood around listening, so one of the nuns hurried me to my room, telling me I was very imprudent. But I was so angry that I did not care what the consequences were, and as I could not sleep I spent the greater part of the night writing down the sermon from memory, and I was able to show this the next day to Monsignor Felten. He had come to see me on hearing all the talk in the town, but after reading the report of the sermon, he could not but agree that I was perfectly justified. Nevertheless I expected to get into trouble, but no doubt the great offensive going on on the Western Front, and the negotiations with the Russian revolutionaries, took up everybody's attention, as I was let alone.

I had received a visit in the previous autumn

from Princess Josephine,[1] but an interpreter had been present at our interview, and, however happy I was to receive the King's sister, I was determined not to subject her again to the indignity of being treated with suspicion. So when she wrote saying that she had asked once more to visit me, and, at the same time, the Governor applied to the hospital to know at what hour the visit would take place so that the interpreter might be sent, I wrote to him saying that unless her Royal Highness were allowed to come alone, I preferred going without the honour of her visit. The result was that the Princess came by herself, and our interview, in which she spoke of her deep love for her country and her "dear brother", was very consoling to me.

Daily the papers announced the tonnage sunk by the submarines, declaring that England would soon be forced to come to terms. She was still considered the arch-enemy; cartoons appeared in the papers calling her "the blood-sucker of the world". On a map of the universe the drawing showed an octopus in the place of London, whose tentacles stretched to all the British possessions, and even to those places which she did not yet possess, but was supposed to covet, among which was Calais! Another cartoon asked Germany if England should be allowed to make Belgium her "Aufmarschgebiet" (a jumping-off place), from which to destroy German industry, and on this map the Channel tunnel led to railways going into the heart of the manu-

[1] Princess Charles of Hohenzollern, sister of King Albert

facturing district of the Rhineland and Alsace, whose towns were shown burning in the distance. The "Hymn of Hate" and other songs were distributed to the soldiers, but I never heard them sing them, and doubt that many of them were foolish enough to be taken in by this childish nonsense. All those who had been in contact with the population in France and Belgium had begun to have an independent judgment, and in any case they were too war-weary to desire anything but the end of hostilities. Some of them said openly that they preferred being at the front to coming home and hearing nothing but complaints and quarrels.

Food was so scarce and hard to get that the people spent their time trying to procure the necessities of life. I admired their ingenuity, and wondered if the Allies would have done nearly as well in such straits. Nettles were collected and woven into a sort of worsted; I was given some to mend my stockings, and I still possess a ball of it. Tablecloths, blinds, and all linen that was not a bare necessity, were collected for clothing children and especially newborn babies, as cotton, of course, was not to be had. To procure any garment, a card was necessary, and this limited the buyer to two shirts and two handkerchiefs at a time. Professors of natural history put notices in the papers to say that on certain days they would go into the woods and explain to all who liked to accompany them which of the many sorts of mushroom or fungi were edible. "Coffee" and "tea" were made out of hawthorn-berries and other plants from the hedgerow; a substitute for starch was made out of the horse-chestnut, and for soap from ivy-leaves and wood ashes. The kernels of fruit, as well as beechmast, were collected by school-children and crushed in mills to extract the oil. But the bread was the greatest problem; every sort of thing was put in it except flour. It reminded me of a slice of bread that my father, who had been attached to the Belgian Legation in Paris in 1871, had kept from the siege, and that was composed chiefly of chopped straw and plaster. The thing the Germans seemed to feel the want of most, was fat. "Fett-karten", or cards which gave right to so much butter, margarine, or one of the "Ersatz" so-called, allowed of such a small portion per head that the people used to discuss whether they would use it all in one day or try to eke it out during the week. Of course, the sick and the feeble suffered greatly. Here, as everywhere, some people managed to procure more than their share, and the "Hamsterer", as they were called (after a small animal which collects big stores of food in its hole underground), were continually being held up to reprobation. But others gave a fine example, and I heard of one lady at least who died literally of inanition because she refused to eat anything but the authorised rations.

So far, I had never had any doubt about the outcome of hostilities. The justice of our cause, the inexcusable German aggression on my peace-loving and innocent country, because no one for an instant believed the lies that the German High Command had spread, to try and justify first the invasion and afterwards the annexation of Belgium, had given me an absolute faith in an Immanent Justice. But when Germany, unable, notwithstanding the many feelers sent out, to get either of the Allies to enter into peace negotiations, determined to play her last card, and began the terrible offensive on the Western Front, I own I felt anxious.

Being hard up for bronze, after seizing on all that was in our homes, such as kitchen utensils, blind- and stair-rods, brass beds, and even musical instruments and door-handles, they had requisitioned the church bells and bronze monuments in our cities. As this still did not suffice, they were obliged to take some bells from their own churches, and when one of these was doomed it was rung, or rather tapped, for several hours before being removed to be converted into cannon. I had heard one of them ringing for hours as I lay in my bed in Münster, and the sound was fearfully depressing. It had been significant that the bell chosen from Cologne Cathedral had been the large one given by the Empress, and named the "Kaiserin". But enough bells were left to be rung for each new "victory", and the sound of them, together with the firing of the cannon, and especially the places in which fighting was going on named in the daily communiqués, struck terror in my heart, until at the end of July I saw that the advance was stopped. The papers said nothing, of course, and the Germans, not knowing the geography of France as I did, were at first unaware that the offensive had been arrested. But I soon realised that they were now in full retreat, although even then the possibility of a speedy peace did not strike me. The messages I received in code in my letters, and reported speeches made by the Chancellor or the High Command, who by now expressed a desire for peace on the basis of a "status quo ante", all made me think that the war would last another year.

But finally the revolution, which had been menacing for long, broke out, and we heard that councils of soldiers, sailors, and workmen were being formed everywhere. I believe these could still have been suppressed, if the administration had shown any energy. But people were weary and underfed, and all the best elements of the nation were at the Front. Besides this, confidence in the Emperor had been lost, and his bombastic speeches only excited ridicule and disgust. I heard much criticism of him, but more especially of those who surrounded him, who were considered both incompetent and unreliable. I heard soon that the officers who went into the town from the hospital put a red badge in their bottonholes, and everyone seemed extremely depressed and anxious. It was reported that an officer in the town had committed suicide in front of a patriotic monument. I don't know if it was that of William I. or of Hindenburg. Big statues of the latter, made in wood, were erected everywhere, and passers-by were requested to subscribe in support of the Red Cross by driving in a nail, so that in time these statues became clothed in iron.

Great excitement was caused by the publishing of the "Fourteen Points" of President Wilson, and these were seized on eagerly by the Germans, who hoped by their means to obtain a "white peace" in which there should be neither conqueror nor conquered. But the events on the Russian Front, and all this talk of peace, were doubtlessly very weakening to the morale of the armies in the field, and Headquarters published on the 15th of October a declaration addressed to the soldiers, of which here is a rough translation:

German soldier, be watchful!
The word Armistice goes through trenches and camps. But we are not there yet.

By some the word is taken for a certitude already; it is understood by others as the long-desired peace. Some think it is no longer necessary to be watchful, brave, and mistrustful of the enemy.

We have not yet arrived so far; no Armistice can be yet, it is still war as before. And it is now necessary to be especially watchful and to persevere bravely.

It is now that you stand on enemy soil, and in Alsace-Lorraine territory, as the defence of your homes. IN A DANGEROUS HOUR THE FATHERLAND SEES IN EACH OF YOU ITS HOPE AND STRENGTH.

At the same time as these patriotic proclamations, many others came from socialistic and revolutionary parties, counselling the Germans to conclude a speedy peace on any terms. A great deal of this propaganda was attributed to Lord Northcliffe, and undoubtedly his publications had a great effect on the war-worn population. When the Chancellor Bethmann-Hollweg had been deposed, the news had been received with a feeling of relief, but when Michaelis was named in his place, everybody seemed to think it was a joke, if rather a sinister one. There seemed to be no one left except Hindenburg in whom the nation felt confidence. The Emperor had practically been put aside, and was only allowed to know what those in power permitted.

During my stay at the Clemens Hospital in Münster, the Empress had come to visit it. Twice already before, her visit had been announced, and they supposed that she had put it off because of her well-known aversion to Catholics. However, this time she came, went through all the wards, and distributed little souvenirs to the wounded soldiers. I lay in bed at the time, but although my window was open, I did not hear any cheering, or notice any enthusiasm during her visit.

At last, after a few days of breathless suspense, we heard that the Armistice had been signed, and almost simultaneously that prisoners of war were to be returned to their respective countries. Frau Manser arrived suddenly to tell me that, the day before, a delegation of soldiers, sailors, and workmen had summoned the Direction to throw the Siegburg prison doors open, threatening them with death if they refused. These revolutionaries had taken the warders' keys and opened all the cells, allowing not only political prisoners, but also the criminals, of whom many were still in the men's house, to escape. Our women, who had known very little about outside events, were so taken by surprise at the idea of being free that they had not dared to stay to claim their property stored away, but had rushed out as they were, and many of them started for Belgium on foot. Others had waited all night in the station, and had frequently been invited to dance by the revolutionaries revelling there, which they, however, had refused. There had been only one violent incident: a warder from the men's house, who had made himself particularly hateful to the prisoners by his cruelty and roughness, had been taken by them and pitched out of the window, where he broke his neck. However, my informant seemed to think that it was the German criminals who were responsible for this.

I wished to leave at once, but remembered my word of honour, and therefore wrote first to the Military Governor, Excellenz von Bötticher, saying that now war was over and I took back my word. Immediately an urgent telephone message came asking me to wait until the General had taken orders about me from the "Soldatenrat" (Council of Soldiers and Workmen). On the next day he sent me a telegram, which I have still in my possession:

"Prinzessin Croÿ ist sofort in Freiheit zu setzen" (Princess Croÿ is to be set free immediately)—signed Government Soldatenrat.

I at once told my nurses that I was going to start for home, but they tried to deter me, saying I was still too weak to travel alone, especially during the Revolution, besides which, orders were posted up that no civilians might take the trains, the latter having to be left free for the military, who had to be got out of occupied territory as soon as possible. That morning only had it dawned on the inhabitants that they in their turn were going to be occupied by the Allies, and the terror was such that many had run away. Some of the servant-girls were missing from the hospital, thus leaving all the work to the nuns. Nevertheless, I persisted in my intention, saying I would go myself down to the town and ask for a permit from the Soldatenrat. Although evidently very frightened, the sister who had nursed me would not let me go alone, and together we left the hospital on foot.

After having been for over three years a prisoner, and unable to move without permission, it is a curious sensation to go out for the first time as one wills. When we arrived at the building where the Council held their meeting, which was guarded by armed men with a red arm-band, I was conducted inside after declaring my business. At a long table sat soldiers, sailors, and workmen, presided over by a young fellow who appeared to be a non-commissioned officer. He had an open, energetic countenance, and waved me forward in a debonair way. When I told him of my wish to return to Belgium he implied that revolution had broken out there also, but I told him I was willing to risk that, and only required a pass for the railway in Germany. "For that you must apply to the civil authorities", said he. "We have left them so far in power in the Town Hall." "Will they give it?" I asked anxiously. "Tell them", said he grandly, "that *I* sent you", as if that sufficed for any emergency. So I started off once more, and we crossed the Square, where crowds of people, chiefly soldiers, seemed hurrying in every direction, and where often I heard them greet each other with the same words, "Der ganze Schwindel ist aus (The whole swindle is over)".

At the Town Hall I was received by a gentleman with a squint, who was *locum tenens* for the Burgomaster, I believe, sitting at a desk with a secretary by his side, and other anxious-looking busy officials coming and going. He evidently belonged to the old *régime,* and said to me with a sour look, "I suppose you are a political prisoner". "I have that honour", I answered cheerfully, upon which he said, "Then you had better go to the Soldatenrat". "I have just come from them", said I, showing my telegram, upon which, after conferring hastily with the secretary, he gave me the desired permission on a corner of my telegram. This was handed to me in silence, and after exchanging long mutual glances with the official, I left, to return for the last time to the hospital. On crossing the Square once more, I heard shouts and whistling behind me. The sister put her hand on my arm and said, "You are being called". I thought at first I was going to be arrested again, and my heart stopped beating; I turned round and waited, while the "President" who had received me at the Council came forward and asked eagerly, "Did you get it?" Silently I showed him my counter-signed telegram, and shaking hands he said in the most friendly manner, "That's all right. Auf Wiedersehen, gute Reise (Good-bye and a good journey to you)."

With great difficulty a taxi had been obtained; they were very rare and the tyres were made of all sorts of "Ersatz", as rubber was no longer to be had. I left a letter with the nuns to show to those of the Allies who might come to the hospital, saying that a prisoner had been kindly treated there, and asking them to treat the sisters kindly in return. By the time I got to Cologne it was evening, and I knew it would be useless to try and travel by night. I endeavoured to get information in the station, but a seething mass of humanity was there, and the officials seemed unable to cope with it or to know anything about the trains. So I turned to the hotel I had stayed at in pre-war times, and was recognised with extreme astonishment by the porter. He told me that no room would be empty until eleven o'clock that night, but I might wait until then in the hall or dining-room. The place was full of officers returning from the war; some arriving by train, others in cars, and others by aeroplane; all looked weary and preoccupied, and although I was the only lady they took little notice of me. At dinner I was asked for my bread-card and meat-card, which, of course, I did not possess, and at last was given a meal which consisted of food not "on the cards". A scrap of meat, which I strongly suspected to be dog, and two potatoes composed the chief part of the meal. Scarcely was dinner over than the officers, many of whom had been sleeping around the room on long settees, got up and brushed themselves down, while the lights went up and a band began to play, and smartly dressed girls from the town came in and began to dance with them. I had no heart to watch dancing, so went for a walk outside in the bitter cold until such time as my room should be ready. The streets, especially in the neighbourhood of the station, had long bands of calico stretched across them, on which were inscribed various messages to the troops. One I was able to read bore the words, "Welcome to our unconquered armies".

At last I got to bed, but coming and going all night made sleep difficult, and at six in the morning I got up and went to Mass in the Cathedral. The darkness inside the great building was only broken by a few candles around one altar, and when I had felt my way up to this I found a small crowd of people, mostly in mourning and some weeping, gathered there. I arrived early at the station to hear that trains towards Belgium might come in later, and I was given a ticket for the frontier for which I did not pay, my permit on the telegraph-form sufficing. It was bitterly cold, but I dared not leave the station, as no one knew when the train would come, and I feared to miss it. Crowds of people were waiting on different platforms, and many of them were talking French or Flemish. I found out that these were either released prisoners, or those worthless members of the population who had accepted to work for the enemy for money. Many of these, I believe, were prisoners or outcasts, and one young ruffian boasted that he had a pocket full of marks with which to go home and enjoy himself, before a weary woman sitting on her poor packages on the platform. She told me she had lost her all in the war, and did not even know if her husband was still alive, and spoke her disgust at seeing that some were not ashamed to profit by the misery of their countrymen. I indignantly gave the traitor a piece of my mind, and she thanked me, and asked if she might travel with me. I saw an official, whom I took to be the station-master, although he had not his full insignia on, and I asked him urgently to tell me about the trains. He answered confidentially that a train had been signalled from Berlin as going to Spa with the Peace Delegates, but he added, "It is already one hundred minutes late; it will come in on No. X platform, and only stop a few minutes. Wait there and get in it, there will not be much room." So with the poor Frenchwoman I waited on the platform indicated for nearly two hours, feeling by this time very cold and hungry.

At last the train came in, and a gentleman with a white band around his arm leaned out of one of the carriages. Seeing that I wished to get in the train, he helped me, and I discovered that several official personages were there. They were on their way to Spa, and seemed surprised to see me. The first, a tall grey-haired man, with a refined face, asked me how I, a foreigner, happened to be in Germany. When I told him that I had been a prisoner there for over three years, he said at once anxiously, "May I ask, have you been humanely treated?" Notwithstanding all the care at the hospital, I was still extremely thin and ill-looking, and, showing him my hands, I tried to tell him quietly what had been the conditions under which we had lived. He looked pained at my recital, but said, "This is still going on for my country-people; great numbers are dying slowly of hunger here. If you see anyone in authority in your country, tell them that unless the blockade is raised it will mean death to thousands of innocent people. You know as I do that it is the innocent who suffer: the sick, the aged, the children are all underfed: a blockade is a cruel arm against the weak." I promised to transmit the message if I should be able, a promise which I kept within a short time of my arrival in Brussels. I gave an account of the conversation to our Queen, who had just arrived back in her polluted palace, and saw her wonder at my interceding for the enemy.

At last the train stopped at the frontier, and the poor woman, who had managed to get into the same car as myself, told me she wished to enquire for a trunk containing all that she had been able to save from her home, and which she had been told was in Herbestal. While I questioned two soldiers standing on the long platform, a train went slowly by behind us, but I did not notice it in the noise and confusion of the station, and was surprised when the soldiers caught my arm and took shelter behind a partition. They explained that the troops in the passing train were revolutionaries, a "red train" they called it, and were firing at any loyal soldiers or "Kaisertreue" troops they saw. Several shots had been fired in our direction without my realising any danger. When this train had disappeared I got up again into my place, and we crept slowly on in the direction of Liège. We came to a standstill at last in the dark between two stations, and on a neighbouring line another train was also stopped. We could hear it rather than see it, as there were no lights, but a polished voice asked in French, "Where is that train going?" and I answered, "To Spa, I believe; where must I change for Brussels?" My unseen interlocutor asked in a surprised tone, "Is that a lady?" and on my answering, said, "This train is going to Brussels; you had better get in here". There was no platform; I was weak and afraid to climb down on to the metals, but, my companions helping, I was lifted with my luggage across to the other train.

The carriage into which I was pulled was already overcrowded with soldiers returning from captivity. Some were French, some Belgian, all were in rags, but merry and hospitable. My first friend cleared a corner of the carriage for me, and tried to arrange a screen as the windows were broken. We were soon under way again, going slowly and stopping every now and then to allow trains on their way to Germany to pass. The latter were crowded in an unbelievable fashion; cars, on which were guns, aeroplanes, and other material, were filled also with men, hanging or sitting on the guns, and lying even on the tops of the carriages. I heard that some who had lain there had had their heads dashed off at the entrance to a tunnel. The driver and guards of the train were still German, and several German soldiers were on board, and some of these joined in and sang national airs of France and Belgium with our soldiers. The latter brought condensed milk and army biscuits out of their knapsacks, and, seeing I had none, shared with me generously. A kindly French *poilu*, in an incredibly ragged costume, got down at one of the frequent stops and obtained some boiling water, which he mixed with a tin of condensed milk, and handed to me with a biscuit, saying, "The lady shall drink first". So I sat in my corner leaning against a canvas hold-all—no cushions of any sort were left in the train—and tried to eat the hard army biscuit in the darkness, while a lively conversation went on all around me.

My fellow-traveller told me that his parents lived in Brussels, and that he was an only son. For trying to escape from his camp he had been sent for punishment to the prison at Paderborn, where for a year he had not been allowed to correspond with his home. I could see that he belonged to the upper class, and he gave me details of his prison life which showed that we, at Siegburg, had nothing to envy from the prisoners of Paderborn. He told me that when he left the Kommandant had said to him, "Now the war is over I hope that you in Belgium will learn to forgive and forget". He said that he had answered, "Sir, in Belgium we have not yet forgotten the Duke of Alva; there is time for you".

At last, a little before daybreak, we got to Louvain, where the train stopped. On the platform wood fires were burning, and soldiers, prisoners, refugees of all sorts, were standing around them trying to warm themselves. I saw several priests, as well as a few women, and all the occupants of our train soon joined these groups, but I was too weak and weary to move, and was grateful for having room at last to lie down in the deserted carriage, where I must have gone to sleep. A little later I was awakened by my Belgian fellow-traveller, who said, "According to the terms of the Armistice three days' march must be left between the armies, so this train, being a German one, cannot continue to Brussels. We are all, therefore, starting on foot. Will you come?" I told him it was impossible, but as the engine had been taken off the train, I could not stay alone in the station, so I said I would go to an hotel. My companion suggested trying to find some sort of conveyance to take me to Brussels. I agreed eagerly, begging him, if he could, to hire a carriage for me and come too. He went off, and I saw that all those who had been in the train had already disappeared, leaving only some German soldiers who were starting for home. Alongside the railway the German army was marching, and I watched it curiously. The men marched steadily in silence with set faces and covered with dust, dragging all sorts of conveyances loaded with booty of every description.

After a very long wait my companion came back and told me he had tried in vain to find a carriage or cart. He had got the offer from a German soldier of a horse for a small price, but the poor beast was too worn-out to go far without rest. So he proposed taking me to an hotel before searching further. I did not realise how many hours I had been there, and told the kind Samaritan that he had better follow his comrades, and leave me to look after myself, as a long march is easier in company. But he answered quietly that having been wounded previously he did not feel any longer fit to start for Brussels that night, and I realised that he had worn himself out on my behalf. He taking my portmanteau as well as his own hold-all, we left the now deserted station and walked in the gathering dusk down the long, still partly-ruined street, towards the Grand' Place. At the Hôtel Britannique I was received with suspicious looks, and evidently they wondered how a lady could be travelling at such a time. Again I was told that no room would be empty until late that night, and I sat in the hall to wait. It was full of German officers, looking extremely preoccupied and anxious. My kind guide, after depositing my bag, had disappeared.

While waiting until such time as I could get something to eat, I went out into the Grand' Place, and there saw what I took at first to be an English Tommy, spick and span, leaning against a motor-cycle. Some groups of frightened-looking townspeople were watching from doors and windows, while in the distance the long stream of the German army marched steadily by. I went up to him, and asked who he was. He was very small, but stood up proudly, with a steel helmet on his head, and answered, "I am a member of the Belgian motor-cycle division. The German High Command feared that the population might molest their retreating troops, and sent a wireless message to Headquarters of the Belgian Army asking for a military force to be sent to maintain order. So I have come. The rest of us are following."

He was the first free Belgian soldier I had seen, and it was also the first time I had seen our new uniform, so I shook hands with him with feelings it is hard to describe. The confident air with which this tiny fellow stood there watching the long stream of our retreating enemies made me feel, better than anything else, that at last we were victorious. In a moment he was surrounded by cheering townspeople, and I went on my way and soon met a very different group. Scraps of British uniform showed me that these were soldiers; but haggard, ragged, unkempt, they looked more like beggars. One wore a boot on one foot and a slipper on the other. Another had on *sabots* (wooden shoes), and there was but one cap between them. They told me that they were four prisoners of war who had had to work several months for the German Army, until that morning they had been turned out into the street by their captors and told that they were free. Although they had had nothing to eat that day, and judging from their looks very little for a long time, they were cheerful and nonchalant. I found a pastry-cook who was delighted to offer a cup of tea and some rare biscuits to the poor starving men, who, hearing that I had been a companion of Nurse Cavell, all gravely stood up and shook hands with me.

On leaving them I went into the Cathedral, which was lit only by two candles, although many people were praying there, and in the dark one could not see the destruction. A temporary roof had been erected in the place of that burned.

When I returned to the hotel I had a conversation with the proprietor, who allowed me to sit in his office, where there was a tiny stove. As there was neither gas nor electricity left in the town, the only lights were tallow candles stuck on plates and placed in the middle of the tables. At dinner I had a small table to myself, close to the long one where the General Staff were dining. At another table in a corner of the room were one or two young officers with some Red Cross sisters, the only other women in the room. Having promised the kind nuns at Bonn, as well as Monsignor Felten, to give them news of my safe arrival, I thought this was a good occasion to send a letter to Germany, so asked the waiter to enquire if one of the officers would undertake to post one in Cologne. Immediately an officer turned and looking at me said, "On condition that I read the letter first". He sat at the end of the table, and although, like all the others, he wore a very plain uniform with no insignia or decoration, I took him for the General Commanding, as he was treated with great deference by all the others. Having obtained a sheet of paper, I wrote to Monsignor and to the Superior of the Hospital, and passed the letter to a young officer who came forward to fetch it. He carried it to his chief, and together they leaned over the table and read my letter in low tones. When they had finished, the orderly came back, and asked, hesitatingly, "Will you tell us how it comes that you have just left Germany?" I answered that I had left a German prison. He hesitated a moment, and then said, "My chief wishes to know in what condition you left Germany. Is it safe for us to return?"

I saw that they had little information about the revolution, and tried to tell them my impressions of what I had seen in the country. I recounted the scenes in the station where I had waited the day before, especially an incident in the underground passage connecting the different platforms. Here two red-banded guards had stood by a big pile of rifles, etc., disarming the soldiers as they arrived by the various trains. I had stood watching this for some time, seeing the different manner in which each reacted. Some, evidently of advanced opinions, had flung down their rifles and torn off their belts eagerly, others were less willing, and one young fellow, especially, looked at first as though he would refuse to surrender his arms. At last, holding his rifle almost reverently, he stooped and laid it on the pile, and when he stood up again I saw the tears streaming down his cheeks. I endeavoured to give some idea of this to my interlocutor, speaking rather haltingly in German, and I saw that he also was greatly moved. He told me that they had been informed that the Rhine bridge at Cologne had been blown up, and asked if it were true. I told them how I had crossed it on the previous day, and that so far as I knew the revolution was as orderly as possible. They promised to deliver my letter, and received eagerly the German newspapers I gave them, and all saluted me when I left my place.

At last I was shown to a cold and cheerless room, where the sheets had evidently not been changed for weeks. Wrapped in my old travelling-cloak, with my last clean handkerchief under my face, I threw myself on the bed to wait for morning. I heard much coming and going, and at last, some time before midnight, there was a knock at my door, and a voice I knew said, "Is the lady with whom I travelled there?" It was my kind Samaritan, and on my opening the door he informed me that a carriage had just come from Brussels, would be returning before morning, and that two seats were to be had in it. I was thankful, indeed, at the idea of getting on at once, and my fellow-traveller asked my permission to take the other vacant place. We started somewhere about one o'clock in the morning, and drove in the darkness and silence through the frozen land. When we neared Brussels we were suddenly stopped; on looking out of the window I saw by the light of a lantern two German officers in fur-lined coats standing in the sleet, while by their side was a soldier who was evidently extremely drunk. I feared at first that we were all being arrested once more, but one of the officers came forward and told us that we must not approach the station of Schaerbeek, I think, as a train loaded with ammunition had blown up there, and more explosions were expected. Surprised at being warned for our safety, we thanked him and went our way. It was the last I saw of the German Army.

In the distance, as we neared Brussels, we saw fires burning along the railway lines, but we got safely into the silent and utterly deserted streets. After waking the night-watchman in several hotels without being admitted, as all rooms had been requisitioned for the expected Allied armies, at last I found a room, and the carriage turned away with my companion, whom I never saw again. The next day I was fetched by the d'Ursels, and the kind reception they gave me in their old home at Boitsfort helped to make my home-coming less lonely and sad. But at first I was too bewildered and weary to act normally, and having been used so long to remain motionless, it took some time to realise that I was free to move as I would.

That first day while lunching, the door opened, and the son of the house came in who had been absent since the declaration of war. Seeing the happy family greeting made me feel all the more the emptiness and destruction of my home. No one knew if the house still stood, and all I could hear was that the fighting had been violent thereabouts. Neither posts nor telegraph remained; and even the roads had been made impassable during the operations, and must still be encumbered by the advancing armies. But on the next day Comte Hippolyte d'Ursel told me that I *must* find courage to go into Brussels, for I should see a sight I should never forget to the end of my life: the triumphal entry of our King. Seats had been offered us in a house on one of the boulevards, but the crowds were so great that it was only with difficulty I was able to reach the house. Here I was given a chair on a balcony and left, as I thought, alone.

The whole boulevard was a seething mass of humanity, roofs and windows were lined with people, who filled even the trees. At last we heard distant cheering which grew into a roar as it spread up to us, and a motor-car made its way slowly through the crowd. It stopped just before us, and out of it got Burgomaster Max, who was received with wild acclamation. Shortly afterwards he was followed by detachments of all the armies, which were each enthusiastically greeted in turn. Some big guns camouflaged in all colours were in the procession, and banners on which were the names of those places which had seen a specially glorious defence and victory. At last a little pause, and, amidst breathless silence, a group of six on horseback came slowly through the waiting streets. Leading was our Soldier King, with the Queen on a white horse by his side, both wearing simple khaki. Behind came Prince Leopold and the Duke of York, and lastly, the Count of Flanders and his sister, Princess Marie-José, her fair hair making a halo around her face. I had stood up to get a better view, and the emotion which had seized the crowd caught me too. Suddenly what I had taken to be a pillar against which I leant began to shake, and I realised that someone was supporting me. It was a tall French General who stood there, and down whose cheeks the tears were streaming. All around I saw handkerchiefs waving, and none were ashamed to give way to the deep emotion and happiness of the moment. Slowly the procession passed out of sight, going towards the Senate, where the King and Royal Family were received by the Government. One heart seemed to beat in the nation. The efforts to destroy the unity of our people, which the enemy had been multiplying for the last year or two, had not borne fruit then. It needed the lassitude and disappointment following the victory to develop, in the minds of the least experienced and understanding members of our population, seeds of discord and unrest.

As soon as it was possible to leave the house through the dense crowd, I was taken to Comtesse Auguste d'Ursel's, and carried upstairs to rest after the emotion of the morning, while the family downstairs greeted, one by one, those soldier sons and cousins who kept arriving, after fifty-two months of separation and anxiety. My ex-companion of Siegburg, François d'Ursel, who was just eighteen, had also returned from captivity, and the joy of all the family at being reunited was very deep. Suddenly the door of the room where I lay alone opened, and Countess Auguste came in and knelt down by me, asking in a tense voice, "Can you stand a happy surprise?" Seeing my imploring look, she went quickly to the door and pushed in a tall figure in khaki, who at first I could not realise was my brother, Leopold. He had been with his regiment, the Premiers Guides, on their way towards occupation in Germany, when his C.O. had sent him into the town on an errand for the troops. It was owing to this that he had had the happiness to witness the magnificent entry of our Sovereigns and of the triumphal armies into Brussels.

None of my people knew where I was, and it was by the merest coincidence that Leopold had passed in the Rue du Luxembourg and had been recognised and told that I was there. He had only been married a month before, after having deferred his marriage for years. But as the war went on, in every letter I had begged them not to wait on my account, and the wedding had been arranged for the end of October, when none suspected that the big offensive was imminent. Leopold at that time was in liaison with the British Army, and had been given leave from the Ypres front for his wedding. But three days before he was to start, a telegram arrived announcing that all leave was cancelled. By this time relations and friends had gathered in Paris; among them was our brother, Reginald, who had arrived from the Embassy in London, where he filled the post of Secretary our father had held before him. The Marquis de Lespinay, the bride's only brother, had also obtained leave, and was in Paris with his mother and sister. As it was too late to intercept all the guests, they agreed together to post people at the different doors of the church of Ste. Clotilde, where the wedding was to have taken place, and tell them it was put off. But Reginald spared no effort, in the meanwhile, visiting Embassy and military authorities, and telephoning to Headquarters, until at last he obtained five days' leave for Leopold, and telegraphed this good news to his brother at once.

Leopold was sitting in his tent taking down orders from General Merinden when the telegram arrived, and his expression must have shown that something was the matter, as the General at once enquired if he had received bad news. Leopold explained that he had been going to be married in two days' time, when his leave had been cancelled, and now, when it was too late to reach Paris, it had been accorded to him again. The General went on working in silence for a time, but at last he looked up and said, "My car is at the door, if you take it at once you can get to Boulogne in time to catch the Paris express". Hastily seizing some luggage, Leopold sprang into the car after thanking his Chief for the kind thought, and was rushed through the night over roads encumbered with the whole paraphernalia of an army in movement, towards the train, which he caught just as it was leaving the station. He had had to leave all arrangements to his brother and to the bride's family. Next day they were married, and they spent three days at the old home of the bride's mother, which was to be theirs in future, after which Leopold rejoined his regiment and saw no more of his wife for months. Her only brother was killed a week later, while leading his men. He left three young children, and the fourth was born shortly after his death.

From the time Leopold rejoined his regiment they advanced steadily, sweeping the enemy backward until, just before the Armistice, they arrived at Sebourg. From here Leopold came over to Bellignies and found our poor home in a pitiful plight. Several shells had struck it, and not a window was left; all the furniture that had not been stolen was broken and soiled. The gardener and old Amand remained among the ruins. During the last operations five hundred Germans had lived here, chiefly in the cellars, and now English troops were quartered in the house, which did not tend to mend matters. Family papers and archives littered the floors, and were being used to light the fires. Leopold collected as many of these as he could during the hour he was able to spend there, and had them sealed in a case until one of us should be able to return home.

The Château de Sebourg, where Baron de la Grange still remained, was hastily prepared to receive King George, who stayed there before going on to Flanders, where he met King Albert at the Château de Lophem. The old Baron de la Grange had died some time after I had left. His son, who remained alone to defend the population, as far as it was possible, and care for the sick, the wounded, and the refugees, had suffered greatly in health. He lived to be reunited to his children and grandchildren, but this strong and comparatively young man died in 1919, worn out by the privations and anxiety he had endured.

A few days after the "Joyeuse Entrée" I was ordered to the palace, and as no motor-cars were left belonging to the Belgian population, the Spanish Ambassador kindly lent me his to take me there. I was received by the Queen in a small apartment which had been hastily prepared for her Majesty; the rest of the palace had been used as a Red Cross hospital, and each of its windows still bore the Geneva Cross in its panes. I had been lent clothing by various friends in which to appear before the Queen, but I had become so thin that nothing fitted, and I must have looked like a scarecrow in my borrowed plumes. But one was beyond caring for such matters, and I doubt if the Queen thought much more about it just then than I did, although in normal times she is so well-dressed. She showed deep feeling and understanding when questioning me, and, on hearing that I had no news of my brother Reginald, after thinking for a moment, but without saying a word, she went and sat at her desk, where she wrote for a few minutes. On coming back to me she said in her gentle voice, "I hope . . . I think, you will see your brother soon." That same evening he received a telegram in London, saying that the Queen wished him to be sent to Brussels at once, and he arrived two days later in the car with the Military Attaché, Col. Matton.

I was listened to with absorbed interest by her Majesty while I told her about our prisoners, their courage, and the deep loyalty with which they had borne privations and captivity. I gave her the work which had been made by the united efforts of so many of these women at Siegburg, together with a dedication written by Mademoiselle Tandel:

Hommage:

>Sur cette toile, quelques points
>Qu'en tremblant, tissèrent nos mains
>Lorsque nous écrasait la chaîne,
>Ne sont point dignes, noble Reine,
>Du sourire de Ton regard!
>Sans grâce, sans beauté, sans art,

> Oserons-nous t'en faire hommage?
> Te diront-ils que Ton image
> Fut notre étoile dans la nuit?
> Celle qu'on adore et qu'on suit
> Parce que son front d'or éclaire
> Les routes du Devoir austère,
> Et fait luire auprès de l'Honneur
> Tant de grâce et tant de douceur,
> Qu'en la regardant la souffrance
> N'est plus qu'un rayon d'espérance.
> S'ils te disent, ces humbles fils,
> Combien dans nos cruels périls
> Leur trame fut d'amour mêlée,
> Alors d'une caresse ailée
> Peut-être passeront tes mains
> Sur la toile et ces quelques points!

The Queen expressed pleasure at receiving this homage from the prisoners, and kept me long talking, until she observed that I was too fatigued to continue, when she helped me to rise with the true comprehension of suffering which distinguishes the experienced nurse.

I had come to Jolimont thinking only to get information about my people and my home, and meaning to leave again at once. But dear Comtesse d'Ursel would not hear of it, and put me to bed and nursed me with the tender affection of a mother. She had had the joy of welcoming back her son, Pierre, who had arrived in Brussels on the day of the King's entry. The other son, who had been married and widowed since she saw him, was lying ill in Flanders, but notwithstanding her anxiety she ministered to all, receiving friends, relations, and officers from the various armies who were passing through Brussels, with her unvarying kindness.

After this I was ordered complete rest, and I have only a vague remembrance of events, as I was so ill at the time and my kind hosts took it in turn to come and watch over me, and tried to make a normal being of me again. At last one day after I had come downstairs, in the middle of breakfast the door opened and the missing son appeared. The joy of all the family to be together again was extreme, and although Georges was far from recovered from his severe illness, he had felt that the home-coming would cure him. While the greetings were going on, someone saw an English officer in the courtyard, and asked me to act as interpreter. On advancing to the open door, suddenly all were surprised to see the newcomer rush forward and greet me warmly. It was Major Preston, whom I had last seen in 1914, when he left Bellignies in disguise to escape! It was by the merest accident that he had applied to this house, of which he did not even know the name. His surprise on recognising me was great, and we both remarked that truth was stranger than fiction.

I was extremely anxious all this time for news of my home, and at last, ill or well, determined to accept General Godley's kind proposal of sending his Aide-de-Camp and car to take me there. The roads were still scarcely passable, and often we had to leave them, and cross through fields after cutting wire and removing obstacles. Shells had been exploded by the retreating armies at the cross-roads, and big holes or craters were still gaping there. Towards evening we turned in at the gates, and saw the lawns all pock-marked with shell-holes, while roofs and walls were torn open. The paneless windows were filled with bits of oiled calico, and shuttered with tarred cardboard, shells and munitions lay everywhere, and dirt and destruction reigned. A British regiment was living here, and I was received by the chaplain and other officers, who told me that the General invited me to dine with him. Again the old feeling I had had at the beginning of the war, of being a character out of *Alice in Wonderland*, came back to me, as I sat at a strange table (ours had disappeared), surrounded by strange faces, in the hall which I had not seen since I parted there from my poor grandmother. The officers were most kind, and I was deeply touched at receiving the following letter before I left next day to go back to Brussels:

>15th Bn. Bedfordshire Rgt.,
>B.E.F.,
>13.12.18.

Your Highness,

Knowing the splendid service that you and your noble family have rendered to our troops, after the retreat from Mons, we wish to thank you.

It is, indeed, a privilege to stay in the home of one who has acted so splendidly, and we are very grateful.

It may be of interest to you to know that this battalion

THE CHÂTEAU DE BELLIGNIES

Photograph taken since its restoration after the war. The tower on the left, which dates from the Middle Ages, contains the hidden staircase.

was in both the advance to, and the retreat from, Mons, and also that it fought the last battle of this war in the forest of Mormal. The best of futures to you and your noble country.—Most gratefully yours,

CHARLES, E. G.,
Lt.-Col.

The dining-room had been rendered uninhabitable by a large shell which had traversed the room above and cut through one of the big oaken beams which supported the ceiling. This shell was still standing unexploded on the floor, and was over a yard high. They told me it would be dangerous to touch it, so I spent the night in its neighbourhood, trusting once more to Providence. Next day, however, some soldiers of the French "Génie" came, and with great precautions removed the shell to the middle of the lawn, where it was exploded, and made one more, and far larger, hole than any that were there.

While sitting in my room next morning I received many of the villagers, and among them a woman who had worked for us formerly, and whose drawn, tragic face made her almost unrecognisable. In 1914 we had received information that her eldest son had been killed, but having no certainty we said nothing to the parents. The second boy was aged seventeen at this time, and was helping at the bakery, and frequently brought our bread. One day, after we had been getting the young men away for some time, this Thomas Sohier asked if we could not send him too, as he was nearly eighteen and anxious to serve his country. Knowing that his only brother was probably killed, we asked him if he had his parents' consent. He answered that his father was willing for him to go, but that his mother was not. We told him he must get permission from both his parents, and then we would help him, but although he came back several times with the same answer, he was still there when I was arrested, and the whole service came to a standstill. Now his poor mother stood before me, saying in a toneless voice, and with dry eyes, "I *had* two sons: Gaston fell with arms in his hand defending himself, but Thomas died of blows and hunger as a civil prisoner at Sedan".

After our arrest all the young men of military age had been sent to various camps and fortresses, and made to work for the Germans. Nothing can conceive of the inhuman treatment and insanitary conditions which reigned at the fortress of Sedan. Of the 300 odd prisoners who worked there, 63 died in one month.[1] These are things which should be known in Germany, and for which those responsible should have been tried and punished by their own countrymen, if they did not want

[1] Mr. J. Schramme, a Belgian lawyer who had been Sheriff of Bruges, published in 1919 a book, which should be widely known, of his experience when a prisoner of war at Sedan. He tells how, of eighteen hostages taken in punishment from the village of Rumigny, where fifteen French soldiers had been hidden and fed by the inhabitants, only three were left alive in March 1918. Often men suffering from typhoid were driven by blows from their straw sleeping-place, and the hospital attendant declared that he himself had buried 732 men since he had been there.

history to hold them up to the opprobrium of the world.

Our church had been shelled, and twelve German soldiers killed in it, their blood still spattered floor and columns. In a confessional sat an old man holding a new-born baby, while at his feet on some straw lay the dead mother. Our Curé had not yet returned from exile. He had been arrested shortly after me, but as nothing could be proved against him, he was sent to Germany as an "undesirable" until the end of the war, and he made the acquaintance there of many of our Belgian patriots, among whom were Burgomaster Max, the Sheriff Monsieur Lemonnier, and M. Delleur, Burgomaster of Boitsfort. The Germans had installed a priest here from one of the villages evacuated on the firing-line, but their troops occupied the whole presbytery with the exception of one room. Monsieur l'Abbé Vallez on his return was named to a new and more important post, but his health was shattered, and he died at the age of forty-eight, an indirect victim of the war.

I saw that the English Army was likely to live for some time yet in Bellignies, and, in any case, I could not have stopped there long in my state of health, without windows or doors, and with the heating and water service broken down. So I returned to Brussels, where my kind friends welcomed me until better times. Here we organised memorial services in honour of our martyrs, of whom 305 had been executed after trial in Belgian territory. Of these,

37 had worked for the Belgian Army, 132 for the English, and 48 for the French; 5 people had been shot for helping soldiers to leave the country, of whom 3 had helped Englishmen. Among all these, 4 were British subjects, 99 were French, and 195 were Belgians. England claimed the body of her national heroine, Nurse Cavell, and fetched it home in 1919. My personal feeling is that if our martyrs had been left where they were laid after their execution, in the little cemetery at the Tir National, the sight of the forty-one graves in this historic spot would have been more impressive. An unnamed grave between those of Miss Cavell and Philippe Baucq was rumoured to be that of a German who had been shot for refusing to fire at the Englishwoman. I do not think there was any truth in this, and I consider that the story I had been told about a German soldier being shot as a traitor for allowing men to escape from Belgium for money is more likely to be true.

Not far off lay Gabrielle Petit, shot, after trial, at the age of twenty-two for having been an active member of the Belgian Intelligence Service. Although in the eyes of our enemies she was a spy, surely all right-minded people will consider that those who work in their *own* country and for their *own* people against a common enemy ought to be known by a more honourable name. This heroic girl had nursed her fiancé, who had been wounded in the battle before Antwerp, and had found a means of smuggling him into Holland, from whence he rejoined the Belgian Army. She had agreed with him as to a means of collecting and forwarding military intelligence, and was able to render good service until she fell into enemy hands. Although during the long months of her detention every means was used to make her speak, her courage never failed her, and she went to her death bravely, without having compromised any of her confederates. She wore a rosette of the national colours, and refused to have her eyes bound at the last, saying, "You will see that a Belgian woman knows how to die for her country". God grant that these sacrifices were not made in vain!

My hope is that *one* good may come out of so much evil, and that some of those who suffered for justice' sake in every nation may work to have the inhuman and unchristian laws of war amended. Surely some distinction can be made between those who act from patriotic and disinterested motives, especially when in their *own land*, and those who betray the hospitality of another nation. The death penalty, at least, should only be applied in very rare cases, and on the most convincing evidence. Who will dare say that many absolutely innocent people were not victims of a blind fanaticism during the war?

The day will come, I firmly believe, when passions are stilled and the conscience of Germany is awakened, so that her people may recognise the injustice and deplore the result of the trial I have described, as well as many others of those which took place in occupied territory. But love for their Fatherland and fear of defeat blinded our enemies' eyes. A great fear also of public opinion, always ready to accuse anyone of "Feindfreundlichkeit", swayed them.

Military authorities will invoke the laws of defence, and the necessity of a terrible sanction to deter people from espionage. But I know from experience that *no* threat will prevent those who act from patriotic motives from persevering in their action, and surely deprivation of liberty is sufficient punishment for this? I know of cases, during the war, where frail women, imprisoned for some trifling misdemeanour, such as receiving a letter from abroad, became active members of an intelligence service as soon as they were released from prison, fully aware of the risks they ran.

No trial should be held without the presence of one or more *independent* witnesses. How this is to be achieved without danger to national defence, it must be the work of jurisconsults or the League of Nations to discover. I have often heard, since the Armistice, the simple words "I am *glad* I suffered; it makes one understand. If it was to begin again, I should act in just the same way." Who will dare maintain that those who gave their lives for their country would say otherwise?

APPENDIX

THE COURT-MARTIAL'S GROUNDS FOR ITS VERDICT

(Translated)

IT appears from to-day's evidence that by the arrest of the accused the police have succeeded in securing at least a number of those persons who for a long time have been active in enabling men fit for military service to reach the enemy's forces.

Either from their own declarations or from the statements made by those on trial with them, the Court holds that the following persons are the principal organisers:

(1) Prince Reginald de Croy, who has unfortunately managed to escape;
(2) Philippe Baucq, architect;
(3) Louise Thulliez, teacher;
(4) Miss Edith Cavell;
(5) Comtesse Jeanne de Belleville;
(6) Louis Severin, chemist.

The conveyance of men to the enemy took place between the period from November 1914 to July 1915, and was carried out by two groups of persons, between whom, however, there was no rigid line of demarcation.

One group, at the head of which were Prince Reginald de Croy and Louise Thulliez, had its principal field of action in the region of Englefontaine, Maroilles, and Bavay, in Northern France, while the second group carried on its operations in the mining region. The work of the two groups consisted especially in discovering stray French and English soldiers as well as mobilisable men, and conducting them to Holland, generally by way of Brussels, so that they might thence join the armies of the Allies.

Reginald de Croÿ put his Château of Bellignies entirely at the disposal of these activities, so that this château may be styled the chief meeting-place on the route to the Front [*sic*] by way of Brussels and Holland. His sister, the Princess de Croÿ, one of the accused, was fully aware of this; she fed and harboured the fugitives, and herself photographed a great number of them, so as to procure them false papers, in which the French and English were passed off as Belgians. The making of the false identity papers was the work of another of the accused, the engineer Capiau, of Wasmes, near Mons, as well as of the chemist Dervaux, of Paturages.

For the men handled by the second group, the lawyer Libiez, of Mons, made out false papers with the help of a seal bearing the name of a non-existent commune. At Brussels the men were hidden in different spots through the agency of Miss Cavell, before being conducted over the frontier to Holland by paid guides specially engaged for this service. By this means she secured the escape of about 250 men. In the arrangements for the rest of the journey she was assisted principally by her fellow-prisoner, the architect Baucq, of Brussels. The stray soldiers thus collected were either unwounded, or else had recovered from their wounds. Some of the men thus taken across the frontier announced their safe arrival in Holland, or even in France. Thus, the accused student, Cayron,[1] as he himself admits quite plausibly, has several times received news

[1] Cayron died after a few months' imprisonment, aged 18.

from the Front from two people, of whom one was his own brother, who had been conducted in this manner to the enemy's forces.

Father Pirsoul (a Jesuit priest) had been the intermediary in this case. In the opinion of the Court, he worked in collaboration with the accused; however, he has made his escape. Severin, also, acknowledges having received similar cards mentioning the arrival of several French soldiers in France, and has often been informed of the safe arrival of soldiers and mobilisable men in Holland.

The Court has no hesitation in declaring that all the accused were perfectly aware that they were helping to conduct stray soldiers and even mobilisable men to the armies of the Allies. Only in the case of the prisoner Libiez does the Court consider that positive proof is not forthcoming.

In the opinion of the Court the intention of the accused, in the whole of their activities, was to furnish reinforcements to the enemy, to the detriment of our own forces.

Inasmuch as it is proved that a great number of the soldiers as well as mobilisable men who have been removed from our control in this manner have crossed the Dutch frontier, that others have even arrived in France and are now fighting against us, the *Court finds established in each case the accomplished fact of having conveyed men to the enemy; in consequence of which all the accused before the Court on this charge are liable to the penalty of the law for this offence, as their premeditation covered the whole action, even if they only played a limited part, according to the duties allotted them, in the various stages of the transfer to the enemy.*

The majority of the accused have admitted their participation in conducting men to the enemy. Those who have not done so have been implicated by the declarations of others of the accused. *Some of the accused have, of course, attempted to limit or to attenuate their admissions. But inasmuch as, according to the quite trustworthy evidence, given upon oath, of the witness, Lieutenant Bergan, the statements were drawn up with scrupulous exactitude, carefully translated, and only signed in each case after having been read over and accepted, the Court is firmly convinced that the statements signed by the accused correspond entirely with their evidence.* As to the contention that any of the accused inculpated themselves unknowingly, there is, in the opinion of the Court, no evidence, and none of the accused made such an assertion.

THE END

A SELECTION OF NEW BOOKS

THE LIFE OF JOSEPH CHAMBERLAIN.
By J. L. GARVIN, Editor of "The Observer". With Illustrations. 8vo.

Vol. I. 1836–1885. From his birth on July 8, 1836, up to the resignation of Mr. Gladstone's Government on June 9, 1885.

Vol. II. 1885–1895. From June 1885, through the struggle for Home Rule, up to the formation of the great Unionist Administration under Lord Salisbury at the end of June 1895, when Joseph Chamberlain became Colonial Secretary.

EGYPT SINCE CROMER.
By LORD LLOYD OF DOLOBRAN, G.C.S.I., formerly High Commissioner for Egypt and the Soudan.

Vol. I. From 1904 to 1919. 8vo.

AUSTRIA OF TO-DAY.
With a Special Chapter on the Austrian Police. By VICTOR WALLACE GERMAINS, author of "The Gathering Storm", "The Tragedy of Winston Churchill", etc. With a Frontispiece. 8vo. 12s. 6d. net.

AN ECONOMIC HISTORY OF SOVIET RUSSIA, 1917–1931.
By LANCELOT LAWTON, author of "The Russian Revolution, 1917–1926". 2 vols. 8vo.

ON ANCIENT CENTRAL ASIAN TRACKS.
By SIR AUREL STEIN, author of "On Alexander's Track to the Indus" and "Ruins of Desert Cathay". With Illustrations. 8vo.

AN INDIAN MONK.
By SHRI PUROHIT SWAMI. With Frontispiece. Crown 8vo. 7s. 6d. net.

An account of a Brahmin's existence written in a style of most engaging simplicity. It gives the reader an admirable insight into the social and spiritual life of India.

MACMILLAN AND CO., LTD., LONDON

A SELECTION OF NEW BOOKS

PEACE AND WAR. A Translation of "La Fin des Aventures" by GUGLIELMO FERRERO. Extra crown 8vo.

Essays and discourses on the supreme importance of peace to the world, written by a highly distinguished historian.

ROME OF THE RENAISSANCE AND TO-DAY. By the Rt. Hon. SIR RENNELL RODD, G.C.B. With 56 Illustrations in gravure from Drawings by HENRY RUSHBURY, A.R.A. Super royal 8vo. 25s. net.

MEMOIRS OF AN ARCHITECT. By SIR REGINALD BLOMFIELD, R.A. With Illustrations. 8vo. 10s. 6d. net.

THE LIFE OF MARY KINGSLEY. By STEPHEN GWYNN. With Illustrations. 8vo.

The publication of Miss Mary Kingsley's "Travels in West Africa" showed her to be a remarkably intrepid traveller and discoverer. She journeyed without white companions in the Wilds of West Africa and became a great authority on that region.

RECOLLECTIONS OF A MAN OF SCIENCEB. By SIR ARTHUR SCHUSTER, F.R.S. With Illustrations. 8vo.

BEETHOVEN AS HE LIVED. By RICHARD SPECHT. Translated by ALFRED KALISCH. 8vo.

This work by a well-known writer in Vienna is neither a biography nor a critical study, but an attempt to produce a portrait of Beethoven by a series of studies of him in different phases of his life and character. It is a book which reaffirms the perennial life of Beethoven.

MACMILLAN AND CO., LTD., LONDON

Lightning Source UK Ltd.
Milton Keynes UK
UKOW05f0942250915

259197UK00001B/37/P